EMPTY CHAIRS

Blessings and peace.

Annelee Woodstrom

By Annelee Woodstrom

EMPTY CHAIRS

Author - Annelee Woodstrom
Publisher - McCleery & Sons Publishing
Cover Design - Lisa Ruebke

International Standard Book Number: 978-1-931916-51-6

Printed in the United States of America

Dedicated to Papa who wanted nothing more than to guide his children while they grew up – but he was taken from them by war, too young.

To Mama who worked so hard, worried and stood by as her children picked their own paths and added new branches to the family tree.

To my family, Roy and Linda, and Linda's Mom, Hilda Bjorge, who is now in her second century. Hilda was 102 on September 10, 2007.

To my granddaughter Freya and her husband Gaurav, grandson Titus and granddaughter Liv. My family gives my life joy, purpose and meaning.

And most especially to my husband Kenny and daughter Sandy who have died, leaving me with memories that have the beauty of roses and they enhance my winter years.

ACKNOWLEDGEMENTS

I am grateful to the following individuals who shared their time and knowledge until the book emerged as the final product of *Empty Chairs*.

I would like to thank Joyce Schlagel who is my neighbor and best friend since 1959. She was there for me during the writing of *War Child* and she made most useful suggestions. Then she listened and recalled with me experiences for *Empty Chairs*.

My thanks to Dick Bernard, who ever since *War Child* has willingly shared his professional expertise, offered suggestions, edited the manuscript and wrote the kind endorsement on the back cover.

I want to thank Linda, my daughter-in-law, granddaughter Freya, Janet Skretvedt, Marilyn Hartman, and Kristi Kuball. They proofread until *Empty Chairs* was in its final stages.

I want to thank Richard L. Gill and Marijo Vick who shared their computer expertise with me.

Last, but certainly not least, I want to thank Roy for his input on how he thought Mom and Dad's childhood and war experiences shaped their views on life. His vast knowledge and recall of cultural and historic events, and his view on coping with the death of loved ones enriched my writing.

Photos and productions of some are the work of Kristi K. Photography, Ada, MN. Lisa Ruebke, Ada, MN designed the cover for *Empty Chairs*.

I know and appreciate the immeasurable value of time and skills the above mentioned were willing to give.

Annelee Woodstrom
Ada, MN
September 2007

FAMILY MEMBERS WHO INFLUENCED MY LIFE

Papa - 1942

Mama - 1944

Uncle Pepp - 1955

Kenny - 1943

In-Laws - Caroline and Andrew Woodstrom - 1966

L to R: Irmgard's friend, Theresa and me, Mama and Irmgard,
Max and Papa - 1941

Top - L to R: Cousin Erna and Cousin Joey - 1940-1942
Middle Left:
Myself at age 17 - 1942-43

Erna, Joey and I were not just cousins - we were friends.

Kenny and our car from 1947-1951.
He bought the car new in 1937.

Theresa - 1947   *John - 1947*

Lower Right:
Annelee and Theresa
- 2000

Upper Left:
Theresa, husband John
and me - 2000

MY FAMILY

Daughter
Sandra Kay
(Sandy) 1952-1978

Kenny and Anneliese - 1945

Titus, Liv, Freya, Roy and Linda - 2001

Granddaughter Freya married
Gaurav Thamann
February 14, 1999

Gaurav and Freya - 2007

Grandma Hilda
(Linda's Mother)

She is now 102.

TABLE OF CONTENTS

PROLOGUE

Frankfurt, Germany – April 6, 1947

"What I am doing here? What will happen to me now?" These questions gripped my mind as I looked around the American Airport in Frankfurt, Germany. Right now, I felt more alone and more disoriented than I had ever felt. Since my fourteenth birthday when I earned my first monthly wages, I had never been without sufficient money to take care of my needs. Now it was 1947, I was almost twenty-one and with less than two marks (two dollars) in my pocket, I was on my way to America to meet my fiancé, Kenny Woodstrom. I questioned myself. Why did I give the American military police officer the three-hundred marks Mama had given me to cover emergencies if they should arise? Silently I reasoned that there was nothing I could have done as the tall officer swaggered toward me with a nightstick under his arm.

He smiled and curtly addressed me in fluent German, *"Guten Tag, Fraulein, sagen Sie mir, haben Sie Deutsches Geld ?"* ("Miss, tell me, do you have any German money?")

I shyly nodded. His brisk tone forestalled any questions while he told me that it was against the American law for an enemy alien to take German money into America. With that, he handed me an official exchange form and explained that the customs office in New York would exchange dollars for the German money he had to confiscate. He held out his white-gloved hand, and I hesitantly placed my money into his palm.

But now I wondered. What could I do if I have to pay for something while I am on the plane? How could I explain? I felt so small and helpless as I stood in the boarding area where the American military police officer had taken me. I wanted to be anywhere else but here! All around me the American personnel stood or sat in groups. I searched the crowd to find a friendly face, but their animated conversations were as meaningless to me as their laughter because my entire English vocabulary consisted of 'I love you -yes -no - hot -cold, and Crookston, Minnesota.' While Kenny had been at my home, we had searched the world map and then the United States map until I found Crookston, in Northern Minnesota, close to the Canadian border. It was the town where Kenny and I would live.

Eighteen months had passed since we said good-bye at the depot where I last saw him in his army uniform. I remembered his deep blue eyes and his smile that captivated me the day I had first met him. Even though we needed a dictionary to communicate because Kenny did not speak German and I did not speak English, he had captured my heart and he had also gained the respect and acceptance of my family. Yet, neither Mama nor Uncle Pepp had ever surmised that Kenny and I would want to marry.

Uncle Pepp, my papa's oldest brother, always told Mama, "Peppi, for me, Kenny's leaving can't be soon enough. When he leaves, Anneliese will get normal again."

Mama and Uncle Pepp were shocked when Kenny with the help of his Congressman, Harold Hagen, obtained permission for us to marry, and shortly after I had my exit permit to enter the United States. While I worked to gain permission to leave Germany, I had not envisioned how difficult it would be for me to leave and venture into the unknown that awaited me in America.

The parting from Grandma, Papa's mama, had given me a glimpse of what lay ahead. Tears were streaming down her wrinkled face as she hugged me and said, *"Anneliese, ich bin alt, und du fliegst soweit fort. Wir werden uns wohl nie mehr wieder sehen. Schreibe oft, und ich werde dich in meine Gebete einschliessen."*(Anneliese, I am old, and you are flying so far away. We probably won't see each other again. Write often. I will keep you in my prayers.)

The final good-byes shared with family, friends and acquaintances had been heart wrenching. My thoughts turned to my twelve-year-old brother Max's tear filled eyes while I hugged him until he squirmed uneasily and slipped out of my embrace. At a loss for better words, I muttered, "Max, be good. Do well in school, and I will send you a soccer ball."

"Oh, boy." he sighed as he scrambled away.

My sisters, eight-year-old Irmgard and sixteen-year-old Theresa, were sobbing while we hugged and then they left the room because they could not bear my final good-bye to Baby Werner. After Baby Werner's birth Mama had been ill and weak, so I had taken care of him for the past eighteen months. I pleaded to let him come to the depot with me, but Mama in her wisdom would not allow it.

Instead she held me tight and kissed me before she blessed me with holy water and said, "Anneliese, I have done all I could to keep you from leaving, I can do no more. You are determined to follow Kenny. All I can do now is give you my blessings and wish you peace. I pray that you will have the future you hope for."

I looked at Mama, and I felt guilty because I saw the despair and pain in her eyes. Today, she looked shorter than her stature of five feet and older than forty-three. Swollen, red-rimmed eyelids paled her azure eyes and tightly drawn face muscles made her face look even gaunter than it had been of late. Her rounded shoulders bent forward, but her movements showed her sheer determination to stay in control while she and I held on to each other in a passionate, final embrace.

Six feet tall, Uncle Pepp, Papa's oldest brother stood straight as a rod while he waited to bid me farewell. I thought I saw an angry, disapproving look in dear Uncle Pepp's eyes.

"I bet you one hundred marks that within two years you will come to your senses." Uncle Pepp grumbled, "I won't send you travel money right away, I will send it only if you promise that you will leave America and come home."

I wanted to say that I would never ask for money from anyone, but I kept silent. That day I had been so confident. Now, as I stood alone in the airport with a few German coins in my pocket, fear and doubts surfaced. What if Uncle Pepp was right?

I recalled his unrelenting warnings. "Anneliese, over there you are an enemy alien because you represent Nazi Germany and the people America had fought against. They won't accept you. Listen to me! Stay home where you are loved and where you are one of us and belong!"

Mama, too, had advised, "The American culture is not the same. You will face so many barriers. You don't speak English and Kenny doesn't speak German. How long will Kenny converse with you with a dictionary in his hands? You are Catholic while Kenny is a Lutheran. How do you think his family will react? You love Bavaria, its woods, hills and mountains but the topography of Minnesota where you will live is flat and it will be foreign to you!"

Their frequent pleading had fallen on deaf ears because I had been so sure that I would prove them wrong. What would I do if I was not accepted by the American people? What if Kenny had changed? He was no longer a soldier, and eighteen months had elapsed since we last saw each other. Were the ten weeks we knew each other sufficient for life-binding marriage vows? Would his parents, his sisters, and the community think of me as the German enemy alien?

While all these questions frightened me, I wanted to run, but Cousin Erna's parting words were a stronger voice, "Anneliese, if you turn back now you will always wonder if running away from all you fought for was the right choice."

My mind drifted back to 1944 when the American armed forces had landed on the Normandy beaches, and Kenny had been destined to fight his way into Germany. At war's end he was stationed in Waldsassen, near my hometown where on July 1, 1945, circumstances not controlled by us had brought us together. So much had changed since the American soldiers conquered our land.

CHAPTER 1

June 6, 1944 - Germany

Regensburg, Bavaria. TELEGRAPH OFFICE. The constant hum of our telegraph machines was interrupted by our supervisor's shout, "Dear God in heaven, the American and British soldiers have landed on the Normandy beaches. The radio announcer said that right now heavy fighting is going on, but our troops surely will drive the Americans back. They will never get past the Siegfried Line. So don't you worry, just get back to work."

That was the beginning of our watch, and we silently questioned, how long could it be before the American armies encircled us from the West and Russia's battalions invaded from the East?

How life had changed since 1939. We had been euphoric and felt that Germany could achieve the 1000 Year Reich when Adolf Hitler and Russia's Stalin signed the Nonaggression Pact of August 1939. Four weeks later, during September 1939, Adolf Hitler commanded our military forces to invade Poland, and during June 1941, to attack Russia and take its resources and people. Our victorious generals sent Polish and Russian prisoners of war, able-bodied men and women by the thousands, to forced labor camps within Germany.

Although the poorly equipped Russian soldiers had been no match for our troops, from 1941 into 1944, they fiercely resisted our armies' onslaught. We heard of the bitter siege of Leningrad's and Moscow's populations. They suffered from starvation, diseases, sub-zero winters, homelessness and death, but they would not surrender. These Russian civilians gave their soldiers time to regroup, attack, and drive the German

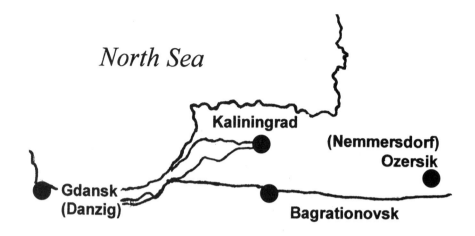

North Sea

Kaliningrad

(Nemmersdorf)
Ozersik

Gdansk
(Danzig)

Bagrationovsk

East Germany

enemy across the Russian borders. As the Russian troops crossed Poland and advanced into eastern Germany, they avenged the suffering their families and loved ones had endured.

At the movie theaters we watched the weekly news. While the movie projectors turned, we saw the Russian subs crisscross the Baltic Sea. They hunted and sank German rescue ships loaded with thousands of wounded soldiers, refugee women and children. The movie reels turned all too slowly as the flames ate away at barns and farm homes. We did not see, but we heard of the atrocities the Russian army executed as they fought in East Prussia and took the Nemmersdorf village. The soldiers, driven by hate, retaliated after three years of starvation, death and all the indignities their families had endured while our troops occupied their towns. Now it was pay-back time! All hell broke loose as the Russian soldiers entered the village Nemmersdorf in East Prussia, (today Mayakovskoye) about 160 miles from the seaport Danzig, (today Gdansk, Poland). Once in Nemmersdorf the Russian soldiers raped the women and girls barely in puberty and then crucified several women on the doors of their barns and family homes. The old men and children of Nemmersdorf were forced to watch as their wives, daughters or sisters died a slow, horrific death. Before their murderous rage was spent, the soldiers shot the children and then they clubbed the old men to death. After our special fighting forces retook the village, they invited reporters from neutral Sweden, Switzerland and Spain and they recorded the horrific carnage as factual. *In 1991, Bernard Fish in his book, NEMMERSDORF OCTOBER 1944, claimed that the massacre was actually set up by Josef Paul Goebbels, 1897-1945 German Nazi propagandist.* [1]

Barely a year ago we had clapped and even cheered at the end of the weekly news, but now the clapping was absent and deep shock and stillness permeated the theater while the audience seemed in deep, oppressive shock. We had a glimpse of what awaited us. We were afraid.

Since 1943, we had also lived with fear of the chaos and disruption the American air raids brought into our lives. Numerous metropolitan and agriculture related areas were subjected to repeated bombing raids. From July 24 through August 2, B-17 Flying Fortress bombers broke through the skies over Hamburg. On the first three nights 780 bombers dropped 2,300 tons of bombs each night. On the fourth night 425 bombers dropped 940 tons. This carpet-bombing of explosive and incendiary bombs caused a fire storm that leveled eight square miles of the city and devoured all the oxygen nearby. Fifty-thousand German civilians died, and as many were injured. 800,000 residents and refugees were now homeless, and all they owned were the clothes they wore.[2]

We prayed in churches and at home, "Please, Father in heaven, have mercy and keep us from the fate of Nemmersdorf and Hamburg. Send the tanks and infantry of the West to take our towns soon."

So we listened to the radio and learned that on the West front, the soldiers gained and lost ground. Our armies and the American invaders suffered heavy casualties, but slowly the American battalions inched forward. They stormed the Siegfried Line, crossed the Rhineland, and put our troops to flight. By April 1945, the American forces had taken most of Germany, but the Americans fought on until they had reached Czechoslovakia where their final objective was the border village, Schlopenhof, in the Sudetenland. Meanwhile, on the eastern front, the Russians had fought unwaveringly until they destroyed our battalions and drove our fragmented forces west, across Russia, across the Polish-German borders deep into the Fatherland. They met the American soldiers who had been waiting for them in Schlopenhof. The war was over!

Germany was soundly defeated, and the Russian and American soldiers shook hands and drank.

CHAPTER 2

Uncertain Peace
April 1945 – Mitterteich, Bavaria

I knew the enemy would reach Mitterteich before they would take Regensburg. I wanted to be with my family and share with them whatever fate held for us when the Russians or the Americans came. So after a night shift at the telegraph office, a co-worker and I left Regensburg without gaining permission from the manager. Our ninety mile trek took seven days. I was glad I had listened to my landlord when he advised, "Anneliese, I will send your belongings to your home, so don't take any baggage with you because it will hinder your travel."

I wore a skirt and blouse, stockings and shoes, and my heavy coat and scarf which kept me warm and dry. I rolled up another blouse and stuffed it in my coat pocket. We walked little used walkways in the woods where we sought safety from the frequent air raids. Because barns burnt easily from enemy fire, we slept in ditches or fields. Like vagabonds we relieved ourselves in ditches or woods and wiped ourselves with grasses. Sometimes we were lucky and we got a ride on a wagon, while at other times we moved past retreating troops at a snails pace. When hunger forced us, we entered villages and searched and begged the farmers for food and water. Within a day after I had made it home, the enemy encircled us from all sides. Barely five kilometers from us, the Russians and Czechs took the Sudetenland and guarded its borders. Mama, whose nickname was Peppi, my sisters, Theresa, fourteen, and Irmgard, six, my brother Max, ten, and I, eighteen were relieved because the American forces broke through and occupied our town. Yet, we were anxious

because chaos was all around us. Since every home was filled beyond
capacity, hundreds of homeless refugees lived outdoors in makeshift tents.
Because they were without electricity and heat, they bathed in the creek,
and relieved themselves in the bushes. The stench of urine and garbage
that clogged ditches and the smell of open fires polluted the air. Poorly
clad children with snarled hair and dirty faces followed the American
soldiers and begged for chocolate and food. After 1942, in order to
propagate the German race Adolf Hitler had ordered the Kinder Land
Vershickung (KLV, Children's Land Evacuation). Four to fourteen year
olds were evacuated to safe areas in south Germany and other locations
while their parents were forced to stay behind. As the metropolitan areas
were frequently bombed, numerous parents died and many of the KLV
children became orphans. After the war these young people became
street people and many prostituted themselves for food and shelter.

Soon, *"German girls sleep with the American soldiers for a chocolate
bar,"* became a much-used phrase.

Mama shook her head and said, "These poor girls have lost everything.
They live on the street because they have no home to go back to. Hunger,
loneliness, and cold are the reasons they sleep with soldiers who
shamelessly take advantage of their plight."

We felt blessed because we still had our home, but we also worried
because we had not heard from Papa since his engineer battalion retreated
from the East front. We could do nothing - we had to wait, just like
thousands of war ravaged families everywhere were waiting to put their
lives in order and hope for lasting peace.

It was April 20, when the C-Company, 357th Infantry Regiment of
the 90th Division, Texas-Oklahoma entered Mitterteich, Bavaria, my
hometown, and interned several hundred German prisoners of war (POW)
in the sports arena. We thought that since we had survived the war, we
could concentrate on getting some normalcy into our lives. But things
got worse. During the early morning hours on April 22, we were
awakened by loud voices and the din of war vehicles that suddenly parked
in our garden. Mama, still in her nightgown, opened the door and she
immediately was confronted by an American officer and an interpreter.

"Ma'am," the interpreter said, "you will have to leave your home
within the hour. So pack some cooking utensils, warm clothes, blankets,

your ID's, towels, your ration cards and money. You and your children are assigned to the former Hitler Youth home in the next block while our soldiers move in here. Your home will be off-limits until the soldiers leave. How long they will stay, I don't know. So just start packing because we will be back soon."

Mama lamented, "We just came back from Dobrigau where we awaited the end of the war. Now we have to leave our home again. When will it end?"

The interpreter shrugged and advised, "Ma'am, you just better get packing before the soldiers come. If you are still here when they arrive, you will leave without anything."

It seemed like the war was still in our land. The whole neighborhood was pulling their wagons to the former Hitler Youth home where every family was assigned a small space for sleeping and stacking personal items. Ten o'clock was mandatory bedtime and we slept on the floor on straw mats. During the nocturnal hours, sleep was interrupted when babies cried or small children had bad dreams while they longed for home and their own beds. The snoring of the elderly and the coughing of the sick awoke the soundest sleepers. Grandpa Schiller, a World War I army officer, swiftly settled complaints and always got his way,

"If you don't like it here," he advised, "you can join the refugees. They will gladly take your space."

Given that option, everyone settled down. But Theresa and I were troubled and we worried when we learned that Mama, who had visited Papa in Berlin, was now four months pregnant. Mama's friend, Anni, and our neighbors reassured Mama, Theresa, and me that we should not panic when a little baby joins us.

"Peppi, we survived the war," Anni consoled, "now we will be here for you and your family until your husband comes home."

A month passed before we were allowed to return home. Max, our brother and Papa's namesake, ran ahead to the shed. We heard him call for Hans, his pet rabbit.

He came running from the shed, "The American soldiers killed Hans," he sobbed, "and the chickens, too."

Mama consoled Max and promised that Uncle Pepp would get him a new rabbit. But we had more immediate concerns because our two goats that supplemented our milk rations were skinny and near death. We fed them and brought them the last of the water in the rain barrel.

"We need to feed them often." Mama concluded, "If they pull through, it will be days before we will get milk."

The disorder in our home was a nightmare, and we worked all day before we had a semblance of order. But we were happy because now we could sleep in our own rooms without anyone telling us what to do. Although the soldiers were gone, we soon found that our home was not our own. Officers still entered at will, brought food and pantomimed that we must prepare a home cooked-meal. They even came at night and carried on with German girls we didn't know or without notice, searched for guns or cameras we had given up weeks ago.

Despite the death of his pet rabbit and the chickens, Max could not still the fascination that the big American trucks, tanks and Jeeps held for him. Since they were parked across the street, he approached the soldiers, admired their vehicles, and stayed near them. He frequently came home with chewing gum and crackers, and he would remark, "I could get a lot more if I could tell them I have two blonde sisters!"

Mama rebuked, "Max, you do that, and you will be home forever."

It was July first when Max, his pockets bursting with chocolates and chewing gum he had highly desired came home flanked by four American officers. One officer spoke fluent German, and he explained that Max had promised they could meet his two blonde sisters and party.

"Mama, we like Max," the officer said. "He is an intelligent boy."

"Oh, no," Mama interjected, "he wasn't so smart today. He should know his sisters don't party."

I felt safe because Mama, her pregnant state quite visible, told the officers that she would stay up and not leave. Such a party was not what the officers had in mind, and they left soon after their arrival to search for a home where they, their food, and their drinks were welcome.

As the officers were leaving, their driver pointed at me and asked, "You, name?"

"Anneliese," I answered and pointed at him, "You?"

He smiled, and his blue eyes sparkled, "Kenny, okay?"

Mama was quite distressed when Kenny, the driver, became a frequent visitor and always politely inquired if we were all right. Mama grumbled,

"Does that man know only one road to Mitterteich? Why does he always end up at our house?"

Theresa and I were amused as Max and Irmgard, whose entire body was covered with impetigo sores were vying for his attention. Since Kenny didn't speak German and we didn't speak English, we used the dictionary and we pantomimed until we thought that we understood each other. One evening a Jeep stopped by our home. As Kenny left the Jeep his passenger moved to the driver's side and drove away. While we still wondered why he came with another driver, Kenny removed a box from his knapsack.

He pointed toward Max, Theresa and me and the kitchen door and commanded, "You. Out! Out!"

All this time he held Mama and Irmgard back. Satisfied that we understood, he nodded and said, "Okay."

We, who had been ousted, waited in the living room and wondered what took so long and what was taking place?

Finally, Mama called us back, "Come, look!"

Except for Irmgard's big blue eyes and her pale lips, her entire body was covered with white gauze.

Mama recalled, "Kenny took a blanket and a pillow from the sofa and he covered the kitchen table. Then he lifted Irmgard unto the table and with motions showed me that I should undress Irmgard and cover her lower body with a towel. He turned his back and looked out the window while I did as he said."

"A few minutes later, he asked, 'Okay?'"

"He turned and took a huge jar of salve out of his knapsack. All the while he talked to Irmgard. She just smiled at him like she always did and said, 'Okay.'"

"He nodded and proceeded to cover every inch of her hair, face, arms and her upper body until all I could see was the white salve."

"Then he turned to me, 'Mama,' he said as he pointed at the towel, motioned to me to finish the lower part of Irmgard's body, cover each sore with the salve, and put the towel back. He then took out two huge rolls of gauze. We covered Irmgard with the gauze and we went through the same procedure as he had shown me. He marked off three days on the calendar and I think he wants to repeat the procedure again.'"

Mama could not stop crying. Kenny walked shyly up to her and said, "Irmgard okay."

He looked at me and said, "*Auf Wiedersehen.*" (See you again). That was the one phrase every American soldier knew. He hurried down, waited a few minutes for the Jeep and waved as they drove off.

Mama shook her head in wonderment, "You know, I couldn't believe it," she uttered, "but Kenny is truly a 'Gentleman Soldier'." From then on, Kenny was indeed dubbed our 'Gentleman Soldier.'

Max had been silent all this time, but now he couldn't contain himself any longer. "Mama, how long will she be like that? May I get my friends and show them the mummy we have in our house?"

"Max," Mama admonished, "you will not bring your friends to look at your sister. She is not a show piece your friends can taunt."

Four days later Mama and Kenny repeated the process, and Irmgard, unlike other children, healed without infection or scars. Kenny didn't seem to know, but unquestionably, there was the beginning of a special bond between Kenny, Mama, and Irmgard. As the impetigo scars disappeared, Irmgard was at Kenny's side as soon as he entered our home. The affection between Kenny and her was evident to us, and as time passed Kenny called Irmgard his 'Second Lady'.

Kenny, true to his nature, was also attentive and caring when Baby Werner was born. There was no medication even for the seriously ill, and giving birth was not considered an illness. Mama gave birth to a baby boy without any medicinal aid to lessen the labor pains.

During the evening hours Kenny came. I called out "Kenny, Mama - baby."

He rushed back to the Jeep, came into the room, walked up to Mama, and handed her a sack, "You," he said.

Surprised, she smiled and motioned for Kenny to open it. He opened the sack and laid a bar of laundry soap on the down cover. We had not seen laundry soap in months. So we watched in awe as he reached for more. There were several oranges - he reached in again, there were some crackers, then packets of coffee and we could hardly wait as he reached in again. There was some powder. It showed eggs on the container, and then Kenny held a small box in his hand.

"Here," he said as he handed Mama the small box. He motioned to

Mama, "Open."

Mama opened it, and aspirin tablets rolled onto the floor. Aspirins were unattainable for home use. Kenny retrieved the precious pills, and he gently hugged Mama.

"Danke schoen, Kenny," (Thank you, Kenny,) she whispered.

"Kenny," Mama reached for the baby and handed him to Kenny. Tenderly, he held the baby and smiled.

A sound behind us made us turn, Uncle Pepp rubbed his eyes, and we became aware that he must have been in the room for some time.

"Peppi Nanni und ich gratulieren," (Peppi, Nanni (Uncle Pepp's wife) and I congratulate you.) Uncle Pepp remarked, *"Es ist ein Junge. Er ist so klein, aber wie koennen unsere Kinder wachsen ohne Nahrungsmittel?"* (It is a boy. He is so little, but how can our children grow without food?) He turned and waved, *"I komme morgen zurueck, so ruhe nun."* (I'll be back tomorrow. So rest now.)

Kenny, too, got up, and they walked out side by side.

It had been July first, Kenny's birthday, when he had entered our lives. Now it was August 29, 1945, and I knew that tonight Kenny had endeared himself to us and even to Uncle Pepp who had stood in the background and had silently witnessed the concern and caring Kenny had for Mama.

CHAPTER 3

Crossing the Border

It was the first week in September when Uncle Pepp came with Grandma, and they shared with us their fears about Aunt Lisbeth and her children's chances of survival in Eger, (today called Cheb) in the former Sudetenland. The Czech's hatred that had been kept in check by the German annexation had now erupted full force against anyone who was German.

Czechoslovakia's combative history was well-known to us since we could see the Bohemian Forest from the hills that surrounded our town. Ferdinand I, of the Habsburg monarchy, ascended to the throne in 1526. The Czechs rebelled in 1618, and they precipitated the Thirty Year War. In 1620, they suffered defeat and for 300 years were ruled by the Austrian Empire. At that time the industrial development was led by the middle classes who were mainly Germans and Jews. The Habsburg monarchy crumbled during World War I, and Eduard Benes founded the multinational State of Czechoslovakia. Although the Czechs were only forty-five percent of the nation, they ruled over and ended economic advancement of the Germans, Slovaks, Poles, and Ukrainians. During September 1938, Adolf Hitler annexed the German-speaking regions of the Sudetenland, and in 1939, he established a protectorate over the Czech lands, while Slovakia became a self-governing republic.

After the war, we heard of the horrific massacre the Czechs who fought Adolf Hitler's annexation had endured. We didn't know the details, but we were told that in 1942 resistance fighters had been trained in England to parachute into Czechoslovakia and assassinate the German

Reichsprotektor Heinrich Heydrich as he rode to his office one morning. Six miles northwest of Prague, the village of Lidice was chosen for reprisal. German troops obliterated the farms and homes, and murdered hundreds of innocent Czechs and deported others to concentration camps before they felt the cleansing of the area was completed.

The Czechs bade their time, but they had not forgotten. The war was over, and now they could vent the anger and hatred that had been kept in check. The systematic, ethnic cleansing of the Sudetenland and the expulsion of all Germans had started.

Uncle Pepp acted quickly. The mayor's secretary, who spoke fluent English, prepared a note for Kenny. The note explained that Papa's and Uncle Pepp's sister, Lisbeth and her three children lived in Eger, and we feared for her and her children's safety.

After Kenny read the note, he struggled for the right words. "I no go Czechoslovakia. I, in Tirschenreuth. We go America." Kenny held up his hands, "ten days."

Uncle Pepp took the news in stride and he pondered, "We must help. Lisbeth is family."

He sent Cousin Erna and me to the border. We walked the eight miles, but as Uncle Pepp had warned us, we stayed away from the border. The refugees who had crossed relived the traumatic, painful hours. The Czechs had seized their farms, the officials took ownership of their business, their money, stocks and bonds while the Czechs soldiers ordered that the Germans would have fifteen minutes, and each family member could take ten kilos of life-time possessions.

"What could one take in fifteen minutes," a refugee lamented. "I couldn't think. I just shook and cried while I gathered all I could in that brief time."

One woman went on, "While I gathered the ten kilos, the Czechs waited and said that we were the lucky ones because we got to leave. If we didn't want to leave, we could stay, go to trial and face the newly established Special People's Court. After that, the Czech soldiers ousted us from our homes, and now we have nowhere to turn."

We experienced their fear for survival as we watched terrified, while a Czech soldier flogged a German man with his leather whip until he collapsed, bleeding profusely. All this cruelty just so he could gain possession of the man's rusty old bike. We realized the power of the victorious warriors and our dependence on their whims of goodness or evil.

We waited anxiously until we heard from Aunt Lisbeth and we were euphoric as she and her children crossed the border. Still shaken by the encounter with the Czechs, she recalled almost verbatim what we had heard.

I searched for the right words in my dictionary and told Kenny that Aunt Lisbeth hoped that somehow, some day, she could bring her furniture and bedding to Uncle Pepp's home.

Kenny listened quietly and all evening he was restless. It took a while, but with the German and English dictionary at our side, I understood. "See you tomorrow, 9:00 a.m."

As he had promised, Kenny and an interpreter came early the next morning. The interpreter explained that Kenny wanted to take me for a long ride.

Mama surmised, "It must be something special that Kenny has in mind for you. Go, have fun. Theresa will help me. I will be all right."

Kenny drove through Waldsassen and as we came near the Sudetenland, he handed me an American uniform.

"Slip the pants on and tuck them into those boots" the interpreter advised, "Wear the jacket like it is yours." His tone became serious as he continued, "Kenny thinks you must see what happens to the German people there because he is afraid that you will cross the border and help your aunt retrieve some of her items. That would be the biggest mistake you and your aunt could ever make. The Czechs would imprison you both, or just being there could cost your lives. Enough said for now. Act like you are an American and let Kenny and me handle whatever comes along. I speak most dialects spoken here, so I will know what the Czechs say and I will respond as needed. I don't think anyone will stop us because they will think we are Americans. Just be quiet and watch, but if they should stop us, don't even move."

Kenny held my hand as we crossed the border. He drove through Eger, and we saw that the Czechs had signs up that already renamed the city of Eger. They named it Cheb. Kenny drove many miles through villages that now had Czech names not familiar to me. I sat still while my teeth chattered and I could barely breathe. How could Kenny bring me here where groups of people were herded into the village or city centers? Women, children, men, young and old were identified by white armbands as Germans. Czechs of all ages, men and women, encircled and hit their captives with their fists or wooden clubs and if they had neither, they kicked them with their boots. They spit on them. Young men fondled women, tore their clothing, and pushed them to the ground. Pools of blood and people screaming in pain or dying by the wayside were left behind. All the while the Czechs were shouting slogans I could not understand, but they surely increased the violent fury these people heaped upon their captives.[3]

I covered my eyes with my hands so I would see no more. But I still could hear the heart-piercing screams of the victims intermingled with shouts and clapping approval of what the speaker said. As Kenny drove through villages and towns, these violent scenes were like flowing lava covering the streets. I could not take anymore of this unchecked violence.

I told the interpreter, *"Ich kann es nicht mehr ansehen, ich will nach Hause."* (I can't watch anymore, I want to go home.)

Kenny made a U-turn, and a Czech shouted, "Thank you, America!"

As soon as we crossed the border, I motioned to Kenny that I needed to stop. I left the Jeep and ran into the woods where I heaved until my stomach ached from dryness. We were on a hill and I could not see what we had just left. From here, the little villages and towns looked strangely quiet and peaceful because the surrounding, century old trees hid that we had just witnessed. Little did we know that what we had just seen was the inhumane treatment and the expulsion of the remainder of what was left of the three million Germans who for centuries had lived in the Sudetenland. Since May 1945, thousands had been killed in mob violence or after hasty trials by the Special Peoples' Court.

Kenny came up to me and tried to take me into his arms, but I could not let anyone touch me after what I had seen. The realization hit me that had I not worn an American uniform and sat next to an American soldier in an American Jeep, I, as a German, would have been forced to wear a white armband for anyone to see. The thought of what would have awaited me made me shiver. The interpreter and Kenny spoke softly while I sat under the tall trees on soft moss holding my body protectively. A few miles east from here people had no power over their lives and for them nothing could ever be the same again.

The interpreter came toward me. I put my hands up, so he stayed a short distance away while he pleaded, "Anneliese, don't blame Kenny or me for what you have just witnessed. Kenny thought you needed to see the existing mayhem. When Kenny's company came into Czechoslovakia the last week of April, it had witnessed atrocities against the wounded German soldiers in the German field hospitals. All Germans feared for their lives. I am half German and half Czech, and luckily Captain Redman needed a translator so I was assigned to him. I owe him my life."

Agitated, he walked back and forth. "If you wonder why the Czechs hate the Germans so, I can tell you. Did you ever hear of the village Lidice in Czechoslovakia?"

"Yes," I said, "I heard some time ago."

"You see, Anneliese," the interpreter shook his head and went on. "I am sure that during the reprisal thousands of innocent people lost their lives because they lived near or in Lidice."

Kenny came toward me, sat near me and gently put his arms around my shoulders.

"Anneliese, you okay?"

We sat while I cried silently, and it was then that I felt his tears on my cheek, and I realized he, too, felt the pain of what we had just witnessed.

We joined the interpreter. "Kenny did this under great risk," he said. "So, please keep this trip to yourself and don't tell anyone what you just saw."

Drained and weak, I just nodded in agreement and then, Kenny, I, and the interpreter rode on in silence. We stopped briefly in Waldsassen, barely three miles from the border, and it seemed we had come to never-never land. People walked in the streets or sat and whiled away time on the park benches. Children ran freely, they laughed and played, and I wondered who knew of the horror that enveloped the German people across the border. I showed Kenny the beautiful, baroque basilica, the all-wooden library where life-size carvings supported the library's balcony, and centuries old paintings embellished the ceiling. We walked through the building where I had taken typing and short hand. I wanted to bring some normalcy back into my life, but today, everything was surreal. The interpreter stayed in Waldsassen while Kenny took me home.

Mama was anxious to hear about our trip, so I told her that we had driven to Waldsassen and the surrounding area. I was glad Kenny could stay for a while longer. Max and Irmgard stayed close to him Mama brought Baby Werner and things slowly became somewhat easier for me. It had been such a horrific experience, but the interpreter had told me that Kenny had put me through this hard day because he loved me.

I knew for sometime that I liked Kenny more than I should. I had fallen in love! There were so many reasons to love him. Kenny was gentle and patient with Max and Irmgard. He held Baby Werner while he was concerned about Mama's health, and he didn't expect special treatment or a party. He liked my family, but I knew he came so he could be near me. I knew now that he worried about my safety, and I thought that he had shown me today how much he loved me. How could that have happened in such a short time?

I had known Kenny now for barely nine weeks, and we were in our garden when he suddenly said in German, *"Anneliese, ich lieben dich. Komm Amerika meine Frau?"* (Anneliese, I love you. Come to America, my wife?)

My heart pounded. So Kenny knew that I loved him. I reached for his hands and said, *"Ja, ja, ich komme zu Amerika, deine Frau."* (Yes, yes, I come to America as your wife.)

I just couldn't tell Mama that Kenny had proposed and I had promised to follow him to America. She had so much to think about. It was easier for me and Kenny to keep our love and our plans for the future as our secret.

On September 19, 1945, the day before my nineteenth birthday, Kenny and I had to say good-bye to each other. Kenny's interpreter told me that Kenny would apply for permission to marry me as soon as he arrived at his home in Crookston, Minnesota. We knew it would not be easy to achieve our goal, but we had not envisioned the almost insurmountable problems that awaited us. America and Germany had not yet signed a peace agreement. Kenny, who had fought for his country and was honorably discharged from the Army, was constantly reminded by officials that I was a German, an enemy alien and that fact alone could stop Kenny's endeavor.

"Forget about that German girl," he was told when he voiced his determination to bring me to America so we could get married. I, on the other hand, had to prove to the German government that I could meet all the legal requirements and all the changes that our most unusual marriage would bring about. Now I had to tell Mama and Uncle Pepp and they were not happy with my decision. They reassured themselves that the American government would not sanction our marriage. So far, it seemed that they were right. My applications for an exit permit and Kenny's application to bring me to America were gathering dust in Washington. Kenny finally contacted Congressman Harold Hagen who lived in Crookston and whom he had known since childhood. Without hesitation, Congressman Hagen promised to bring Kenny's efforts to a closure. We mailed numerous legal documents back and forth and Kenny was required to state under oath that he would never request any financial government assistance for his German fiancé.

I waited and supplied one document after another to satisfy endless requests. Despite all my efforts, nothing moved forward. As months went by, living conditions in Germany deteriorated even more. We existed on meager rations. Refugees kept streaming into town, and Aunt Lisbeth and her children slept on straw covered by a blanket. They lived in what once had been a store room in Uncle Pepp's home. Aunt Lisbeth and I were uncertain of what the future held for us. She wondered when she would have new living quarters, and I counted the months and wondered when I would get my exit permit to join Kenny in America.

CHAPTER 4

The Gift of Love - a Doll House Chair

It was March 1946. Dense rows of tall fir trees had shaded snow patches that stubbornly hung onto the hills, but now the warm spring winds and the long yellow beams of the sun reduced the patches to rivulets of water that trenched their way into the nearby fields. Spring brought a strange calmness to the land. Even the violent rages of the Czechs had ebbed, and for some time now Aunt Lisbeth had heard from refugees who had crossed the border into Cheb that presently the city was relatively quiet. The German homes that the refugees had been forced to leave were still uninhabited, but Gypsies from Hungary and Romania would soon work for the Czechs and live in the vacated homes. When her friends and neighbors crossed over for the second time, Aunt Lisbeth could not be held back any longer.

Uncle Pepp related to Mama, "Peppi, how can I deny Lisbeth? She stood before me and pleaded. 'Pepp, help me just once more, I need to get back to my home. Every night I see it in my dreams and then I wake up on straw. I need bedding and clothes for my children. What could I take in fifteen minutes? I need to get back and see what is left in my home. If you won't help me, I will go alone.' Uncle Pepp shook his head. Lisbeth will go, but I just can't let her do that! The longing for her home consumes her. She doesn't sleep much, and she has lost so much weight.'"

Uncle Pepp outfitted a large hand wagon and he determined that Cousin Joey, his son, and Herbert, who was one of his bakers, and I should go with Aunt Lisbeth. We could help her retrieve clothes and bedding. I had felt sure that Mama would forbid my going across because

I had heard her when she told Uncle Pepp, "Pepp, what are you thinking? Lisbeth is all worn out, and she doesn't think clearly. You want to send Joey, your own son? He is still a boy, barely fourteen. You want to send Anneliese, although she is nineteen, you know how impetuous she acts at times. I know Herbert, your baker, is dependable but is he aware of what you asked of him? Pepp, you are asking too much of me. I worry constantly about my husband who is still a prisoner of war in Russia. I just can't place Anneliese into a dangerous situation."

Uncle Pepp sighed, "Peppi, it isn't a decision I haven't thought about, but Lisbeth is family. If it were you, I would do the same for you and your family. I am sure they will be safe. Even the mayor said that the people who go into their own homes in Czechoslovakia and take just small items like bedding, clothing and dishes have nothing to fear. Peppi, we must do this for Lisbeth."

Mama relented and gave her consent. I felt that there was no way for me to back out. I had to go. I thought of Kenny and the interpreter, and how they had tried to keep me from entering Czechoslovakia ever again. But Kenny was in America and he slept in a good bed, while my aunt and her children spent every night on straw on the floor. I prayed to God that he would keep his guardian angels around us and keep us safe.

The next morning under the cover of darkness, Aunt Lisbeth, Cousin Joey, Herbert and I took a shortcut through the woods and approached the East-West border. Every step I took brought forth the images of what I had seen. I dragged my feet, broke out in a cold sweat as my body shook and I wanted to scream. Yet, I kept still and moved with the pace of the wagon.

Dawn broke as we reached the outskirt of Eger where Aunt Lisbeth had lived. We felt uneasy because Eger the once beautiful, vibrant city had ceased to exist ... Cheb, as it was now officially renamed, was devoid of people. We moved past the rows of empty homes where the branches of the huge chestnut trees hung over the fences that lined the street. The silence of the neighborhood was threatening our courage and yet we were feeling a bitter-sweet joy because we had reached Aunt Lisbeth's home. The hinges of the garden gate screeched as if they wanted to announce our arrival. We quickly entered and hid the wagon under the stone fence that surrounded the house. The bushes and fruit trees looked ominous, and I feared that someone could easily hide there and wait until we entered. I was glad when Aunt Lisbeth locked the door behind her, but now I felt like we were trapped in her home. We could hardly breathe. The air was stale. The furniture was covered with dust, and the walls were bare because the oil paintings that had hung in the hall and in the living and dining rooms were gone. The chandeliers and all the crystal and porcelain had been removed also. I felt foreign in the home where we had spent childhood days after Adolf Hitler annexed the Sudetenland to Germany. Cousin Joey and I had played hide and seek in the same woods where now we feared for our lives.

Aunt Lisbeth never acknowledged the missing pieces. "Pack clothing, bedding, and small utensils." She directed, "After we have taken everything downstairs, Herbert, you load the wagon and secure the load. Joey, take some oil and fix the screeching garden gate hinges before we leave. Everyone, wear all the clothes you can but make sure they won't hinder walking or running should the need arise."

I went into Cousin Reserl's room and there stood my doll house. I remembered how upset I was when before Christmas 1942 Mama told me, "Aunt Lisbeth asked if you would lend them your doll house while you work in Regensburg. During the war, Lisbeth can't get one for little Reserl. They'll take good care of it and you will surely get it back."

I didn't want to part with my doll house, but Mama thought it was the right thing to do so I relented. Childhood memories sprung forth. I was six years old when my doll house stood under the Christmas tree. As I remember, the wooden outside walls were twelve inches high, fifteen inches deep and painted a light-brown. The back wall was three feet long and two inside walls partitioned the rooms. The kitchen was painted off-white, the living room pale blue, and the bedroom walls were green. The doll house had no roof and the front was open, so I could change rooms and furniture to suit the play situation. I loved my doll house because Papa had skillfully sawed the wooden furniture for each room and Mama had painted each piece. The kitchen chairs were four and a half inches high, and Mama had painted two blue flowers on the backrest and seating area of each chair. The yellow center of each flower was set in dark-blue petals that had a light blue edge, a thin stem and several dark-green leaves. Every Christmas, something new was added to the kitchen, living room and bedroom of my doll house.

As I stood there, I sadly looked at it, and the love that still bound me to my doll house burst forth. The doll house was clean. Its colors had faded somewhat. The furniture was nicely arranged and it seemed that it was beckoning me to touch it. Momentarily, I wanted to take it with me, but I knew I could not so I quickly closed the door and helped where I was needed. Cousin Joey and Herbert loaded the wagon until it could hold no more. Upstairs, we peeked out the windows and waited for the guards to pass by. We were tense. Our clothes were damp and no one spoke. So far, we were safe. Now we wondered. Would our luck hold? Would we make it across the border? We bowed our heads and prayed silently for a safe return trip.

Finally, the guards drove by. Their Jeep had barely turned the corner when we moved down the stairs and outside. We paused behind the stone fence and listened. The deserted neighborhood was eerily quiet. Cousin Joey hesitated then opened the garden gate, paused and looked in all directions. He nodded, so we pulled the wagon onto the street. Then we pushed hard while we feared what awaited us on top of the hill. Were the Czechs waiting for us? Since the road down hill was clear, we never braked. We just ran with the wagon until we reached the open fields. Then we gasped for breath and pushed some more until beads of sweat blocked our sight and trickled down onto our chins. We wiped our faces with our sleeves and never looked back until we reached the protective cover of the woods. We had covered two miles by now, and within a mile or so we would be on German ground. So we pushed harder and strained our muscles until they hurt because we knew that our lives could depend on our speed.

At last, we had crossed the border. Everyone scattered to find a spot where we could shed the extra, sweat drenched clothes to throw on the wagon. Then we sought shade under the crowns of the tall trees and we rested our weary, aching bodies and slowly the release of the pent up fear and deep emotions took their toll. We were exhausted, and we couldn't go on just yet, so Aunt Lisbeth sat down beside me and she took my hand.

"Anneliese," she said, "I can never thank you for what you have done for me today. I know you didn't want to cross. Yet you stayed the course and helped me." She reached into her coat pocket and continued, "I saw you looking at your doll house. During the war when we couldn't get one for little Reserl, I had promised your mama that if you lent her your doll house, we would take good care of it and you surely would get it back."

I looked at her, "Aunt Lisbeth," I consoled her, "there is nothing we can do. It is gone."

"Not all of it," she replied while she reached into her coat pocket. "Anneliese, I can't give you your doll house, but I will give you this chair."

I looked at her, dazed. In her hand laid a chair from the kitchen of my doll house. She took my hand and placed the tiny chair in my palm. I couldn't find the words that could express how I felt. Here was my dear aunt who had lost her home. Of all the small treasures that she could or should have taken - she thought of me and gave me a treasure from my childhood days. I hugged her and we wept.

"Danke schoen," I whispered, *"Ich werde nie vergessen was du heute fuer mich getan hast."* (I won't ever forget what you did for me today.)

Cousin Joey and Herbert looked on in silence. We sat, each locked in our own thoughts and feelings until we had gathered enough strength to finish our trek home. Mama had joined Uncle Pepp at the bakery, and they were anxiously waiting for us. When we finally arrived, Uncle Pepp asked,

"What took you so long?"

Before we could answer, Mama interjected, "Pepp wasn't worried, not at all. He just went to Father Neidl and paid for five masses to be read so you would safely return."

"Well," Uncle Pepp admonished, "we surely can't forget to give thanks to God. It was He who watched over you."

Anneliese, Mama said, I will take you home. She had barely closed our garden gate, when I showed her my doll house chair and declared,"No matter where I live, my little chair will always be with me."

"Aunt Lisbeth's devotion should remind you," Mama said, "that despite all the evil and cruelty in the world, we have people like Lisbeth who keep their faith." It was a profound and life affirming insight I'd never forget.

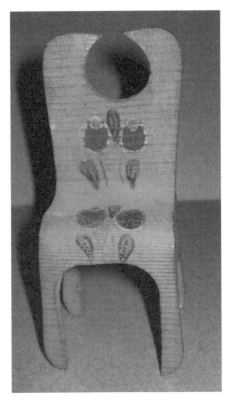

Doll House Chair

CHAPTER 5

Uncontrollable Fear

Two weeks later, there were rumors that the Czechs would soon close the border for good. Aunt Lisbeth wanted to go once more. She was sure we would be safe. Uncle Pepp agreed and he determined that the same crew should go again. I started out with Aunt Lisbeth, Cousin Joey, and Herbert. As we went through the woods and neared the line, I became more apprehensive than ever. I just felt we wouldn't make it this time. All the recent images of horror I had seen revolved in my mind. Even the wheels of the wagon seemed to chant a warning, "You won't make it today! You won't make it today!"

We could see the border and the open field lay straight ahead. No one would stop once we reached the open fields.

"Aunt Lisbeth," I whispered, "before we cross, I'll have to relieve myself over there in these bushes. I will catch up to you."

I left them and disappeared behind a large clump of bushes where I waited until I knew they were in the open field. I started to follow them, but uncontrollable fear overtook me, and I couldn't go on and cross over to the safety of the wagon. I stood still and watched as Aunt Lisbeth and the wagon disappeared into the outskirts of Cheb.

Now I knew I would never cross because I felt the Czechs waiting for me with their clubs raised and their fist coming toward my face. I felt so weak while accusatory thoughts raced through my mind. What a coward I was! I could never measure up to the goodness of my aunt. Never! I was more scared than I had ever been before, and I felt rotten as thoughts of doom plagued my mind. What will I do if they don't make it back? How can I explain that I am here, and they are in Czechoslovakia? I walked back and forth until I noted the path my walking had made. I found a large tree and I hid from view. Silently, I prayed and asked God to keep their guardian angels near them and protect them from harm.

I had waited in the woods for several hours, and I began to despair and fear for their safe return when far in the distance I saw a small, black speck. It came closer! It was a wagon loaded with boxes, clothes and utensils. I saw that Aunt Lisbeth was pulling hard in front, and Cousin Joey and Herbert were hidden from view pushing as hard as they could. Relief swept through me, and I crossed the border without a thought and took my place next to Aunt Lisbeth and pulled hard. When we were across, we sat down on a patch of grass.

"Anneliese, where have you been?" Cousin Joey reproached, "We needed you, but you just never showed. How could you do that?"

Instantly, Aunt Lisbeth admonished, "Joey, Herbert, you will not say a word to Anneliese or anyone about her staying behind. She just got scared and she found that she couldn't cross alone. I thought we did wrong when we didn't wait for her. I bet neither one of us would cross the border onto the open field alone. Remember, when we cross, we draw strength from each other. Joey, Herbert, tell me would you cross alone? Show me right now that you can." Neither Cousin Joey nor Herbert moved. "Well, we have our answer. Not even the two of you would try it. So let's keep what happened here today between us. Now we will rest for a few minutes, and then we will go home. I will not come back to Cheb or my home, not ever again. I can't take it anymore."

Then, realizing the finality of it all, Aunt Lisbeth covered her face with her hands while she rocked back and forth and wailed. We huddled around her, wishing we could take her pain, but we remained silent since there were no words to make what happened to her all right. We waited until she could cry no more, and we helped her up. Resolutely she took the front handle of the wagon, and somberly we walked on until we were home.

Mama and Uncle Pepp were both moved and relieved that Aunt Lisbeth was trying to free herself from the home that had held her life experiences.

Uncle Pepp took her in his arms while she wept. "Lisbeth," he said, "we'll get you through this. This damn war has brought nothing but death, hate, and misery. We are alive and you are safe. That's the only good thing."

I stood there ashamed. I knew that I would have to live with knowing that I failed Aunt Lisbeth, and I could not measure up to her bravery and goodness. I knew intuitively Cousin Joey and Herbert would not tell that I stayed behind at the border. I thought of Grandma, who had once told me, "Anneliese, don't ever think you get away with things you shouldn't do. You may think you got away without punishment, but you will learn it isn't so. The deed will mark your soul and you will carry the guilt with you as long as you live."

Years would pass before Aunt Lisbeth would be able to live in her own home. Uncle Pepp traded on the black market so they could furnish the rooms in her new home. Time passed slowly, Aunt Lisbeth's husband, Uncle Anton, was a prisoner of war until 1951. After he came home, he lived in a world of his own, and he blamed everyone for not salvaging his home in the Sudetenland. Aunt Lisbeth died on October 28, 1978. Uncle Anton and Reserl died several years later.

Aunt Lisbeth

CHAPTER 6

1947 - Leaving Germany

During 1946 into 1947, numerous documents requested by the American immigration office seemed to lead nowhere. Finally, during March 1947, the exit permit, which was the final document, was in my possession. My departure day was scheduled for April 6th, 1947, the Monday after Easter. The eighteen months of working and waiting were over, and I could leave from the Frankfurt Airport. Cousin Erna who had come with me to Frankfurt had left and after a short wait at the airport, I boarded the plane. Within minutes, the plane climbed to heights unknown to me. The sudden change from the destruction of the land below to the sky's peaceful immensity made me feel like a tiny speck in the universe. White puffy clouds floated silently below while others reached up to another heaven. I wondered if in His magnificent creations God was looking down in disapproval at the humankind who mutilated, killed and destroyed the earth. The stewardesses interrupted the flow of my thinking while they served delicacies I hadn't seen or tasted in years. A full stomach and the steady humming of the propellers lulled me into a deep sleep. Hours later a passenger shook me gently.

"Newfoundland," he gestured downward.

I understood that we were landing because I had studied the flight route that would bring me to America. After refueling, the passenger next to me tried to draw me into a conversation, but after several fruitless attempts we fell silent. Again, I was reminded of my inability to function on my own. Unashamedly, I let the tears flow. I reached for a handkerchief, and I felt the small package Cousin Erna had given me while we said good-bye. I feverishly tore the paper, opened the box, and her golden necklace with a heart shaped pendant lay in my hand. The pendant opened easily, and Cousin Erna's likeness smiled at me. I missed her and my family already. Longing for home, the change of hours, the hum of the propellers made me doze.

The stewardess who took care of me throughout the flight touched my shoulder and pointed at the window. "America," she said, "Welcome to America."

She stayed by my side while the shoreline of New York skyscrapers, and endless rows of homes kept me spellbound. Out of habit I searched for bombed-out city sections until I recalled that I had come to a land where there was peace. The stewardess collected my luggage, smiled and motioned for me to stay back until the last passenger had departed. Then she motioned, "Come."

With my first step onto American soil, I looked for Kenny in a boisterous group waving and shouting at us. But Kenny was not among them. The stewardess reassuringly stroked my arm. "You, okay?"

I nodded and she led me into a huge hall where uniformed officials checked suitcases and stamped papers. Uncertainty gripped me full force as the official took my bags from the stewardess who smiled, waved, and left. While one officer inspected my bags, another scrutinized my exit permit and entrance documents. He seemed satisfied as he shoved several forms toward me.

"Sign." he ordered and waited.

I couldn't read the documents, so I looked around for help, but the officer became impatient, "Sign," he repeated more forcefully. Reluctantly, I signed.

He looked at my signature and exclaimed, "NO, no, no! In America you are not Anneliese."

He reached for a blank paper. He was deep in thought while he paused and finally he printed with great flourish A N N E L E E. His voice rose as he slowly sounded out each letter "A N N E L E E."

Was he talking about my name? My heart pounded and with all the courage I could muster, I protested, "NO, no, Anneliese."

The official sighed, and his manner became conciliatory. He walked around his desk, pointed his index finger at me, and said slowly, "No!

You America - nix Anneliese." His long index finger almost touched my nose, "You, Annelee, understand?"

Did I understand? Not knowing what to do, I again looked at the officials nearby who somberly watched our exchange but remained silent. I shivered as I took the pen and signed. Tears trickled down my checks. With a few strokes, here, in America, Anneliese was no more. My given German name had disappeared, and my American name had come into existence. I silently wondered, was this the only change I would encounter?

Before I could reflect more deeply on what just happened, a German speaking custom official approached me, "Fraulein, your fiancé Kenneth Woodstrom is waiting impatiently behind this door. All we need from you now is the fifty dollar immigration entry fee."

Finally, something would go my way. I handed the official my U.S. Money Exchange Form. "Another counterfeit!" he exclaimed. "Where did you get this?"

I told him about my encounter with the American military police officer at the Frankfurt Airport. My three hundred marks were in Frankfurt, and I was here with the form. Several officers conferred briefly, and they paged Kenny. I waited anxiously until finally Kenny rushed toward me.

"My Anneliese, Anneliese, you are finally here!"

I threw myself into his wide open arms, and we hugged and kissed and clung to each other. As he released me, he urged, "Come, we leave."

"No, Kenny," I said and pointed at my counterfeit form. "No dollars!"

The German speaking customs officer who stood near me lost his authoritative composure, and Kenny later often recalled with glee what he had said, "Here is your bride. She is a foreigner, but like women anywhere, she too needs your money."

Kenny was displeased with the official's explanation of why I was penniless but he paid the fee. What are you doing? I wanted to ask the official as he held me back and addressed Kenny, "Mr. Woodstrom, you must return to the waiting room until we have processed all the necessary forms. It will take a while longer because we don't process an enemy alien everyday, you know."

The big iron gate clanged shut behind Kenny and I felt afraid and frustrated. Why had they taken Kenny away from me? With an infuriating, casual demeanor, the official glanced at me while he stamped page after page of official documents. At last, he handed me a sheet.

"Sign American name here," he instructed. "Annelee, okay?"

I couldn't read nor understand what I had just signed. I just wanted to get away and be with Kenny.

The gate that had separated us opened. I grabbed my bags and stepped into the outside world where Kenny was waiting. The tension of the past days and hours drained away, oblivious of my surroundings, I flung myself into his open arms and sobbed, "Kenny! Kenny!"

I felt weak, yet safe and happy as I pressed my head against his chest until my sobs subsided.

Kenny enveloped me in his arms. "Anneliese, my Anneliese," he whispered. He looked at me. He caressed my face and kissed my tear-streaked checks and asked, "Mama, okay?"

"Good." I replied.

"Taxi? Taxi, mister?" The strange abrupt voice of a taxi driver invaded our world. "Downtown, mister?"

Without waiting, the cab driver jumped out of his cab, opened the trunk, placed my wicker suitcase in its cavity and shut the trunk with a thump. He stepped up, opened the back door, and, with a flowing motion of his free arm, helped me into the back seat. All the while he chewed on a soggy stub of a cigar and talked in rapid-fire staccato to Kenny without missing a beat.

He moved his vehicle through a network of streets. I felt overwhelmed by the constant changes. As New York's skyscrapers dwarfed us, I wondered if the occupants of the top floors of these towers had the clouds for neighbors. At times the panorama of the buildings seemed almost close enough to touch, yet seconds later a kaleidoscopic view passed by. Kenny had sat silently beside me as he watched my reactions to what I saw. Everything here was untouched by war. People entered or left buildings while a stream of cars and trucks moved smoothly in their lanes. There were no beggars or homeless people. The area was not patrolled by police, and no one asked for our ID's. Kenny reached for my hands and cupped them over a small, velveteen box.

"Anneliese," he said and motioned, "open."

I opened the box slowly. Kenny took the gold band set off by a small, sparkling diamond, knelt on the floor of the cab and took my hand in his.

"Anneliese, I love you." He asked in half English-German, "you my Frau?"

I reached for him. *"Ja, ja, Kenny, ich werde deine Frau."*(Yes, yes, Kenny, I will become your wife.)

He placed the ring on my finger, kissed me gently and promised. "We okay."

The driver meanwhile had whipped into the driveway of a hotel and came to a smooth stop. The stop and go traffic and the foreign sounding voices of well-dressed people overwhelmed me. I realized Kenny was the only person I knew in America and I would have to depend on him for everything. My heart pounded as the elevator took us to Kenny's room, and I thought this is the first time I am alone with Kenny, the civilian who looks so sharp and handsome in his gray, pin-striped suit. What will happen now? Will he hold me and kiss me, will he take me to bed, or will he wait until we are married as I had promised Mama?

Kenny closed the door softly. He took me in his arms and kissed me, longingly. Yet, he pushed me gently away, folded the coverlet of the bed back, and motioned for me to lie down and rest. Tiredness overtook me. Feeling secure, I slept soundly until Kenny awoke me.

"Come," he said, and on his tablet he wrote. "Hunger?"

He knows a German word, I thought and I nodded.

The hotel dining room and the meal were a new experience for me. Kenny selected the food, a chicken dinner, hard rolls, coffee and dessert. I couldn't eat all that was before me since my stomach tolerated only small amounts of food. While the waiter carried leftover food away, I thought of Mama. She could have fed our family for days with all the uneaten food that was removed from the tables around us.

Later we boarded a train to Washington, D.C. and as I searched my dictionary and translated the words Kenny had written on a tablet, I learned that his parents were waiting for us in Washington, D.C. Apprehension gripped me. So far I had survived the flight and the immigration officials, now a life-changing event awaited me. What if Kenny's parents don't like me? If only Mama, Uncle Pepp, or Cousin Erna were here with me, but I knew I would have to face them with Kenny at my side.

My fears were quickly eliminated when Kenny's parents, who were waiting at a bed and breakfast home, hugged me and said, "Welcome, Anneliese!"

They took us to their suite and eagerly questioned Kenny while I sat listening without understanding. The clock showed after midnight, but in Germany it was 7:15 a.m. My whole body ached. Frequently I jerked fighting sleep. Kenny's mother came to my side and led me to a bedroom. I felt lonesome and I could not stop the tears that I had held back for so long. Kenny's mother rubbed my back and I fell asleep.

The next morning, April 8, Kenny woke me. He carried a tray laden with eggs, bacon, hard rolls, butter, honey, coffee, cream and sugar, which momentarily reminded me of our meager breakfast at home. A slice of bread and a semblance of coffee or tea was all we could have because we saved our weekly two cups of skim milk rations for Baby Werner. Kenny, dressed in his gray suit, a white shirt and a blue tie wrote on his tablet, car, Washington, Congressman Hagen.

I met the Honorable Congressman Harold Hagen and members of his staff who had worked so tirelessly to secure my arrival. I learned that they had even set our wedding date. The ceremony was arranged for 5:00 p.m. on April 8, 1947. Since Congressman Hagen did not know who should perform the ceremony, he had engaged a Lutheran minister, a Catholic priest, and a Justice of the peace to stand by. Congressman Hagen's secretary, Fay Child and an interpreter drove us to the Arlington courthouse to secure our marriage license.

Before we entered the courthouse, he cautioned, "Kenny, since Anneliese is an enemy alien, it could take hours before all the documents are ready for signatures."

The courthouse office was old and small. On one side of the wall was a long, wooden bench where I sat and waited while the men filled out forms. The clerk climbed a ladder, reached for a book and read specific passages while Kenny and Fay Child listened. The men approached me, and the clerk pointed at the discrepancies of my name.

"Exit permit, Anneliese Solch?" the clerk questioned. "Entry form, Annelee Solch?"

I confidently explained to the interpreter, "Anneliese in Germany, okay. But in America, the immigration officer had said that I must sign Annelee, always. "

The men conferred, and they were satisfied with my explanation of how Annelee came into existence. The clerk showed me the official German document in which Mama had given me permission to come to America and marry Kenny.

"You are not twenty-one until September," the translator went on as the clerk pointed at the blank line below Mama's signature. "You have no death certificate for your papa. His signature must be right here. It is the law!"

Kenny explained that Papa was a prisoner of war in Russia, and we had not heard about his whereabouts since 1945. The clerk motioned for the men to follow him. Fay Child talked on the phone while Kenny and the clerk looked through books and at times shouted phrases that Fay Child repeated to someone on the line. Kenny came up to me, "Come", he motioned.

"Back to Washington," the translator explained, "Congressman Hagen will make it right. He is working on a rider so either parent's signature would be legal if one of the parents was probably alive but not able to sign."

Late into the evening all documents were in order. Since the priest, the Lutheran minister and the Justice of the peace had left for other appointments, Congressman Hagen found a Presbyterian minister who lived in Arlington Virginia, and we were married at 10:00 p.m. The happiness I should have felt was lacking because the minister spoke English, and the words that I repeated had no meaning for me. After an eighteen month struggle to gain permission to marry, the ceremony lasted barely fifteen minutes, and Kenny and I were husband and wife. The wedding had not been what I had dreamt of during my teen-age years. I always envisioned a big wedding with all the dress and pomp customary in the Solch clan. I envisioned Uncle Pepp's black carriage pulled by two *Schimmel* (white horses). My fiancé and I would throw out nickels and dimes to the children who ran along the carriage wishing us a long, happy life. The flower girls and family would meet us before we entered the courthouse for the civil ceremony. Then we would walk across to the Catholic Church where Father Neidl would unite me in marriage to the man I loved and vowed to honor and obey while my family, relatives, acquaintances and townspeople looked on. After dinner, the invited guests would enjoy coffee, pastries, cakes and tortes from Uncle Pepp's bakery. After a cold plate supper, we would have danced until way after midnight.

The war had changed all that. In a fifteen minute ceremony that had been arranged in great haste with Kenny's parents and Mr. Child as witnesses, Kenny and I realized our dream and became husband and wife. We returned briefly to Mr. Child's home where all the office workers had been waiting to congratulate us and also celebrate their own achievement. Tomorrow Kenny's and my files could be marked closed.

It was after midnight when we finally were alone in our own room. Kenny realized that I was physically and emotionally exhausted. All that had transpired made me weepy. My husband held me gently, and we consummated our marriage before we fell into a deep sleep in each other's arms.

CHAPTER 7

1947 – Crookston, Minnesota

It was the morning after our wedding night and right after breakfast we were to leave Washington. I felt apprehensive as Kenny started our 1936 Ford. He had shown me a map pointing at a city.

"Rochelle, Illinois." He tried to explain, "Sister Helen, two days."

Now I would meet Helen who had written to me in Germany where I had translated her letters as well as I could. Kenny kept his eyes on the road and often reached for my hand, and I eagerly clasped onto his while our backseat passengers, his parents, talked quietly. One thing hadn't changed as yet. Whether I was in Germany or America when I was with Kenny, I always had a mother near me.

After Kenny had driven for quite some time, I wondered when we would approach an exit to the Autobahn. In Germany, Adolf Hitler's Autobahn had employed thousands of long-term, unemployed workers and at the same time he had increased his power a hundred fold. Throughout Germany, the Autobahn was started in 1934, and it consisted of beautiful, divided four-lane roads that skirted villages, cities and metropolitan areas.

I pointed at the two-way roadway, "Autobahn?" Kenny shook his head, "America no Autobahn."

Unlike our Autobahn, the two-way roadway had stop signs at every crosswalk. In cities and in small farm communities, speed depended on the farm machinery or the livestock crossing the road. Stop, wait, go - stop. Driving on hilly roads demanded skill from the driver and patience from the passengers. The double yellow markings on the lanes and the No Passing signs would often be numerous and they caused frayed nerves when traffic came to an undesignated stop. The road demanded Kenny's attention, so I counted the different traffic signs and watched the landscapes. I thought, *Hier in America ist alles so gross.* (Here, in America, everything is so large.) The expanse of the landscape was the same for hours since in America a state was often larger than a European country. Whenever we stopped for food, I did what I could not have imagined two weeks ago. I hoped for small food portions because my stomach felt frequently queasy when I ate more than what I had been used to for the past five years.

The jukebox at the restaurant was a new experience for me. Each table held a miniature box that displayed the top ten songs, and there was no shortage of customers spending dimes while listening to their favorite tunes. Families or friends dined together, but it was not frowned upon if a lone person took a table or booth and receded from view behind a newspaper. Clothing and physical shapes of the guests varied throughout the restaurant. Across from us were several men who talked across tables. They were young and slim and wore shirts or jackets with red inscriptions on the sleeves or across the back. Other men were in work clothes, mainly blue cotton shirts and pants. Men dressed in suits accented by white shirts and a primary color tie that blended well and gave a professional appearance. The women wore skirts and color contrasting blouses, or they wore dresses that tightly hugged the bodice. Warm coats and hats could be seen here and there. I wondered if anyone suspected that my tailored black coat was made from Kenny's army blanket, which Mama had dyed over and over in hot water that the neighbors had donated. Our tailor changed the blanket into a princess-style coat. We laid an old bed sheet on the grass, waited for rain and hoped that the sun would bleach the cotton while it dried. Then Theresa cut the good pieces of the bed sheet and sewed the stylish blouse I wore. Kenny had bought me a new coat in New York, but when things were not familiar to me, I felt more comfortable in something from home.

Late afternoon as the blue sky changed slowly to twilight, Kenny's parents watched for a restaurant near a motel. Spying one we finally pulled into a motel, left the car, and the men brought the suitcases to our rooms. After supper we walked through the town's park where children were batting at a small ball and ran.

"Baseball," Dad explained.

"*Max spielt Fussball gut,*" (Max is a good soccer player), I said. I hoped Dad understood what I said. He nodded, "Yes, yes."

As we retired for the night, Kenny's mother hugged me and it was easier than I had thought. As they turned to leave, I said, "Good night, Ma. Good night, Dad."

Exhaustion overtook me as soon as we entered our room. Kenny understood and he looked at his watch.

"8:00 p.m. in America. Mitterteich 3:00 a.m. Mama, Theresa, Max," Kenny pantomimed, "all sleep."

All day long I had fought the longing to talk with someone who understood what I said, so I could share all I had seen. Now I longed for home and my daily, familiar routine where my family depended on me. My heart pounded, I felt unsettled, and homesickness overtook me.

Kenny shook his head, "Me, dummkopf," he sighed.

I managed a smile, "Ja, ja."

He held me gently, he kissed me, we made love and I fell asleep in his arms. The next morning, another day of travel began. Paging through my German-English dictionary I tried to converse with Kenny and his parents, but when a simple phrase or sentence was not fully understood, we found silence was a better travel companion. The landscape's emerging spring colors were vibrant and I wished that I had more knowledge about the topography and history of the states we had traveled through. However, each state and each town with its brick and wooden houses remained just a part of the many miles we covered.

It was twilight when we arrived in Rochelle. Helen came running from the wooden home, holding onto five-year-old Gary's hand, while her husband Ray carried two-year-old Denny. They greeted us and ushered us inside where Helen's father-in-law was waiting. He greeted me in German, and he told me that the families were happy because Kenny could finally bring his German girl home. It was good to hear words I could understand, and little Denny reached out to me and told me in a deep voice, "Denny Schabacker." I loved little Denny instantly because whenever I hugged him, I felt the hug was also for Baby Werner who was so far away.

It was at Helen's home where I realized Kenny's and Helen's family were devout Lutherans. They prayed before each meal and everyone attended the Sunday morning service. The Lutheran liturgy was quite different, and during the service I began to miss the familiar Catholic Latin hymns and prayers of my faith. I thought of Mama and how she had tried to make me think.

"Anneliese, how will you resolve your religious differences? You are so confident, but believe me, it would not be the first time religious differences mushroomed into problems that ended an otherwise good marriage."

Before we left for church, Helen placed meat and potatoes in her gas oven. As we arrived home, dinner had cooked to perfection! Everything was so different from the Sunday dinner preparations at home. On Sunday, Mama and most housewives attended the 7:00 a.m. service. Papa went to High Mass at 9:00 a.m. Theresa and I attended the 11:00 a.m. children's service. During peace time, while we were at church, Mama worked hard and prepared Papa's favorite meal, potato dumplings, filled rouladen, and a cucumber, spinach or a green bean salad. During the war, it was uncertain and extremely difficult to know what a Sunday dinner would be. We stood in line for hours for grocery items and, all too often, meal preparation depended on the availability of our meager rations.

After Helen had served dinner, the men sat around the table and played cards while the women did the dishes, filled coffee pots and prepared food trays. Before I could guess how the women would spend the afternoon, friends of the family stopped by. I was introduced and within minutes another table and chairs were brought in. The women joined the men and partners were chosen. My father-in-law made it clear that I would be his partner and he would check my card playing skills.

I couldn't believe it! How could women, especially married women with small children, play cards on Sunday? I had been brought up to understand that women played chess and games like old maid and black cat with their children-but never on Sunday. Decent women knew their place at home, and only bar maids played cards whenever men wanted their company. I tried to imagine Mama's and Uncle Pepp's reaction if they saw me holding all these cards. We played a game called whist, and another was called five hundred. During the short supper break, eating took place in such a hurry. Dishes clanged and while they were stacked, new partners were chosen, and immediately a new game called canasta had everyone's attention.   Now it was past midnight, and I still didn't know one rule from another, but with Dad's expertise we had won several games. I thought that God must forgive them for playing cards on Sunday because the laughter during the games was surely good for the soul. Ever since I came to America, my bones ached from tiredness and I wanted sleep. It was 7:30 a.m. in Germany when the games were finally over. After their friends left, Dad, Helen and Kenny still replayed several moves they thought could have been better.

We left Helen's home early Monday morning. Kenny showed me the map and circled Crookston. As we left the industrial areas and bare fields of Illinois behind us, a beautiful, scenic vista came into view. Throughout Wisconsin and on to Minnesota, the river banks of the mighty Mississippi hugged the highway closely. It took miles and an everlasting search in my dictionary before I could comprehend what Kenny tried to tell me.

"Anneliese, Mississippi starts in Minnesota, Itasca State Park, so small," he said, gesturing to make a point.

During the evening hours we crossed from St. Paul into the sister city, Minneapolis. "St. Paul, capital of Minnesota."

I held a flashlight and searched in my dictionary said, *"Oh, St. Paul Hauptstadt, (capital) of Minnesota."*

Kenny nodded, "Okay."

To assure good travel time, we stopped for food only when the car needed refueling, and now we were closing in on our final destination. A beautiful spring day had lost its vibrant colors as night hid the rolling countryside.

Ken's parents and I had been sleeping when Kenny announced joyfully, "Crookston!"

We drove into the city for several blocks before Kenny stopped and said, "Home, Anneliese."

It was after midnight, and the street lights illuminated the silhouette of a white, wooden house with its yard sloping unto the sidewalk Groggily, I walked up several steps, and we by-passed the front porch. Four large pillars supported a slanted roof in a quaint American style and gave protection from the elements of nature to anyone who entered.

Last night, Kenny had said, "Anneliese, Crookston, we live upstairs. Okay?"

I was too tired to fetch the dictionary, so I said, "Okay."

I had no idea where upstairs or downstairs was. It could have been next door or miles away. Now I would learn where upstairs was and where we would live. A curved cement pathway led to a side door. Dad turned and made a cross on my forehead, said a short prayer and bid me to enter. With Kenny at my side, we stepped into a narrow, cozy kitchen that was enlarged by a small pantry

We lived upstairs.

to the right. On the kitchen wall next to the pantry were white, metal kitchen cupboards with a built-in sink, and an open doorway led to a large dining room. Ma motioned for me to choose a place by the round dining room table that was set for four. She uncovered a food tray filled with sandwiches and cookies and poured tea from a thermos.

While I wondered who brought the food, Kenny said, "Agnes, sister."

Dad sorted through the mail like he was looking for something. Suddenly, he pointed at a newspaper article and exclaimed, "Here!"

Kenny assumed that Congressman Hagen's office released the information.

Crookston GI; German Bride
Overcome Red Tape to Wed

WASHINGTON (AP) Kenneth Woodstrom and his German bride, the former Anneliese Solch of Mitterteich, Germany, head for Crookston, Minn., today with a joint hope – no more red tape.

It took more than a year of correspondence, telephoning

and cabling among Woodstrom, Rep. Hagen (R-MN), the state department and the American consul in Germany before Miss Solch got her visa to come to the United States. Woodstrom, a former corporal, was with one of the first units to hit the Normandy beach on D-Day. He met his future wife when the fighting was over.

"BEING ANNOYED"

He was then with the occupational forces and she was bringing in food to German prisoners of war. Later, he went to her aid when she was "being annoyed" by some soldiers. From then on, he saw her often.

When he left for home, he said he would send for her right away and they would be married as soon as she arrived. He sent for her – but she didn't come. There were some papers to be cleared first.

"OFFICIAL CLEARANCE"

Running into a stone wall, Woodstrom contacted Rep. Hagen and later came to Washington in an attempt to get an official clearance from the State Department. The months went by and various papers went back and forth across the Atlantic – but always something else was needed. The State Department finally gave its approval for a visa, but an exit permit had to be obtained. That took two months more.

At last, however, all regulations were complied with, and she left by air from Frankfurt, Germany for the United States. Woodstrom met her in New York Sunday when the plane landed. He took her to dinner, of which she later said:

"When I sat down to that first dinner in New York, I saw more food in front of me that I would have for a week in Germany. I couldn't eat it all."

Later, they came to Washington and decided to be married in nearby Arlington, VA., but there was more red tape. She was only 20 years old and Virginia law says a girl under 21 must have her father's consent, if he is living, before a marriage license can be issued.

She explained that her father was a German soldier who had been captured by the Russians, but she didn't know if he was alive or dead.

"BIG MOMENT"

Hagen's secretary, Fay Child, rushed back to the office to get the visa and other papers that indicated the mother's consent for the marriage. That did the trick and an hour later they were married in a Presbyterian parsonage. Present were Woodstrom's parents, Mr. and Mrs. Andrew Woodstrom, who had driven from Crookston.

The bride is frankly awed by the American way of life. "I am going to write the folks in Germany about the wonderful things in America, but I know they won't believe it," she said. "It's just like a fairyland here."

Kenny showed me the article, but pointed at several phrases in the article, shook his head and said, "No, no."

I didn't understand. If I wanted to know what this article said, I would have to learn what each word meant. It was way after midnight, and I knew that reading the English language would be easier than trying to speak it. After reading a word, I always failed miserably whenever I tried to pronounce it.

Kenny's mom stood up and said. "Sleep well."

We bade each other, "Good Night."

Kenny put his arm around my shoulders, said "Now upstairs," and led me through the kitchen and up the steep, narrow stairway. There, to the left was the kitchen. It had slanted attic walls, a long, narrow, one pane window, and next to the window stood two white metal cabinets stacked on top of each other. A table with curved chrome legs and two chairs were pushed against the wall. I thought of our kitchen in Germany where two large French windows and a huge lamp brightened the kitchen day or night. We took our meals around a large table with its six matching chairs. The china cabinet with colored glass insets held the dishes, and all the cleaning utensils were hidden in a large cupboard near the sink. The stove and a side cupboard for pots and pans were adjacent to the sink. The inside wall held a sofa, a small round table loaded with books and the local newspaper while the easy chair nearby was Papa's favorite for relaxation.

Kenny pointed at the living room, bare and unfurnished. A few steps across the narrow hallway led to the bedroom at the right. It was furnished with a double bed and a dresser that was built to fit under the slanted attic wall. One could not stand up where the outside walls and ceiling met.

I realized that in Germany our foyer and kitchen were bigger than this upstairs apartment. The sparse, small living area shocked me and made me feel uneasy. I wondered how long would we live here? While Kenny had been at our home, I had never once given a thought to where we would live in America.

I watched as Kenny made room for my luggage. He was so at home. I tried to feel relieved that we had our own apartment but the bareness and strangeness of everything oppressed me. I knew it would be a long time before I would send photos to Mama and Uncle Pepp.

Uncle Pepp would certainly shake his head and mutter, "For this she left Germany? She could have done better with any Bavarian man."

Shame overtook my thoughts. I loved Kenny and I vowed we would work toward a good life. Whenever all the changes that had taken place overwhelmed me, homesickness surfaced, and I felt isolated and alone. Periodically drowning in uncertainty and fear, I held on to Kenny and I hoped and prayed that we would survive together.

As always, Kenny understood and he tried to cajole, "Anneliese, it will be better soon."

CHAPTER 8

Facing New Challenges

The next morning several decisions had already been made by Kenny and his parents. To avoid confusion, they would call me by my American name, 'Annelee.' Now I knew that I had left my family, my given name and my past in Germany. From now on Annelee would live in America, and Anneliese would exist with Mama in Germany.

Kenny and I eventually would purchase new furniture for our apartment. For now it was important that Kenny, who was an expert mechanic, would return to his repair shop immediately. Spring in the Red River Valley kept farm-related business places on call day and night. The farmers needed their machinery running so they could seed their fertile land. I was frequently alone, and since I was unfamiliar with the American way of life, my in-laws suggested that Kenny and I should join them for meals.

I met Kenny's sisters. Agnes was married to Reverend Fellger who was the minister of the church Kenny's family attended. Irene lived in Grand Forks where her husband Hans attended the university. Their little girl, Kathy would hold up three fingers so I could understand her age. As soon as it became known that we were with Kenny's parents, relatives, friends and acquaintances came to meet me. I struggled for days before I finally accepted the fact that it would take time before I would remember new faces and associate them with names that were foreign to me. The language barrier became more evident with each day. I began to understand what Mama had tried to tell me all along, "Anneliese, you don't speak English. How will you communicate?"

Oh, how wise I was then. I always responded, "Mama, Kenny and I will manage."

Right now, when it came to communicating, I was reduced to the level of a two-year-old. The little ones who would come over with their parents could converse better than I. They looked at me in puzzlement, and they would try to help me with phrases of their own when I could not respond to their mother's questions. To offset my inability of conversing with visitors, I wrote to Mama and my family almost daily. There was so much to share:

Dear Mama, Theresa, Max and Irmgard. A hug for Werner,

I hope everyone is well and survival is getting easier with each day. I wish you could be here with me! Mama, it is true: in America there seems to be no need to wait in line for anything, and no one is hungry here, ever. My mother-in-law doesn't go out and buy groceries because the grocer brings them right to her home. Every morning the milk man delivers his products. He drives up in a white vehicle that probably holds a hundred milk and small cream bottles. Ma puts her empty bottles and money out on the porch. She leaves an order for what she needs. The milk man fills her order and drives on.

Mama, there is one thing I can hardly believe. Most of the houses here are built of wood throughout. Every room is always heated and I am never cold. The inside walls are wooden, and the walls are decorated with beautifully designed wallpaper. It looks nice, but how long will that paper last? The roofs of their homes are not slate; they are covered with asbestos tile. How will these roofs hold the snow? If an enemy should ever bomb here, there would be no need to go to the basement for shelter because these houses would fall and burn like cinder boxes.

Kenny and I live upstairs. We have a kitchen, living room, and a bedroom. The bathroom is used by the whole family.

I try to learn English, but it is hard without a teacher and just the dictionary and newspapers as my guide. When I listen to the people, at first they speak slowly but loud, and then suddenly they talk so fast that I am still six words behind and lost. I think most of the time it would be safe to just say, "Yes, yes," but I am not sure. I feel so dumb so often.

Have you heard anything of Papa's whereabouts? I think of him every day and worry.

I love and miss all of you always, your Anneliese

My lack of understanding of the easiest phrases caused daily confusion. One afternoon Ma came upstairs with a beautifully wrapped, belated wedding gift. I wanted to wait for Kenny so we could open it together, but she motioned that I should open it now. I eagerly removed the wrappings and looked bewildered at the beautiful walnut chest that contained a silver plated dinner service for eight.

She said, "From us."

"Thank you, thank you," I said, while I thought, *Wer ist uns? Wo habe ich diese Leute kennengelenrnt? (*Who are us? Where did I meet these people?)

After Kenny came home, I showed him the gift and he asked, "Another wedding gift?"

"Yes, yes," I pointed at the walnut chest, "from us."

Kenny took my hands, shook his head, and searched for words.

"No, Annelee," he pointed toward me, "you" and then he pointed toward himself "I", he struggled and he held me close and said again, "Annelee, Kenny, we are us!"

I understood. But I still wondered who gave us that beautiful gift? Kenny found the card that had fallen under the table while I had eagerly opened the gift. The card contained a verse and was signed, Love, Ma and Dad.

Whenever I thought my English had improved, an unexpected incident would shake my confidence. One day, I was home alone resting on the sofa downstairs when suddenly, a tall man stood before me. I was frightened because he emphasized the same phrase over and over while he motioned toward the basement. Finally, he shrugged and left. But within minutes he returned with Ma whom he had met outside. She introduced the stranger, and he gently shook my hand. "Come," he said.

I meekly followed him to the basement where he showed me what a meter man does. My determination not to embarrass Kenny or his parents ever again had caused me to become overly cautious, I suppose.

Several days after I had met the meter man, Ma attended a funeral service. So I locked every door and window and decided our living room windows needed cleaning. Since I couldn't clean the outside panes from within, I crawled onto the slanted front porch roof, and as I pressed on the window frame, the latch fell, and I suddenly found myself locked out. I tried, but I could not get to the ground from the roof. As the funeral procession approached, I rested my hands in my lap and remained motionless. But when the mourners returned from the interment service, they looked up, waved and smiled.

I imagined their conversations, *"Schau mal, das Deutsche Maedchen sitzt auf dem Dach!"* (Look, the German girl is sitting on the roof.)

By the time Kenny and his dad came, we had the cleanest windows in town, but my self-esteem had evaporated also. Kenny brought a ladder and he helped me down. Since the windows and doors were securely locked from within, Ma and several neighbors watched while Dad and Kenny removed the side door hinges so we could enter the house. At that moment, all I wanted was a bridge across the ocean so I could go home.

Whenever my adjustment progress resulted in anxiety, homesickness and depression, Kenny took me for a drive. He loved Minnesota's Red River Valley, and spring was his favorite season. Kenny tried to familiarize me with the crops that looked like lush, green carpets spread out over endless acres. We stopped at several farm homes, and the owners proudly showed us their farmsteads. Young men who had returned from the war helped their parents on the family farm, while other young men talked about newly acquired land that they were determined to make their own homestead on.

I knew of no one in Germany who could have purchased two-hundred acres of land after World War II. Most farm land and homes were owned by the same family for generations. Grandma's farm land, bakery and home had been in the Solch family for centuries. Papa had inherited some land and in 1934 our home was built. If peacetime were here to stay, our home would stand for centuries more. The basement was poured cement with the outside walls reinforced with granite stones. The whole structure of our home from the first and the second floor to the attic were brick walls, but no one would know that because the outside brick was hidden under stucco that was painted pink. The inside brick walls were covered with plaster. Each room was first painted in a

1945

solid color, and then the painters stepped on big ladders and used rubber rollers inlaid with decorative patterns that brought forth beautiful, different designs that would fit the function of each room. We had a big garden with berry bushes, fruit trees, flowers and vegetables. There was room for us to play, pick berries and weed the vegetables and flowers.

But as the war intensified in 1943, authorities assigned space to bombed-out families, and each home and apartment owner had to share space with people they had never met or seen before. The upstairs of our home was occupied by a family, and they took in their parents and a sister who had lost their homes and possessions during air raids.

Despite these limitations forced upon us by the war, I loved the scenic, familiar views where in the east, west, north or south, century old evergreens surrounded the villages nestled on the hills. Church steeples pointed toward the sky and the red, slated roofs of the farm homes greeted me when I looked out my bedroom windows. While I waited for my passport, I walked miles through the woods on century old paths that connected one village to another. In the winter I skied from the hills onto the meadows and reveled in guiding the ski poles through the blanket of powdery snow. Even when we were hungry or cold, or wondering where Papa was, I found solace in the woods and hills, and I could cope for another day. But so far, the beauty and the productiveness of the unbroken flatness of the Red River Valley heartland that was now my home escaped me. I knew that for Kenny, there was no land, nor state, more beautiful than Minnesota.

Summer vacation in Minnesota was get-together time for the family and friends, so I decided it was time that I would leave Ma's tutelage and start housekeeping. Activities that were simple for everyone else became daily challenges for me. Anything I bought in the grocery store I selected by picture on the package or can, otherwise selecting items led to confusion and frustration. *Mehl* was called flour, *Eier*/eggs, *Schmalz*/ Crisco, *Waschpulver*/ laundry soap. The list was endless. The only meat item at the meat market that had the same name was the *Wieners*, but even then I encountered problems when someone called them hotdogs. *Rindfleisch* was called beef, *Schweinefleisch* was pork, *Huenchen* became chicken,' and *Fleischwurst* became bologna. Without fail, I bought more than we needed. I hoarded food for storage because the war and the lack of food had left their indelible mark. One morning I waited for the milkman. When he handed me a pound of butter, he watched, wide-eyed because tears were streaming down my cheeks while I held my purchase close to me. How could he know that a pound of butter was a miracle for me? Since 1943, our weekly butter rations for each adult had been fifty grams (barely two ounces) and since most other ingredients were lacking also, meal preparation was at a constant, experimental stage.

Here again, in America nothing was the same. Grams became ounces, while liters became quarts and pints. Heating the oven changed from baking at low, medium or high temperatures to degrees. All these unfamiliar changes caused several disastrous meals. Canned goods had not yet been introduced in war torn Germany. Canned soups, vegetables, pork chops or wieners with mashed or fried potatoes were soon meals I could handle.

Just as I thought my adjustment to the American way of life was advancing, even if it were at turtle speed, dreadful stumbling blocks emerged full force. My throat hurt, I was feverish, and my tonsils were infected to the point where I could not swallow anything. But with effort and pain, a few drops of liquid could be swallowed. Kenny rushed me to the local throat specialist who hospitalized me immediately.

My hoarse voice and my severely limited language skills frustrated the doctor, "Kenny," he asked, "what on earth did they do to her tonsils in Germany? Her tonsils are cut in sections like a lemon, and they are shriveled like a dried prune. I will have to remove them as soon as the penicillin treatment takes care of the infection."

Kenny had no idea why my tonsils were in such a mangled shape. He pantomimed, and with the aid of my dictionary, I soon understood what I would have to endure. I had suffered through three tonsil infections in Germany, and the thought of what occurred during such a surgery made me weak and weepy. I felt helpless because I could not tell Kenny or the doctor that I didn't know how I would go through such pain again.

It was during July 1934, I was almost eight years old when the first acute tonsil infection introduced me to tonsil lancing. After all home remedy treatments had failed, Papa had fetched Dr. Durocher, and they entered my bedroom.

"I'm glad you are home, Max. There is only one thing I can do. Anneliese's tonsils are infected throughout. I will have to lance them today before they burst and poison her system," I remember the doctor telling Papa.

I screamed, "No, no, Papa. Please let me gargle, and I will get well on my own."

"Anneliese," Papa said, "it must be done. When it is over, you will get well more quickly."

"Max," the doctor interjected, "I will paint her tonsils with iodine. Then within a few minutes I can lance."

He and Papa placed me onto a kitchen chair, and Mama held my hands to my sides while I wiggled and pushed my feet against Papa and Dr. Durocher. My throat hurt, and my screams were barely a whispered protest. All the while I was no match for the strength of the two men, and they soon had me encased in a huge bed sheet. Papa pushed his bent knee across my legs, and the doctor ordered,

"Anneliese, now open your mouth and sit still. You don't want my knife to slip and make a cut on your cheek or on your face."

His chubby fingers pressed my cheeks while pain exploded in my mouth and it opened. I hurt all over while Papa's hands held me in his vice like grip. My whole body jerked as the doctor made two quick cuts with his sharp knife. Blood and puss spurted into the pan that Mama held to my chin, and she pounded on my shoulder blades with the palm of her free hand. A putrid odor permeated the room. My throat burned and the excruciating pain wedged there made me feel weak. Mama and Papa released me from the bed sheet and placed me in my bed. I wished that I could die right now because then Mama and Papa would feel sorry for what they let happen to me. I didn't care that they stroked my back and spoke words of comfort.

Mama informed me, "It is over. Now clear your throat often so healing can begin."

Uncle Pepp and Cousin Erna came to visit me. Cousin Erna brought me a beautiful diary, and Uncle Pepp gave me a box of chocolate. I suspected he didn't feel sorry for me either because he said,

"I never worried about you at all. I knew all along that weeds don't die. They just wilt for a while and then they come back better than ever."

I again endured the same procedure during 1936 and 1941 so I knew well what was in store for me. It frustrated me that I could not ask questions nor could I explain to Kenny or the doctor why I was apprehensive. I would do anything to avoid a tonsil lancing. Then the time came. I could not believe it. Within the hour the doctor had completed my tonsillectomy. The medicines they gave me had kept me relaxed to the point where I didn't care what was done to me. Now I was sitting up in a hospital bed, and the doctor said that he would release me to Kenny's care within a day and tonsil infections would be history.

CHAPTER 9

Little Sammy

While I recuperated, I sat frequently on the front porch. One afternoon, a little boy came up the steps. I guessed he was about four or five years old. He wore cowboy boots, and his black, curly hair covered part of his forehead. Big, brown eyes held my gaze, and he stood still, his little lips sternly pursed.

He watched me intently as he came closer and said, "I am Sammy. Are you Kenny's German lady?"

I guessed he was talking about Kenny and me so I nodded.

He took a small play pistol from his pants pocket and pointed it at me. "I am Sammy and I am Jew," he stated defiantly. "Do you kill Jews? Bang!"

I didn't understand his words, but I surmised he was talking about shooting someone.

"No, no," I held his hand and pointed his pistol downward. "No, no, Sammy?"

He sighed and stood still holding his toy pistol downward, he looked me over as if he wanted to make up his mind. Was she an enemy or was she okay? Suddenly he waved and left.

His mother who lived near Kenny's garage told Kenny. "Sammy saw your wife today. Would you believe it? He asked her if she killed Jews. He told us that she didn't. Apparently the boy added, 'She didn't even like my pistol. I think she is nice.'"

For the next few days, whenever I sat on the porch my little visitor stopped by and we fell into the same ritual, "Hi, I am Sammy."

"Hi, I am Annelee."

I motioned for him to join me on my cushion. We waited for the mailman, the milkman, and one day I took him upstairs and made cocoa. We sat opposite each other and drank it. After a while, he thanked me and left.

Sammy's visits became one bright spot in my life. His mom told Kenny, "At first, Sammy was just curious about Kenny's lady from Germany, but now he has taken a liking to her and he tells us, 'I am going to see Annelee.'"

His visits were now an almost daily occurrence. Sammy knocked, greeted Ma and then boomed, "Annelee, I am here."

His cowboy boots met each step as he clumped his way upstairs. He came into the living room, plopped himself next to me on the sofa and focused his eyes on my knitting. His little fingers traced the mitten until they reached the white rows of stitches that spelled 'Sammy.'

"Mine," he smiled and he cuddled up to me.

"Yes, yes, for Sammy," I assured him.

We could not converse like we would have liked, but we had a bond between us that had come from nowhere. I needed to knit mittens for Sammy, and he needed to come and visit Kenny's lady.

Sammy now stopped also at Kenny's garage, and his mother said, "Kenny, I guess he wants to gain your good will also. We hear all the time about red mittens that have his name on them so everyone will know they are his mittens. Ever since he visited Annelee at your home, we have a hard time to keep Sammy home."

"The language barrier bothers Annelee," Kenny explained. "She can't converse with adults the way she would like, but she feels comfortable with Sammy so just let him come."

I was also knitting Christmas gifts for my family in Germany, but whenever Sammy came his mittens took on priority.

CHAPTER 10

Same Holidays - Different Customs

Winter came full force, Sammy's frequent absence, and the approaching holidays were chief reasons for my increasing loneliness and homesickness. Even during the war years when we were without sufficient heat and hot water, the Bavarian winters could not compare to the bitter cold temperatures that were taken in stride by every native Minnesotan. I had never even heard of a blizzard, and now I had experienced several winter blizzards with seventy-mile-per-hour winds, or wind chill temperatures fifty to seventy degrees below zero. Snow banks were five to eight feet high. They isolated man from beasts on the farms, and they blocked access to homes, roads and highways.

In Bavaria, we had rain and sometimes even a momentary trace of snow before Christmas, but here it was extremely cold even during November. It was 27 degrees below zero during the week of Thanksgiving. During such nights, when the wind howled and pitched snow against the windows and walls and the house cracked when the outside cold penetrated the heated inside rooms, sleep evaded me. My thoughts crossed deep into Siberia where we assumed Papa was a prisoner of war. The German prisoners of war who had been released told that thousands of their comrades had been forced to work in mines or on road construction. During the days and nights when ice and snow locked everyone inside, the prisoners clad in their tattered uniforms huddled together as the ice coated walls within robbed them of the warmth and protection their makeshift shelters had offered during the summer days. Throughout Russia, thousands of prisoners succumbed during the Siberian winter's fifty below temperatures and hip-deep snow. It was established that of the 147,000 German troops taken as prisoners of war in Stalingrad, less than 10,000 had survived. I lay awake and wondered. Did Papa work outdoors and survive the Siberian ice storms? Did he suffer hunger, harsh treatment? Was he powerless against the merciless forces of man and nature? Then I prayed,

"Please God, if Papa suffers, hear his prayers and shield him from harm or take him to heaven."

I loved Papa and I missed him every day. At times my dreams held me captive in the air raid shelters where the constant drone of the bombers with the deafening sound hitting their mark paralyzed me or made me run for safety. Kenny stopped me from running, held me tight, and stroked my hair until I quit shaking, and I fell into a troubled sleep. Kenny understood because he too was plagued by dreams that returned him momentarily to the hellish eleven months he had spent on the front fighting the German enemy, fighting to live. I could imagine how he must have felt when his first sergeant, who had become a good friend, was killed one morning.

Kenny and I lived with the past invading our daily lives, but we could help each other because we understood that war on the frontline or the bombs raining from the heavens did not differentiate who should live or who should die.

As Thanksgiving Day neared, Irene, Kenny's sister, her husband Hans, and three-year-old Kathy came home. I had become accustomed to the availability of food, but the food preparations for the American Thanksgiving celebration were new to me and held my attention. *Erntedank Fest* (Thanksgiving) in Germany was nothing like this. During October, farmers brought baskets filled with items they had harvested to be blessed by the priest, and then the baskets were given to the poor. These gifts were placed at the foot of the outdoor altar that had been erected near the church. During the service, prayers of thanks were offered for the bountiful harvest, and then everyone went home to a regular Sunday dinner.

In contrast, since Wednesday afternoon Irene and Ma kept busy until the pies were out of the oven, and the aroma of freshly brewed coffee lured everyone to the kitchen where we sampled the gooey pecan and cinnamon rolls. Early Thursday morning the fourteen pound turkey stuffed with bread dressing almost filled the oven space. The pumpkin and the mince meat pies and the rolls were now stored in the pantry. I had never heard of sweet potatoes, but Dad told anyone who would listen.

"The turkey is good, but the mashed sweet potatoes are my favorite. There is nothing better."

Kenny's sister, Agnes, and her husband, Reverend Fellger, joined us after the church service. Ma worked quietly as she prepared the mashed potatoes, the giblet gravy, added two kinds of green salads, jellied cranberry sauce and relishes. Agnes and I set the table, and we were told to watch the coffee in the big percolator. The Reverend gave the Thanksgiving table prayer. We had so much to be thankful for. We were well, we had each other, and Kenny's and Dad's business was growing.

Finally the big turkey wonderfully browned was brought to the table. It was tradition that Dad cut the turkey. The succulent slices and the savory smell of the stuffing and gravy made everyone anxious to dig in. I could not help but think of my loved ones at home. How little they had, and yet I knew they were thankful every day for just being alive. Today no one was in a hurry to leave the table. After we carried the dinner dishes to the sink, the pies were cut and served with double dollops of whipped cream and coffee. Since the Reverend was present, cards stayed in the cupboard. The men settled down in the living room where they discussed town and national events while we did the dishes. Ma took care of the leftovers and held back what would be served for supper.

After everything was back in place, we paid attention to little Kathy because she could hardly contain her excitement. She was impatiently waiting for Santa Claus because he brought presents on Christmas Eve. I couldn't understand it. What did Santa Claus have to do with Christmas?

Ever since I could remember, in Germany Saint Nicholas visited homes and schools on December 6, his names day. He checked his golden and black book which showed whether children had been nice or naughty since his last visit. Depending on behavior, there were small gifts for those who had been good while naughty children would feel the willow switch of Knecht Ruprecht who was Saint Nicholas's helper. After December 6, only the memory of Saint Nicholas remained. Now we concentrated on the coming of the Christ Child on December 24. On

Christmas Eve, we were blessed with gifts and gave gifts to our loved ones because the Christ Child was born on this day. I wondered if I could cling to my celebration of Christmas or, would I, too, wait for Santa Claus even though I knew better. Again, I remembered that Mama had tried to tell me how difficult it was to live in another land and adhere to its customs.

As Kenny's family prepared for the Christmas season, I found that many Christmas customs that had been so dear to me were not known here. In 1947, no one, not even the churches, had Advent wreaths, while in Germany the assembling of an Advent wreath was a family project. In Germany the children ventured out to the nearby woods where we selected and cut the flawless evergreen branches. While we watched, Mama shaped the wreath. She wound a wide, red ribbon near the candles and secured the ribbon streamers on the ceiling hook. On the first Advent Sunday during twilight time, we watched the clock in anticipation. At dusk Mama lit the first Advent candle and the small flame struck a special glow within us. The wreath's shadow reflected on the kitchen ceiling, and we waited until Mama hummed the pitch of the first Advent hymn. I joined in but it was Mama's and Theresa's clear voices that affirmed our longing for Christmas.

On one of the milder winter days, Kenny and I selected Christmas presents for my family in Germany. We bought Crisco and coffee for Mama, a toy for little Werner, a football for Max, and a little doll for Irmgard. I looked for an Advent calendar for the children, but I learned that Advent calendars were not yet known nor used in America. Besides working on Sammy's mittens, I had finished a wool sweater and Norwegian mittens for Theresa and a cap and scarf for Cousin Erna. Kenny suggested that we add three pairs of the sheerest nylons for Mama, Theresa and Cousin Erna. We wrapped all items in clothing that American friends and acquaintances had given for my German family. How I wished that there would be room in the box for me because I knew that only a family reunion with Papa and me could surpass the happiness that my family would feel when they received our gifts.

When I asked Kenny what we could get for little Sammy, he shook his head, "Sammy's family goes to the synagogue in Grand Forks. No Christmas for Sammy."

I worked feverishly and finished the mittens before Christmas. I wrapped them in plain, red paper and hid them under a sofa pillow.

Anxiously I waited for Sammy's visit. He looked puzzled as he came toward the sofa and I was not knitting. He sat down and his big, brown eyes gazed steadily at me but he stayed silent. I couldn't wait any longer.

"Here Sammy," I said, "for you."

He eagerly reached for the small box, tore the wrappings and opened it.

"My mittens!" He called out as he slipped them on.

He touched the white stitches, "Sammy," he sang out.

He never took his mittens off, hugged me and pleaded, "I'll go and show Mom, okay? Thank you, Annelee."

His boots barely touched the steps. I watched as he ran toward home his arms high in the air and his hands covered by the mittens waved back and forth.

For me Sammy's happiness was bittersweet and I vowed that I would knit another pair of mittens for my little brother, Werner. I hoped that by next Christmas when he was going on four, little Werner would love his mittens, but pensively I wondered if he would still remember me?

The weekend before Christmas, Irene came with little Kathy and both were singing,

"You better watch out, you better not cry,

Better not pout, I'm telling you why,

Santa Claus is coming to town"

Kathy could hardly sit still while Ma and Irene trimmed the upper part of the Christmas tree, and then they placed wrapped packages on the tree skirt below. Irene helped Kathy with her letter to Santa Claus. I remembered when we were children how Theresa and I wrote our wish letters and after darkness set in, we put them on the window sills. Before we went to sleep, we listened and we were sure we heard angels at the window pane and they took our letters to heaven.

I watched and thought how differently they do things here. Homesickness gripped me with an intensity I had not known before, and memories sprang forth like an avalanche. In Germany about three weeks before Christmas, the Christmas tree was far from our minds. But all century old traditions that had originated in certain areas of Germany were still handed down to family members. Mama who observed all traditions fetched the small manger from the attic and she reminded us, "The amount of straw for the manger and the decorations for Baby Jesus' linen shirt depend on your behavior. If you make your bed and keep your room neat, complete your homework, and keep the 8:00 p.m. bedtime, you will be able to place many straws in the manger bed. That way Baby Jesus will be lying in a soft bed. For extra good behavior, that means no quarreling or taking toys without permission, you will earn a silver or gold star which you may place on the linen shirt."

We tried to be good because we competed with our cousins for the softest manger and the most beautiful shirt Baby Jesus could wear. We were also good for another reason that lurked ahead on Christmas Eve. We had to follow one more tradition which existed in several regions of Germany. Even Mama didn't like this tradition because she thought it was not Christian.

"Pepp," Mama inquired, "Why scare the children half to death? Isn't Knecht Rruprecht enough?"

"Well, Peppi, it doesn't hurt to keep a tradition going." Uncle Pepp declared. "Children forget sooner than you think."

Mama tried to prepare us, so she told us what she had learned from her grandma about the legend of the Christmas Specht who had lived centuries ago. The Christmas Specht, who was also known as the Christmas witch, was once a woman of great beauty and riches, but she was mean and a miser. She would never help the poor or share her riches with the sick and elderly. She used the orphan children to work for her during the day and deep into the night so she could add to her riches. After she died, God banished her to earth where she must show her now disfigured, ugly self during the Christmas Season. She must beg for food scraps, and sleep in gardens, barns or work sheds. Hopefully, the Christmas Specht's plight reminded us to be thankful for our blessings and share with the needy.

Right after December 6, Saint Nicholas Day, we avoided going into Uncle Pepp's big storage shed or his garden because we knew that the Christmas Specht was waiting. Since Christmas Eve was a fasting day, Mama served the traditional carp dinner and she collected leftovers and fish bones and placed them on a large plate.

"Anneliese, make sure you place the fish bones under Uncle Pepp's fruit trees," she advised. "If you don't, the Specht will curse the trees and they won't bear fruit next fall. Watch out for her sickles. They are good for cutting grass and weeds, but you don't want them near your face. The Specht is obsessed with these sickles and she sharpens them constantly. Whatever you do, leave enough bones under each tree and enough leftovers for the Specht."

As soon as dinner was over, Uncle Pepp took Cousin Erna and me to meet the Specht. He ordered, "When she is finished with her rituals, she will take your plates and check the food scraps. That's your chance to get away. Then cousins Hans and Lisl will take their turn. Theresa and little Cousin Joey won't go in with you since they are too young, but we will stay near. I met the Specht when I was young. That was enough for me."

Cousin Hans was quiet as we approached the storage shed. All around us was the quiet fear of the onlooker while we, the condemned, stood frozen in tableau waiting. In this stillness, I had a pounding urge to scream, but I did not because I feared the Specht's wrath.

Cousin Erna broke the spell. She said, "Hans, you open the garden gate and keep it open, so we can get away quickly."

Hans stepped up to the gate. Just then we heard the eerie sounds of two sickles screeching out against each other. I stood frozen, brittle with fear. A tall rangy figure, its body hidden by flowing black rags, hopped back and forth and around scrapping the sickles without a pause while an eerie sound surrounded us. The Specht hopped closer, until I looked into her steel gray eyes. Tangy grayish-white strands of hair hid her face. Her long, crooked nose and the ugly blackness of missing teeth gave the figure a ghastly appearance. She scraped the sickles together incessantly, and she followed our every move. I hoped Cousin Erna was beside me, but I couldn't take my eyes off the Specht. Driven by fright, I ran from tree to tree and placed the fish bones near each trunk. It seemed forever before the Specht saw my outstretched arm and hopped closer. My throat and mouth were parched. My hands felt ice cold, and I stood shaking uncontrollably with fear as she touched my hand. She momentarily took the plate, stepped up to a tree and nestled the plate in the fork of a tree branch. Sprightly she hopped back and she encircled me. Cousin Erna came to my side, she thrust her plate forward, and the

Specht, never leaving us out of reach, took it. We slowly moved backwards. Our eyes were fixed on the Specht until we came upon the open garden gate and we passed through it. Never looking back, we ran until we had reached the bakery. We sat down on the steps and imagined Hans and Lisl's fear as we listened to the sickles screeching in the distance. Cousin Erna and I sighed deeply. We had done everything as planned. Tonight the Christ Child would surely bless us with gifts.

While we had wrestled with the Specht in Uncle Pepp's garden, the forester delivered our Christmas tree. The tree was always special to us because during several of our summer Sunday walks we searched the forest until we finally found our special Christmas tree. It was Papa's job to place the tree in the living room where Mama could decorate it behind the closed door. When we came home, Mama shooed us off to bed for our Christmas Eve nap. The streets and homes in the neighborhood were quiet now, and throughout the town and in the villages, children took their Christmas Eve naps or at least were anxiously but quietly waiting. Theresa and I discovered a book on our bed covers. We feverishly read, hoping the hours of waiting would go by faster.

After the traditional bratwurst and sauerkraut supper, we washed and dried the dishes. As the first clang of the Christmas bell sounded, we scurried into the hallway and into the living room where we stood still in awe. We finally saw the tree we had selected during our summer walks decorated and bathed in a festive glow of wax candles. While we adjusted to the candle light, Papa read the Christmas story. At last, Mama called our names, and we received presents that reminded us of the Christ Child's birth. There were games and new clothes for everyone. Our dolls in their buggies or cribs had several new outfits. I was seven when a miniature grocery store with glassed-in-display windows was added to the doll house. We played house for hours. We shopped in the play store for carrots, potatoes, lettuce, loaves of bread, buns and chickens all shaped in miniature likeness out of delicious marzipan. Small candies represented coffee beans, yellow beans, peas, and rice. All that could be purchased with tiny chocolate coins that were wrapped in gold or silver paper. We refrained from eating the goodies because we knew that we would have to wait until New Year's Day before we would have spending money to buy replacements. On Christmas Eve, we could play and stay up as late as we wanted. When the time came, we readied ourselves for the Midnight Mass, and then we sat by the window. Out toward the hills, we watched for the first flicker of a villager's Christmas lantern. Like the glowworm during the summer night, one lantern upon another flickered boldly until a river of lit lanterns streamed from the hills into the city as groups of villagers proclaimed with strong voices,

"Christ is born! Hallelujah!"

Into the town they came, singing, praising. As they passed our home, we joined the procession to the church. At midnight, the church bells rang out, beckoning everyone to come and celebrate the birth of the Christ Child. During the mass, we waited for the highlight of the season. The organist played the organ chords until they burst forth and the choir sang the first stanza of the song that no one had sung throughout the Christmas season, Franz Gruber's *Silent Night*. I shivered because the special moment had finally come. Mama and Papa moved toward us and held our hands, and with all the worshipers, we sang the final two stanzas of *Silent Night*.

Aglow with happiness, we wished each other a blessed Christmas.

This was Christmas! We had received the Christ Child's blessings and joy and thankfulness filled our hearts.

It seemed to me that in America, Santa Claus overshadowed the real meaning of Christmas. I wished that I could tell Kenny, his family, but most of all little Kathy about Christmas in Germany, and how it had been for me. But here, it was the magical figure of Santa Claus who brought Christmas presents.

Christmas Eve came and Kenny's present was a surprise he had secured right after Thanksgiving Day. It was 4:00 p.m. when the phone rang and Kenny said, "Annelee for you,"

I didn't understand. Everyone knew that I couldn't speak English. Reluctantly I took the receiver, and then I heard Mama, *"Anneliese, Froehliche Weihnachten,"* (Merry Christmas,) she said. *"Wir alle sehnen uns danach dich wiederzusehen."* (Everyone here longs to see you again.)

"Mama! Mama," I called out. *"Ich sehne mich nach dir. Ich sehne mich nach Euch allen."* (I long to see you. I long to see everyone)

Her voice faded in the interference that sounded like a sea shell's ocean waves.

I could barely hear Mama, *"Anneliese, Ich gebe dir Theresa und alle, und dann spreche ich wieder mit dir."* (Anneliese, I will give you to Theresa and everyone, and then I will speak with you again.)

After Theresa, the conversations with Max, Irmgard, Cousin Erna, and Uncle Pepp were tearful wishes for a blessed Christmas, and even Uncle Pepp told me that he missed me.

Mama came back on the line, *"Das Telefon ist ein schlechter Ersatz fuer dich. Ich Liebe dich."* (The telephone is a poor substitute for you. I love you.) Her voice trembled, *"Wo ist Kenny?"* (Where is Kenny?)

I handed him the phone. Kenny listened, while his eyes were clouded with tears. "Ja, ja, good Mama," he said. "Annelee okay. You okay, Mama? I love you, Mama."

He motioned for me to come close and everyone shouted, *"Froehliche Weihnachten. Auf Wiedersehen."* (A blessed Christmas! Good bye.)

My family, so close for a few minutes, was gone and emptiness was all around me. It had been so good to hear their voices, but now I longed to be near them. Especially now, when in Germany it was time to go to the Midnight Mass. I sobbed uncontrollably while Kenny held me in his arms.

The remaining hours of Christmas Eve were a blur, and Ma and Dad decided that we should open the presents on Christmas Day. I knew that Kenny meant to give me the best Christmas present ever, but he too realized that the phone call had been a mistake. My legs felt weak as we walked upstairs into our bedroom. Suddenly the enormity of what I had done hit me with sledgehammer force. I ran to the bathroom. My head ached! My stomach churned, and bile stuck in my throat. I felt sick. I wanted to be home with Mama and my family and celebrate Christmas with them. I wanted their warmth, their love, and their arms around me. Kenny helped me undress and get into bed. He held me gently while sobs shook my body. Mama, Theresa, Max, little Irmgard and Baby Werner, even Uncle Pepp and Cousin Erna floated in and out of my thoughts and I knew I could not touch them.

Throughout the Christmas Season I had felt the gap, but I always pushed the differences of customs and the absence of my Catholic faith aside. I missed the familiarity of friends and acquaintances. I missed chatting with them where and when we met. I had met people here, but

I could never ask them, "Remember how much fun we had in school? Do you know where Maria is? Did she marry Hans? Is your brother still in Russia?"

We had no recall of each others' past because we had not shared it. Only Kenny had been with my family, only he had seen where and how we lived.

Now I recalled how Mama in desperation had pleaded, "Anneliese, you are not listening, and you don't envision what you will have to cope with. I have watched you while you were growing up into the young woman you have become. I know how deeply you love our land. The woods seem to renew your spirit and diminish what is bothering you. But in America, in Minnesota, the weather, the land and woods are different than what you know. You won't be able to share your feelings since you can't express yourself. You will be so alone. The one person you know in that great, big land is Kenny, whom you have known as a soldier for ten weeks. Will he understand when you are homesick, and will he give you the support you need? Think, please think! Will having Kenny at your side be enough to make your life complete. You demand so much of life! To fill your needs, you need your family, and you need to draw strength from your land and your woods. You need what you love so much. Anneliese, will you have all that in America?"

Finally, I understood. Why hadn't I listened to Mama? Was this Christmas Season truly the first time I heard her words? Why had I shut her out when she spoke to me? Whenever I missed my family while I worked in Regensburg, I could go home as soon as I had several days off, but now it could be years before I could see my family again. This time my homesickness was not of short duration, it stretched into weeks. The long winter nights were frequently sleepless, and the bitter cold January days seemed never ending. After Kenny left for work, within the hour I had washed the breakfast dishes, made the bed, and swept the floors. Music, knitting or reading filled my idle hours. Reading the newspaper or a magazine article became a laborious task. With the English-German Dictionary and my spiral notebook in front of me, I copied each sentence and then I deciphered the meaning of each word. If I was lucky, I finally had a sentence that I could understand. With this type of learning, frustration took over and frequently I threw the dictionary and the newspaper and thought, I will never learn that language! How can I be sure that after I know the meaning and the spelling, I will also master the pronunciation of each word?

Another stumbling block for conversations was the homonyms. Take for instance, lone - loan, mourning - morning, sight - cite, insight - incite, new – knew, idle - idol, need - knead. Even the typewriter that Kenny bought for me had the letters *a .q. z* and t on different keys in different rows. In Germany I had easily typed one hundred ten words a minute without a mistake. Now I finger picked my way. Kenny, too, felt frustrated, because daily life and simple tasks had road blocks we had not envisioned.

New Year's Eve was a quiet celebration. Sammy came on New Year's Day and he wished us a Happy New Year. I quickly got my billfold and gave Sammy twenty-five cents. Sammy's eyes were saucer-like.

"Mine?" He looked at the quarter and at Kenny, "Thank you, Annelee," he said. "I'll show my mom."

"You really like Sammy," Kenny remarked, "but you don't have to pay him for wishing us New Year happiness."

It took some time before Kenny understood that in Germany New Year's Day was a favorite holiday for children. While adults celebrated New Year's Eve, the children waited anxiously for New Year's morning because we went from house to house and offered wishes for *"Ein Gesegnetes Neues Jahr"* (A Blessed New Year.) By noon we had received *fuenf Pfennig* (nickels), *zehn Pfenning* (dimes), and *fuenfundzwanzig Pfennig (*quarters) to keep as spending money for quite some time. Kenny thought children in Germany had a good start into the New Year, but neither his family nor anyone he knew had ever heard of the custom.

Kenny pondered, "I better explain to Sammy's mom why he came home with a quarter."

I soon learned that even during Adolf Hitler's time we had celebrated several Christian dates that were hardly noticed in America. In Bavaria, on the evening before the day of Epiphany, we carried water, white chalk, salt and incense to the evening service where the priest blessed these items. Then head of the household inscribed *19 - C + M + B – 40 Caspar, Melchior, Balthazar* the names of the Three Wise Men and the given year on the top board of each entrance door. After that, no one, not even family, relatives, or friends, could cross the door's threshold unless they were at peace with the home's inhabitants. Epiphany was observed strictly as the day when ill feelings were put aside, and quarrels among family members and friends were resolved.

I wrote to Mama and wished her a blessed name day. Again, I learned that Kenny's family and friends had never heard of anyone celebrating their given name. In Germany, St. Josef's day was and still is celebrated on March 19, as a church holiday. On that day, Uncle Joseph whose nickname was Pepp, and Mama Josefa, whose nickname was Peppi, celebrated their name day. Theresa and I collected flowers that were blooming in the hills. We pinned the flowers on the edges of the damask table cloth and centered a vase of forget-me-nots on the table top. All this time, Mama fussed with dinner preparations because everything had to be just right.

There is one Saint Josef's Sunday I will always remember. Mama's special name day dinner was now stone cold, because Papa who had left for the High Mass didn't come home. Most wives who had a Josef in the family were probably facing the same fate. It had been customary for decades that after the Saint Josef's Day High Mass the men met in the pubs and toasted every Josef present. That Sunday we waited for Papa to come home and celebrate Mama's name day with us. When we had waited for almost an hour, Mama decided that we would eat before the special dinner was as spoiled as her mood. Then Mama sat near the window looking out to spot Papa when, suddenly, Theresa and I heard terribly off-key singing. I wanted to see who could sing so loud and so off key, but Mama slammed the kitchen window shut with a force that made the glass rattle. Papa and Uncle Pepp had reached the entrance while their singing echoed throughout the house.

They stomped up the stairs, entered the kitchen and stood before Mama. They bowed awkwardly and tried to kiss her hand. They missed and said,

"A most blessed Saint Josef's Day to you, my dear. We came to toast you and celebrate your name day."

I had never heard or seen Uncle Pepp or Papa so tipsy and I knew they were in big trouble with Mama.

"There will be no toast," Mama ordered. "It will be coffee for you and Max."

Uncle Pepp addressed us *"Hier sind fuenfundzwanzig Pfennig, Anneliese, Theresa,"* he chuckled. *"Geh' zum Buchka fuer ice cream."* (I'll give you twenty-five cents go to Buchka's for ice cream.)

I really loved ice cream, but today I didn't want any ice cream. I wanted to stay home, listen and watch because Uncle Pepp and Papa were in trouble. But I knew that wouldn't happen because Mama turned to me and said, "Anneliese, Theresa, leave now, buy a treat and visit with Grandma for a while."

It was different in America. On March 19, in Crookston, the snow banks on the side of the highways and roads were still higher than the cars. I longed for spring, and a month later, on our First Wedding Anniversary, April 8, spring finally had Father Winter on the run. It was still cold but the grass was turning green. Crocuses and tulips broke through the ground and through the patches of snow that were left here and there.

Farmers afflicted by spring fever checked their fields. Sugar beet farmers itched for the day when the black earth was dry enough to hold their huge seeders while they planted the seeds in straight, narrow rows in section after section of land. The grain farmers planted the seeds of grains and soy beans, and the dairy farmers hoped their alfalfa fields had survived another year as they readied their fields for oats and corn. All the while, each farmer hoped for suitable weather and a good harvest.

Holy Week was upon us. Kenny and I looked at the biography book and photos of Therese Neumann who lived in Konnersreuth, Bavaria, four miles from my home town. I brought the book with me to America because even as a child I had been in awe of the woman who came to the local nursery during spring. Adults and children alike would gather at a distance, watch and comment on the purchases Therese made. Everyone knew she bought flowers and plants that would bring birds and butterflies to her garden. That was befitting Therese because even though the Catholic Church had not yet declared her a Saint we felt that we stood in the presence of one.[4]

Every year, it was observed by many people that Therese Nemann suffered from stigmata during Holy Week. During the same season she said that she had Visions of the Passion. From Maundy Thursday until

Easter morning she endured the suffering of Jesus. During her visions, she said that she walked with Jesus from Gethsemane to Golgotha. Linguists observed and confirmed her accurate usage of Aramaic and other foreign languages she had never learned, and they were astounded by her extra-ordinary visions of Gospel events including architecture, dress and manners. Father Hepfner would tell us her

Right: Visitors in Konners-reuth, Good Friday, 1950. The crowds are so thick that the Neumann home is not yet in sight. American soldiers in the foreground.

Good Friday, 1959. Visitors stream to the Neumann home despite the pouring rain.

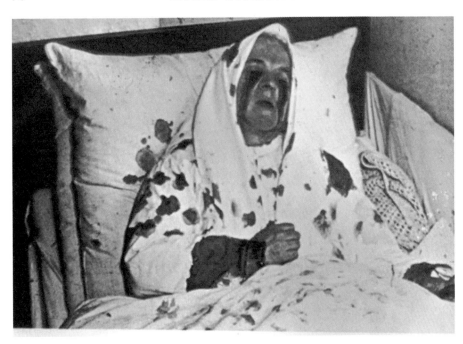

Good Friday, 1953. After the vision of Jesus' death.

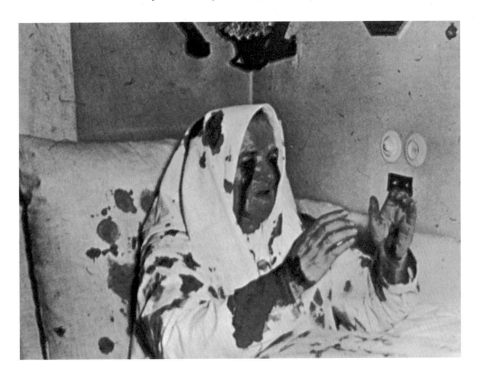

Good Friday, 1957, in front of the Neumann home.

story during religious instructions.

Therese Neumann was born into a deeply devout Christian family, and as a child the villagers knew her as Resl. She was the first of eleven children (of whom one died shortly after birth. Although Resl was intelligent and industrious and her report card upon leaving school stated that she was very good in most subjects, the poverty of the family with its many children forced them to hire Resl out to work on a farm. It was 1919 after World War I when a fire broke out on a neighboring farm. While Resl sought to rescue the animals, a burning rafter fell and severely injured her spine. She was paralyzed for four years, and she was completely dependent on her family who now cared for her and incurred additional expenses for her medical care. By mid-March of 1919, her condition was further aggravated by blindness. During April 1923, Resl prayed to Saint Theresa of Avila. She fell asleep and dreamt that someone was touching her pillow. She woke up and found that she apparently miraculously had regained her sight. Her family was overjoyed as she recognized each member and made comments on their physical changes that had taken place while she had been blind. However, the pain in her paralyzed limbs kept her bedridden.

Two years later, on May 17, 1925, Resl was said to have told her

parents and Father Naber, who was the parish priest and her confidant.
*"I saw a beautiful light, and a voice came out of the light, and it asked
me if I wanted to be cured. I answered, 'It is all right, because I believe
it came from God and God is the one best fitted to decide.' The voice
asked again, 'Would you like to get up this day and walk and take care of
yourself again?' I answered, 'I want anything and everything that comes
from God. I am happy with my family, the flowers, and the birds, as well
as with any suffering he sends. What I like most of all is our dear Savior
himself.'"*

*Then Resl recalled that the voice told her, 'You can walk, but you still
will have very much and very long to suffer and no doctor can help you
either. Only through suffering can you best work out your desire and
your vocation to be a victim and thereby help the work of the priests.
Through suffering you will gain more souls than through the most brilliant
sermons' 'Who is this?' The voice did not say.'"*

After Resl's conversation with the voice, it was decided to drop her
nickname and call her by the name of her name saint, Theresa of Avila.
Since there were several Theresa's in the village already, Resl became
Therese Neumann. Adolf Hitler had Therese Neumann watched and
examined by his trusted and highly qualified physicians and scientists,
while she was guarded around the clock by German S.S. officers. Hitler
wanted proof that her Catholic home church, her priest, Father Naber,
her family, and the bishop made fraudulent claims. Father Naber had
stated under oath that in 1926 Therese experienced an ever increasing
aversion for food and drink. Then from September 1927 for a period of
thirty-five years, until her death in 1962, Therese Neumann's only
nourishment was daily Communion. Throughout each day, Adolf Hitler's
doctors subjected Therese to numerous exams. Despite these intense
efforts, they could not bring charges of fraud against Therese or the church
officials because the doctors found all claims to be true and valid.

It was the week after Easter 1936, and I looked forward to my tenth
birthday, when Uncle Pepp had been invited by Father Neidl to observe
Therese Neumann during her stigmata. Webster's' New Collegiate
Dictionary defines stigmata as resembling the wounds of the crucified
Christ and Visions of Passions.

"Like everyone else, I had read and heard about her stigmatization, the wounds of Christ on her hands, on her feet, and on the left side," Uncle Pepp recalled. "I tell you, Max, I didn't believe it before I went to Konnersreuth during Holy Week, but I just can't change what I saw."

He shook his head, "Seeing her head, eyes, hands, feet and left side bleeding and caked with blood was . . . frightening. Her suffering began on Holy Thursday after the Last Supper and ended on Good Friday with the vision of the burial."

Father Neidl explained that the hour of death was 1:00 p.m. and it coincided with the death hour marked in Jerusalem. There the clock is two hours ahead of the German time during that season of the year; it is 3:00 p.m. in Jerusalem.

Ever since Uncle Pepp told what he saw in Konnersreuth, I understood why during Holy week crowds from all over the world came through our town on their way to view the stigmatization of Therese Neumann.

I recalled that on the night of April 19, 1945, the enemy was closing in, so we had left home and searched for shelter in Dobrigau. The artillery fire in the northeast became more intense, and suddenly Konnersreuth was in flames. Huge billows of smoke rose and hid the fate of the village and its inhabitants. Weeks later we learned that fifty farms were lost to the huge, monstrous fire, but the church and Therese's home were saved. After World War II, Therese's fame had spread across Germany and 12,000 American, British and French soldiers came during Holy Week and witnessed Therese's stigmatization and Passion Visions. Kenny learned about Therese Neumann because he drove several officers to Konnersreuth. Ever since, he had been sorry he did not go in to witness Therese Neumann's suffering. At the time he had reasoned that he was a Lutheran, and Martin Luther himself did not believe in such miracles.

Kenny tried to explain that another Catholic holiday we celebrated was the Corpus Christi Procession. Although it is celebrated on the first Thursday after Pentecost in many Catholic dioceses throughout the world, Kenny's family did not know of it. Even while the living conditions were still chaotic, most Catholic Church members in Bavaria partook in the yearly Corpus Christi Procession. (*Fronleichnam.*) After Pentecost Monday, the farmers carried small wooden crosses decorated with pussy willow sprigs that had been blessed by the priest. They and their family placed the crosses on the northeast corner of their fields. On Thursday morning, cut grass hid the streets while cut silver birches and evergreen garlands decorated the outside walls of homes, and the window sills held statues of saints. Right after the High Mass the church bells rang. The congregation stood still and waited solemnly while four honor carriers maneuvered the gold embossed festival canopy until Father Neidl stood in the center. Father Neidl wore a white frock hidden under a vibrant gold-colored habit, and the white, gold-embossed Corpus Christi stole hung over his shoulders. His arms bent forward and his hands hugged the large golden monstrance to his bosom. Two rows of altar boys wore carrot-red ankle length gowns covered by knee-length white tops set off by a red collar. At intervals, they swung covered incense burners until the canopy and the choir members in their long choir robes were engulfed in grayish-white smoke. Able-bodied church elders carried wooden posts or flags of their organizations. The First Communicant girls dressed in white and the boys dressed in black suits walked reverently behind the canopy. The town's band played hymns, and the congregation joined in hymn singing and praying. The procession encircled the nearby fields and stopped at the four home altars that had been owned by the same families for centuries. These altars, ten to twelve feet high, covered the front outside wall, and their ornamentation often surpassed the regional chapel altars. The earthen floor of each altar was hidden under a flower carpet that depicted Christian symbols. After the Epistle was read, prayers for a plentiful harvest were offered.

The Corpus Christi celebration had been an important part in my life. I missed the familiar church related festivities that had been my heritage since childhood. I wondered what else I did not know about daily living in my new homeland.

Right after Holy Week, Kenny came home with Sammy's mom and little Sammy who carried a beautifully wrapped box. He handed it to me.

"Annelee, from me and my mom," he said. "We are moving to Chicago, a real big town. I came to say thank you and good-bye."

I didn't want Sammy to leave, so I opened the candy box and let him pick.

"I like truffles," he told Kenny who helped him find what he wanted.

His mom hugged me. "You have been good for Sammy," she said. "He loves you."

I knelt down by Sammy, "You are a good boy," I said, "I won't forget you."

"I will take my mittens to Chicago," he replied. "So you come to Chicago."

"We must leave. Jacob is waiting for us," his mom told Sammy, "now wave good-bye to everybody."

With every step he took, we heard Sammy's good-byes. I already missed his clumping up the stairs. My heart ached and I cried softly.

Kenny reasoned, "Chicago is better for

My Grandma's family.

Sammy, big synagogue, good school, cousins, uncle and aunts, family."

Lacking Sammy's visits, I spent a great deal of time learning new words. As my language skills improved, my confidence grew. I ventured out and shopped in the nearby grocery store for our daily needs and spent time with my sister-in-law Agnes who lived across town. She and her husband drove everywhere in their shiny 1948 Chevrolet, which they had purchased for $2,500. Every member of the congregation, every member of his immediate family, and even Agnes called her husband Reverend because he was the minister of St. Paul's Lutheran Church. Agnes and Reverend were new parents, and little Dale was introduced to the women of the congregation at what everyone called a shower. There again, I searched for the word shower in the dictionary, and I almost wished that I had not looked. How could one word have so many meanings? "Shower n. 1. a brief fall of rain, hail, or snow. 2. a hard shower, a gentle shower, a shower of tears, a shower of sparks from an engine." At last I found the definition I was looking for: "shower U.S. a party for giving presents to a woman about to be married, have a baby." I wondered how many people in America really knew the many definitions the word 'shower' had.

CHAPTER 11

Faith of My Childhood

It was now May. Reverend, Agnes and Kenny suggested that it was time for me to experience fishing at Maple Lake, their favorite lake resort near Crookston.

Kenny thought he would purchase a family fishing license when the clerk asked, "Kenny, aren't you the fellow who married a German girl out in Washington and brought her home?"

"Yes, I did. Now I want a license so I can take her fishing."

"Well, Kenny, there is a problem. I can give you a license, but your wife is still classified as an enemy alien, and an enemy alien can't fish in our lakes. You can purchase a license for yourself. Your wife can hold the fishing rod, but she can't pull the fish in. You will have to do that."

Kenny asked, "Can she eat the fish after I cook it?"

The clerk replied, "I don't think there is a law against that."

Kenny never purchased a license that day and after that incident, I never liked the thought of fishing.

A few days later, I didn't feel well. Since my periods had always been as irregular as the weather, Kenny and I were elated when I found that I was pregnant, and we would be parents. We were happy, but I was also scared when our obstetrician didn't share our happiness. He told Kenny that my body was not ready to carry a child. I weighed ninety-four pounds and within a month I was down to eighty-nine pounds. By the end of June I felt better, but I still couldn't stand the smell of cooking food. Kenny brought me malted milk, chicken in the basket with French fries, a hamburger, coffee and ice cream. Slowly I gained weight. The men hoped for a boy, but Ma and I just hoped the baby would be healthy. Kenny bought me a sewing machine, and I sewed cotton diapers, baby blankets and little pillow cases. I wrote to Mama that during January 1949, she would be a Grandma, and little Werner, going on four, would be an uncle. As my baby moved within me, I realized that I had to deal with a concern that up to now we had postponed.

"Annelee, have you thought in what faith you will rear your baby?" Ma asked. "Will the baby be baptized in the Lutheran or Catholic faith?"

I knew that Kenny and his family lived for and served their church. Ma belonged to the Lutheran Ladies Aid, and Dad was the appointed church treasurer. He and Kenny supported their church weekly to fulfill their yearly, monetary pledge. In Germany, even while Adolf Hitler was in power, churches were supported through taxes. The Catholic and Lutheran districts received yearly sums from the government determined by the size of their congregations. There still was an offering of pocket change during each mass that was given to charity causes selected by the bishop. I realized that if I joined the Lutheran church I would have to deal with several changes that would start soon after our baby's birth.

I was one month old when I was baptized. After that I rarely entered church. When I was five, I was puzzled. "Uncle Pepp," I asked, "can I go to church with Cousin Erna?"

"No," he replied, "you must wait until next year."

"I don't want to wait. I want to go right now!"

"That won't happen. You will have to wait because that's the way it has always been," he added, "and that's the way it will be for you, too."

I wanted to go to church because Cousin Erna, who was in third grade, had just told me that she had studied for her first confession.

"When I am ready," Cousin Erna explained, "I will enter a confession booth that looks like the front of a little house. The priest sits in there behind a wooden partition. When I step into that little wooden house, I can kneel down. There is a wire screen about the size of a small window, and the priest is listening on the other side of that screen. I tell him about all the bad things I have done. He gives me penance, and all my sins will be forgiven until I sin again. Father Ziller said that after our first confession, we should confess once a week."

"Cousin Erna," I asked dumbfounded, "when do you sin that much?"

"I don't really sin that much," Cousin Erna explained. "The more I go to confession, the better it is for me." She went on, "You see, if I should die and I don't have too many sins, I won't have to stay in purgatory very long."

Now I was determined to watch her first confession and I told Papa, "I want to go to mass with you or Mama on Sunday. Then, when she is ready I want to watch Cousin Erna's first confession."

"Anneliese, you can't come to church with us because you are not old enough. You will be able to go to children's mass next year—after you enter school," Papa resolved patiently.

"But I want to go now! Why can't I go now?"

"The mass and many other prayers are in Latin. You wouldn't understand what's going on," Papa added, "but you will after you learn Latin during religious instruction."

I found church attendance was quite different in America. Babies and small children attended the Sunday services with their parents. Boys and girls alike colored papers, some became restless and cried until one of the parents finally took them downstairs so the worshipers could return their concentration to the words of the minister. I felt bad for these little ones. It was just too long to sit still. These same pre-school children had already sat through an hour of religious instruction before they came to the church service.

I tried to tell Kenny how different the Lutheran church services were for me. I missed the familiar Latin hymns, the beautiful Latin prayers and the almost professional, large choir. Back in Germany, I could understand the sermons, and I could partake in the service. Now I sat still and listened intently because I wanted to understand so I could decide what I should do.

Since my decision would affect our lives, Kenny said, "Annelee, I am not going to tell you what you should do, but it would only be fair if you learned what my faith is all about before you decide."

I agreed and attended weekly lessons with Reverend Fellger since he was the most qualified and knowledgeable to prepare me. As the weeks passed, I became more troubled and confused because I found that what I learned in the Catholic schools, in church, from Mama and Papa and the Catholic community was more part of me than I had ever realized. In

Germany, everyday, morning, at noon and evening the Angelus bells tolled for people to pause and recite the Angelus in memory of the announcement by a angel Gabriel to virgin Mary of her conception of Christ. From first grade on, throughout the school year, it was understood that all students attended the daily morning service before we started our school day, and Sunday services could not be missed.

It was during third grade that Father Hepfner, the priest for the elementary grades, admonished during the religious instruction class, "Break the Third Commandment, and you will have committed a mortal sin. You will go to hell and eternally suffer."

I asked Cousin Erna, "If I don't go to church for just one Sunday and I am really not sick, do you believe I will go to hell forever?"

"You know what Father Hepfner said." Cousin Erna sighed, "You'd better go to church on Sundays. I don't want for you to go to hell."

"There must be a lot of people who won't go to heaven, like Uncle Baptist and Aunt Lena because they never go to church."

"Anneliese," Cousin Erna cut in, "just go to church. Believe me, purgatory is enough for you or me."

The next Sunday I didn't go to church. I took Theresa with me, and we went to Aunt Lena's house instead. On Monday and all week long I dreaded God's punishment, but nothing happened so I took a repeat the next two Sundays. But then, Uncle Baptist did something worse than tell God — he told Mama.

Mama was furious. When I pointed an accusing finger at Theresa that after all she could have gone to church if she wanted to, Mama cut me short and told me.

"Don't you point a finger at Theresa. Look at your pointed index finger, only one finger points at her but three are pointing back at you."

So, Mama said that meant it was more my fault. When Papa came home and Mama told him, he asked me,

"Anneliese, why do you question all the time? You must have faith. When you go to church just to be saved, you are not there for the right reason."

I didn't understand that, but I had another question I couldn't understand either. "Papa, religion is so hard. Why do I have to be religious, when I don't understand it?"

"What don't you understand?"

"How can there be three gods in Godhead, like God the Father, Jesus, God's Son, and the Holy Ghost? Father Hepfner taught us about that. I don't understand it, but I won't ask him because he gets angry when you question what he says."

"Anneliese, let me think for a day or two. I will see how I can answer your question so you can understand. By the way, for skipping Sunday service, you will not go on Sunday hikes with us. You will be staying home for three Sunday afternoons."

I was sure Papa didn't know the answer to my question, but after supper he said, "Anneliese, Theresa, listen." He placed a mirror in front of me, "You told me that you can't understand how God the Father, Jesus, and the Holy Ghost could be contained in God as one. Well, if we use a mirror, maybe it will help you understand God's Trinity."

He lifted the mirror up until we could see his image smiling at us. "Now join me. Anneliese, you stay here on my right, Theresa, you come close to my left. See? Now we have three reflections in the mirror. If we were the same size and shape, we would be three identical persons in the mirror. Now come and stand right behind me and hold on to me. You would see just my image, but we are still three, you are just holding on to me. Peek out just a little and you see we are three. You move back. We are still three, but I can see only one image. Anneliese, had you lived hundreds of years ago when mirrors didn't exist, would you have believed one looking glass could hold the image of three people at once?"

"No, Papa, I don't think so."

"You see, back then you would have had to take the invention of a mirror on faith, just like you have to take the Holy Trinity on faith." Papa concluded, "I don't know how much this helped you. You always question so much. When it comes to religion, there are some things you must believe because our church says so. Do you understand?"

"Yes, Papa."

I loved Papa because most of the time he could tell me what I wanted to know and when he couldn't, he always said, "That's the way it is and that will be that." Then I knew it was so.

How I wished that Papa would be here with me now because he would have an answer. The Lutheran doctrines were easier to understand,

and I could find similarities to what I had been taught, yet, I could not move away from the faith that tied me to my homeland and my family.

Kenny understood and he told the Reverend that I still was unsure and he should wait until I would ask him to continue instructions. Right now, all I wanted was to concentrate on having a healthy baby that we could place in the little crib in our bedroom.

During early October, Kenny and I spent an afternoon at the Itasca State Park. I loved the woods. We drove past groves of maple trees where their red crowns momentarily overshadowed the green firs that broke the various shades of red here and there while the silver birches, their leaves in shades of yellow, gave a golden glow to nature's autumn canvas. We stopped at the Indian mounds near the buffalo ranges, and Kenny told me that we stood on historic, sacred ground. I marveled at the size and clearness of the lakes where the sky and trees reflected their colors. The tall majestic Norway Red Pine at Preacher's Grove rustled softly in the wind, and the large, clear lakes contrasted the narrow, shallow Mississippi River I could finally walk across. On our way to Bemidji, Kenny told me the legend of Paul Bunyan and his Blue Ox. He was the mythical King of the lumberjacks who was born in Bemidji, Minnesota and a statue of his actual size at his birth stands now at the shoreline of Lake Bemidji. All the while I had thought Paul Bunyan was a friend of Kenny's whom we would visit at his home. The next morning I was angry with myself because I so readily assumed that I understood who Paul Bunyan was.

When Agnes came, frustrated, I cried out, "When will I ever learn English and understand what's going on?"

"Annelee, you will understand English when you dream in English." Agnes assured me. "Don't worry so much, you understand more each day."

Several weeks later, it was after midnight, and Kenny and I were sound asleep. Suddenly, I sat up and shook Kenny. "Kenny! Kenny! Wake up!"

Kenny was startled, "What is it, Annelee? Are you sick?"

"No, no, Kenny, I just dreamt in English!" I shouted. "I just dreamt in English!"

"That's nice." Kenny mumbled. "That's nice. Now let's go back to sleep!"

The next morning I complained, "You don't even care if I ever learn English."

"Annelee, please understand." Kenny pleaded. "I slept so soundly. I dream in English every night."

I thought Paul Bunyan was a friend – was I surprised!

CHAPTER 12

1948 - 1952 – We are a Family

Christmas was two weeks away. I weighed 116 pounds, and I tired easily so we stayed close to home. On December 19 as day was breaking, my labor pains became intense and Kenny rushed me to the hospital. After more hours of labor, our Sunday child, Roy, six pounds, eight ounces, was born. Roy was a beautiful baby. His big blue eyes looked at Kenny and me. I touched his fingers which he opened and closed and he curled his little toes under to the soles of his feet. Our doctor was almost as happy as Kenny and I.

"For being over three weeks early," he said, "he is a fine looking boy. Everything is in order and he certainly has good lungs. But next time, remember, the babies I deliver are usually born on Monday."

That was the truth. It was common knowledge that all the perspective mothers who were almost ready to have their babies had a Monday morning admittance day. The doctor induced labor. The expectant mothers walked the halls, and the delivery room's door opened and closed. Happy new fathers stood by the nursery window. They admired their new family member, shared information and congratulated each other. By midnight the halls were empty. Tired nurses called Monday the "Baby Day."

Roy and I spent Christmas and New Year's Day in the hospital, and after three long weeks, we could finally join Kenny in our apartment. Roy, like all little babies who are wanted and loved, changed our daily life and its routines. Oh, the power these little ones have! Now, nightly sleep interruptions were the norm, and work, meals and leisure hours during the day were adapted to the baby's needs and cries. Each day when Kenny came home from work, he could hardly wait to hold his son.

"How is my little fellow?" Kenny would sing out, "How did Mommy treat you today?"

Roy sucked his little fist and tried to get his legs up to his chin then gurgled and smiled. Kenny would place Roy on the floor and lay down beside him. I watched my husband, who had fought for eleven months in long and horrific war battles, glow and go soft. Kenny cooed and made faces, until he coaxed smiles and sounds from this little boy who had come from him and carried on his ancestor's family name. Happiness made our eyes shine as our baby boy reached for Daddy's hand and held onto his fingers.

I loved the clean scent of lotions and powder that emanated from Roy right after he had his bath. I too was happy to hold, to change, sing to and hug little Roy. Truly, these were the golden hours and days because I, Kenny and little Roy were a family and we were content. I now rarely minded the winter weather because life had meaning and Kenny and I were building toward our future. We took lots of photos as Roy smiled and learned to sit up. Now his grandma in Germany and his uncles and aunts could share in Roy's growth and development.

There was only one problem still unresolved, and I wanted to bring it to a conclusion. I knew that everyone was waiting for Roy's baptism, but in whose faith Kenny's or mine? I knew how important it was to have both parents united and attending church services together. I was baptized in the Catholic faith but I grew up, left home, and I spent the war years in Regensburg. The air raids, suffering and untimely deaths caused me to frequently doubt the existence of a loving God. To tell the truth, even during my adolescence, I fluctuated from daily church attendance, partaking in confession and communion while I questioned several rules the church asked me to adhere to. Why could I not eat my fifty grams of meat on Friday, the fish day for Catholics, when the meat had not been available during the week? From 1944 into the chaos of 1945 when we worked sixty to seventy hours a week, church attendance was limited to Christmas and Easter.

Kenny's family members were devout Lutherans and Kenny's faith was solid. I reasoned that such an example of faith would be beneficial to Roy, and I surely could learn to respect and believe in the Lutheran doctrine. I shared my decision with Kenny.

"Annelee," he said, "I prayed that you would make the right decision for you, and I am so thankful that we will be a family united in faith."

Much of what I learned about the Lutheran faith I could accept without a doubt. Roy was baptized on February 6, 1949, by my brother-in-law, the Reverend C.J. Fellger, and I became a member of St. Paul's Lutheran Church, in Crookston. I wrote Mama after my decision was a fact and as I recall, she answered,

> Dear Anneliese and Kenny,
>
> Thank you for sharing your decision to join the Lutheran Church. Anneliese, you asked me if I feel you made the right decision. My dear, if you feel it is right for you and your family that is what matters. I will NOT tell Uncle Pepp or anyone because they still haven't accepted the fact that you are living in America. Aunt Nanni says that Pepp still looks out the window every morning like he is waiting for you because you would take a stand and argue his point of view. Just think what he would do with the fact that you left the Catholic Church and that now you are a Lutheran. I best leave that alone. No news about Papa.
>
> We love and miss you so much, every day! Everyone is well.
>
> Mama

Spring slowly gave in to summer. Everyone talked about the grain fields and sugar beets, but I still missed the woods and meadows we had at home. I dreamt how far I could take Roy into the hills and woods, or walk along the creek and come home through the meadows filled with wild, fragrant flowers. Here in Crookston, I had the sidewalk or the narrow side streets where I pushed the buggy for an afternoon outing or for a visit with Agnes. We compared the development of our boys, Dale and Roy, and we shared what we learned about being a parent. One day, at dinner time, Kenny came home and he handed me a sheet of paper.

With the help of my dictionary I deciphered,

"Annelee, I asked Mom to take care of Roy tonight. We are asked to visit a family. Their son, Don, was wounded in Germany and his eyesight was also severely impaired. He had been released from the hospital with a German shepherd guide dog. The dog was trained in German obedience words so the family hopes that you can help. The dog's name is Fritz."

I was afraid of German shepherd dogs, since they were so protective of their masters, and I wondered what awaited me. As Kenny and I entered the living room of the beautifully furnished Victorian home, I wanted to turn and run. Don, a haggard-looking young man, sat in a wheel chair near his hospital bed and he held the leather leash of his guide dog.

The dog growled and stood up, and it took all the courage I could master, "*Fritz, setz dich!*" (Fritz, sit down.) I commanded while I moved my arm with a cutting motion toward the floor.

Fritz suddenly wagged his tail, whimpered, sat down and did not move from his master's side. I knew the dog understood my command so I approached the young man. As I came closer, I could see that his face and his right arm were disfigured by ugly scars. I knew he had been wounded in Germany during the final days of the war. He held out his hand which I took and I wanted to say, "*Bitte vergebe meiner nation was sie zu ihnen getan haben.*" *(*Please forgive my nation for what it did to you.) But all I could muster was, "I am so sorry. I am so sorry."

Don pulled me close with his good arm, "No, no," he said, "it was the war! It was the war."

Don's parents joined us while I spoke and translated each command. "*Fuss, setz dich!*" (Heel, sit down) "*Leg Dich! Lauf!*" (Lie down! Run!)

Don and I drilled the commands several times, and Fritz seemed to relax as he followed us. Don and his parents were most grateful, and Fritz wagged his tail and whimpered.

"*Guter Fritz!*" (Good dog!) I exclaimed while I patted him.

I felt for Fritz. He seemed to have the same problem learning English as I did. Don tired easily so Kenny and I promised we would come back whenever we were needed. Once again, the war and all its horror had returned to Kenny and me. I felt uneasy for the rest of the evening and into the night. Whenever we saw someone like Don, we were thankful that Kenny had come through eleven months of fighting without being wounded severely. We knew that at times Kenny's breathing became more labored and his stomach would bother him. But he felt that every soldier came home with some ailment caused by war. With over the counter medication for breathing and a momentary soft food diet we could handle what he called his war afflictions. Then I thought of Papa, Don, and all the soldiers and their families who still were held captive by the consequences of war. Why did people who had never seen each other and had never caused hurt to anyone maim each other in the name of war? Sleep evaded me that night, and the memories of the war would not be still.

We did visit Don several times, and within weeks he and Fritz had bonded and they worked together as a team. The loving, professional care Don had at home elicited a great change in everyone, but mainly in Don. He gained weight. He could walk Fritz by himself, and his positive attitude put everyone at ease. He told us that he would return to the Veteran's Hospital out east for additional surgeries, but he was glad to be home, and he felt that he was on the path to healing inside and out.

Thanksgiving 1949 was a week away when Roy stood up and took his first wobbly steps. We coaxed with applause and little rewards, and he soon mastered walking. I also learned that we would spend Thanksgiving with Kenny's sister Helen and her family in Rochelle, Illinois. Kenny told me to pack for three days, and as we rose on Wednesday morning, at 3:30 a.m. it was twenty-seven degrees below. Kenny scraped the ice from the windows of our 1936 Ford, while I rechecked the suitcase. Ma and I shared the back seat with Roy who slept in his buggy. Dad was the navigator, and Kenny drove in the morning darkness on snow covered roads.

As I remember, we drove on two-way roads to Minneapolis, Eau Claire, Rockford, Rochelle, Illinois. It was stop and start at every cross walk in the small towns and metropolitan areas. Whenever there were other cars or a truck ahead, we could not pass since traffic was coming against us at all times. Infrequently, Kenny drove at top speed, 55 miles per hour. Since we were confined in such a cramped space, I couldn't remember when I had been so tired. The motion under the drive shaft hump, which went from the front to the back of the car's floor, made my legs tingle and ache. This caused me to shift my legs from left to the right, then to the side, but nothing brought relief. Roy slept a great deal, and as long as I took care of his needs he never cried. At long last, during the morning hours of Thanksgiving Day, we had reached our destination. Church attendance, the traditional Thanksgiving dinner, visiting and card playing filled our days.

Since it snowed on Saturday, Kenny and Dad shortened our stay and we left early because Monday was a work day. I still was tired and I dreaded the return trip, but I was happy when we entered our little apartment and readied ourselves for bed.

"Kenny," I asked, "why did we take such a long, hard trip? Helen and her family were visiting during July."

Kenny looked at me surprised. "Annelee, we will go again next year."

I could not believe it. We will make the same trip next year? I thought of Mama and how she longed to be with me. She would have liked to meet her first grandchild, but I knew that we couldn't afford the cost of a plane ticket. Mama wrote frequently that in Germany living conditions had not changed for the better, but had they had gotten worse since I had left. Now more changes seemed in store for Mama because for several months now Theresa had dated a young man from Poland. They had chosen June 10, 1950 for their wedding.

Mama wrote that Uncle Pepp was perplexed. She recalled that he asked, "What is it with your girls? Why can't they find a nice Bavarian man? Anneliese left and lives in America. Will that Polish fellow after he marries Theresa immigrate and live in America too?"

"Pepp, you know that even as a child Theresa was and she still is a homebody. She wouldn't go for a sleep over, she wouldn't go to summer camp and she wouldn't spend a weekend at Aunt Lorie's home. Matter of fact, did she stay with Cousin Erna for even one night? She promised me that after she married John, she would still live with me at home while John would work in Amberg. So let's keep peace and relax."

I imagined briefly how good it would be if my sister Theresa would come to America and live near me - but I knew she would never leave Mama.

A few days later Kenny came home, "I have a surprise for you," he announced, beaming with pride. "Ma will watch Roy. Come, we must go."

"Where are we going?"

We drove across town, "Close your eyes," Kenny commanded. "Now look."

Three new homes, all built in the same style, were ahead of me. Kenny stopped at the first home, shut the car off, elbowed the car door open, ran up the four steps, and opened the front door.

"Come Annelee, come look!" he shouted, "This can be our home!"

Caught up by his excitement, I ran to his side. "This is wonderful!" I called out.

Most people would have seen a typical, new, two bedrooms home adequate for a young family, but for me this was heaven. We stood in the living room and we walked the narrow hallway that led to the two bedrooms. A small, narrow bathroom was in the corner. The smell of newness, the shiny, varnished wooden floors in the main rooms, the off-white linoleum floor in the kitchen, the white cupboards with a built in sink and a big refrigerator completed the newly introduced kitchen triangle. The stove was mid-center, and the refrigerator and cupboards were placed on the opposite side, rectangular to the stove. From the kitchen window we could overlook a huge backyard that ended at the bank of the Red Lake River. The basement could be reached from the kitchen and the side door to outside. I could hardly breathe. To have this home, and for the first time be alone, on our own, what more could I wish for?

"Annelee, if we buy this home," Kenny cautioned, "It will cost eight thousand dollars, we will have fifty-five dollars a month mortgage payments, and around sixty dollars a year property taxes, so you may not be able to go home for a few more years."

All I could momentarily think of was *"Unser Heim. Unser Heim!* (Our home. Our home!)

Right now, I lived only in the present, and the future looked better than ever. During July 1950, we moved our few belongings into our home and we were welcomed by our neighbors. Libby and Jack came with their son, four-year-old Gary; Jean and Clark brought their two children, Michael, five, and Susan, three. Evelyn and Mac lived across the street with their three children Gary, six, Susan, five and Mark, four.

They told us that they were glad we didn't add another Gary or Susan to the neighborhood since there was enough confusion already. They instantly accepted us as their neighbors. When I inquired about the neighbors next door, they hesitated.

"The Bocks? They are retired," Evelyn explained. "Don't step on their manicured lawn and that goes for little Roy, too. Be sure you don't leave toys or any other unsightly things on your own lawn."

"Will they tolerate my 1936 Ford?" Kenny interjected as he pointed at their brand-new car.

"If you'll keep it clean and shiny it might do," Libby pondered.

Further up the street lived Marie who came with little Dean, her three-year-old son. As time passed, we became neighborhood friends. We watched each other's children, and I haltingly partook in discussions as I became more fluent in English. Roy had playmates and Kenny had friends close by.

I was happy, and I wrote Mama how good I felt because, finally, Kenny and I could live as husband and wife in our own home where we cared for our baby and watched over his development and growth. I sent her the house plan and shared with her my wonderment over all the new appliances it contained. The home came with a built-in refrigerator and a washing machine in the basement. The furnace never needed attention. All we had to do was set the thermostat and each room was equally warm. Wood or coal never darkened our kitchen floor.

Kenny's cousin, Alton, and his wife Ruth came for a visit and stayed overnight. Ruth was as kind as she was beautiful. Intuitively, I knew she liked me, and I surely was drawn to her.

After breakfast, while the men were outside, Ruth asked, "Annelee where did you get that sofa and that chair?"

I confided that it came from my in-laws. They meant well, but I hoped to replace that dark brown unit with something more fitting as soon as we could afford it.

"I have been saving for months," I responded, "but a new unit is so expensive. So far I saved fifty-five dollars."

She suggested, "Why don't we recover it? You pay for the material and I will show you what we can do with those ancient pieces. I will come back tomorrow, and I'll take you to the upholstery and fabric shop.

Grand Forks is twenty-five miles from here, but their big selection and
low prices can't be matched anywhere within the area. Don't tell Kenny.
We'll surprise him."

"What will your help cost?" I asked shyly.

"A good meal," she laughed, "and seeing Kenny's face when we
have the sofa dismantled."

I was ready to back out, "Oh, no!"

"Don't worry. We can do it."

Ruth then told Alton and Kenny, "Tomorrow, I am taking Annelee to
Grand Forks. She needs to get out more."

The next morning we drove to Grand Forks. I had never seen Ruth
in action. We bought horse hair, linen, tacks, little nails, rope, three
wooden buttons, and fifteen yards of beautiful upholstery material with
silver-gray background black and white thread variations throughout.
During each transaction, Ruth bartered with the saleswoman, and she
promised that the store could display a photo of the finished product.
Finally, both women seemed satisfied, and we left.

"Tomorrow, after Kenny leaves for work, I'll come to your home,
but don't tell Kenny," she cautioned. "We'll have the sofa apart by the
time he comes home. I'll leave everything in the pickup. If Kenny asks
you what we bought, just say, 'it's a surprise for tomorrow.'"

During the evening hours, I prepared a casserole, potatoes, and
vegetables for tomorrow's meal, and all the while I wondered how Kenny
would react to the changes that awaited him.

Ruth arrived shortly after Kenny had left. She stopped the pickup
and came in with an old tarp. She surveyed the room, moved the chairs
and end tables, and within minutes, the tarp hid the living room floor.

"Come," she motioned. We went outside and Ruth climbed onto the
back of the pickup. She handed me a huge tool box that I dragged up the
front steps and into the living room. Ruth followed me, carrying the
sawhorses which she spaced carefully on the tarp, and then she placed
several long boards across the sawhorses.

"Annelee," Ruth directed, "take this end of the sofa."

With her lead, we lifted the sofa onto the boards. She reached for the
tack remover, and rip, rip, the upholstery was off the backrest and the
inside cotton batting was exposed.

"Oh, dear God, what have I done?" I whispered, "Kenny will never forgive me."

Ruth was unmoved. She started to remove the padding, and she asked me to do the same while she sorted what we could use again and what was useless.

The pickup, the boards and all the activities had aroused Libby's curiosity and she walked in, "Annelee," she asked, "What are you doing?"

"We are creating a new sofa that will fit in this new home." Ruth explained.

"Oh, dear," Libby muttered. "Annelee, if you want, I'll watch Roy for you. You can keep Gary for me sometime. What does Kenny say to all this?'

"It's a surprise," Ruth laughed, pointed at the clock and added, "and it will happen any minute now."

"Oh, no," Libby sighed, "I'll take Roy and leave right now."

Just then Kenny came in and gasped, "Ruth, what is all this?"

"Kenny, you and Annelee need a better looking sofa, and when I am done, you will have it."

"It surely doesn't look like it to me," Kenny protested. "Just look at all the loose cotton batting and the dust."

"Let's eat," Ruth pushed Kenny forward to the kitchen. We ate.

Kenny rested in his easy chair and his hands gripped it like he wanted to protect it from Ruth's chopping block. When it was time to leave, he said, "Annelee, I saw Libby with Roy and she said that you had a surprise for me. Well, I'll say, that was putting it mildly. See you tonight."

By evening Ruth and I were down to the springs. "We can saw the rounded arms off, but Kenny will have to help with tying the springs. I will show him how." Ruth promised. "Tomorrow I will bring our neighbor's son with me, and he will help with the new arms."

When Kenny came home that evening and saw what we had done, he asked, "Annelee, what possessed you to do this?" He went on, pleading, "Before I will tie these old springs, listen to me! I don't know yet how we can do it, but if you will quit this, I will see what we can do about a new sofa."

"No, Kenny. I saved money. I got material. Ruth is good! We will have a new sofa."

The next morning Ruth came with her helper. They measured wood, cut and pounded, and by noon one side of the sofa had lost its 1920 appearance and the straight arm style of 1950 had emerged. Within the next few days, the sofa took shape and useable padding covered the springs and back. Now even Kenny showed interest in the progress. Libby, Jean, and Evelyn stopped in, and they, too, were amazed as they saw the transformation taking place. While Ruth cut and sewed the new cover, I helped tug and pull the fabric in place. Now the men kidded us that they would hire us out to upholster other people's dilapidated sofas and chairs.

With the covered, oblong buttons, the decorative cording around its edges, and two padded cushions fitting in the space where formerly there had been three, the sofa looked grand. Even its scuffed legs were hidden under a new, lined skirt just like the expensive sofas had in the furniture stores. Kenny didn't complain at all when we tackled his chair. We matched the chair's design to the sofa and even he had to admit that our sofa and chair were more beautiful than what we could have afforded on our limited budget.

Kenny wanted to pay Ruth. But she declined, "No, Kenny, don't spoil what I did for you. It is a gift from me to you." With a twinkle in her eye, she added, "If you really feel that you must do something, maybe some day you can look at our pickup and see what it needs to start during the winter."

I had learned a great deal from Ruth, and I was glad that she was my friend. She never thought about what needed to be done. She just went ahead and did what was necessary.

"When Ruth worked

Our new sofa.

for the dairy company in Crookston," Kenny recalled, "she put the men to shame. She lifted the heavy milk cans on and off the trucks as well or better than the men. The foreman liked her because when she worked, the men never voiced a complaint."

May 1952 ended. I wasn't feeling well, but soon I wouldn't mind because another life-changing event was ahead for Kenny and me. We were so happy when our doctor confirmed that I was pregnant. Roy, besides having playmates of his own age, would also have a little sister or brother.

Our 1936 Ford, still shiny and clean, needed a lot of replacement parts and tires. Kenny and his Dad worked out a deal. Kenny could sell the 1936 Ford for $175 to a neighbor, and Dad suggested that we could use the money as the down payment for an almost new 1951 Ford four-door passenger car we could buy for $1,500, Dad would lend us the money, and Kenny could pay it off with whatever monthly payments we could spare. On Sundays, Kenny would switch off with Dad for church service, dinner and supper hours. I was reluctant to give away so much of Kenny's meager free hours.

"Annelee," Kenny explained, "we need a safe car. We also have a new baby coming. This is the only way we can manage all of it at the same time."

I felt caught. Yes, I was happy with our new home, a newer car, and best of all a new baby. But all of this was costing so much!

"Kenny, we are paying double," I argued. "You are paying the owed money back with work, but we also lose the precious little free time we have now. Is a new car worth all that?"

"Annelee, to provide a nice home for you was important to me because that's what you were used to in Germany."

Kenny wanted to give me more than he should. But now the limited time we had and my condition curtailed our summer activities to a minimum. We drove short distances to Maple Lake, Lake Bemidji, and for a special treat, to Itasca State Park. The Bavarian woods and hills did not seem to pull at me as they had, so the periods of homesickness were less frequent and not as intense in longing. Mama and I were in touch more often, and Kenny and I couldn't believe it when she wrote,

Dear Anneliese, Kenny, and a hug for little Roy,

I hope this letter will find you well while you wait
for the day when the new baby will join your family.
Anneliese, you won't believe the commotion one of
your photos has caused. It is the one taken at Itasca
Park where you stand in front of an Indian Chief's
tepee. The chief is dressed ceremonial attire. He has
his arm around your shoulder and you smile at him.
Werner, without my knowledge, brought the photo
to school for "show and tell" time. He proudly
announced that this was the place where his sister
lived in America. Of course, he loved the commotion
the photo caused and he passed the photo to everyone
who wanted to see his sister and her Indian Chief.
Now some ill-advised busy bodies have you married
to an Indian Chief, and you live in that tepee in the
woods. Others can't wait to tease me when I am in
town. Irmgard, Max and Theresa are not pleased with
Werner and the rumors he caused. They work
overtime showing photos of your family and your
home. No more photos of the Indian Chief! By the
way, he really is stately.

We love and miss you, always,

Mama, Theresa, Max, Irmgard, and Werner

Kenny loved the letter, but I knew Mama. I could imagine the comical
effect Werner's show and tell had on my family. There were periods
when the war experiences moved to the background because all around
us everything seemed so vibrant, and everyone had work. Buildings and
new homes were going up, and life was good until...

CHAPTER 13

The Accident

It was Saturday, October 10, 1952. Roy was going on four in December. It was a beautiful fall evening. Roy and Gary were quietly playing on the living room floor with their little cars and tractors. I was sitting on the sofa, knitting a baby blanket, and Kenny was in the bathroom shaving.

The phone rang. It was Libby. "Annelee, please call me when you send Gary home. I will watch for him."

"May he stay for a while longer? I will call you and watch from here when he leaves."

Gary came up to me. "Roy hurts," he stammered.

I rushed toward the kitchen and Kenny came right behind me. He lifted Roy up and set him on the kitchen stool.

"Roy," he coaxed softly, "tell me, where do you hurt?"

"It doesn't hurt anymore," Roy said.

"What did hurt?" Kenny asked as he looked at Roy's eye. The eye lid and the surrounding skin were pinkish red where Roy had rubbed.

As I looked around, I saw it and I uttered, "Kenny, they opened the bottle with the ice pick!"

"Yes," Gary said. "We got the ice pick!"

"It doesn't hurt anymore," Roy said. "All gone."

Kenny looked at Roy's eye. It seemed fine. Even the slight redness around the eye was disappearing. I was drained and shaken. I sent Gary home, and I sat by Roy after I had readied him for bed. He seemed fine. We said his prayers. While I read him a story, he fell asleep.

When I came out of the bedroom, Kenny was pacing the floor. "Roy came to me and asked if I would open the Coke bottle." Kenny said his voice filled with pain. "I opened the bottle with the can opener that's attached to the ice pick, and I laid it on the top of the cupboard. The boys apparently closed the bottle again. They must have gotten the ice pick to reopen it, and it must have slipped. Annelee, I thank God because we were incredibly lucky. It could have been so terrible. I will throw that ice pick, and we will never have one in our home, ever! That was just too close!"

We were relieved that we had bypassed a terribly close accident. I awoke on Sunday morning as Kenny left to open the filling station at 6:00 a.m. Roy started to moan and cried out in his sleep. I rushed to his bedside, he rubbed his left eye, and his moans became more intense while I gently removed his hand from his eye and opened the lid. I shook and felt faint. Roy's eye was a clouded mass, and he tried to push my hand away. I carried my baby to the phone with me and dialed.

"Kenny, it is Roy's eye. Come home!"

I called the ophthalmologist at his home and begged him to come to his office and help my little boy. Kenny drove up, held Roy while I grabbed a short robe, and we drove off desperately.

The ophthalmologist waited by the clinic door. He reached for Roy. "I will give him a shot," he said, soothing us. "It will relieve his pain, and then I will be able to examine his eye in depth. You wait right here."

Thoughts exploded in my mind. How could I sleep when Roy was so sick? He said it didn't hurt! How could an eye that looks like that not hurt? Why didn't I cover his right eye with my hand and ask him if he could see me? All the 'ifs' crowded my mind, and I had no answer. My whole body ached, and I felt powerless to help my son to be well again. All the while Kenny sat near me, I touched his hands, and he looked down while tears trickled down unto his shirt. We were utterly quiet while the minutes crawled into an hour. At long last the doctor motioned for us to come closer. Roy was deep asleep, quiet for now.

"Kenny, tell me how did Roy injure his eye?"

We relived the night and this morning's horror. The doctor shook his head. "If I tried to hit the cornea like Roy did, I would need precision tools to achieve it. I want you to know that even if you had brought Roy in last night, I could not have saved his sight in that eye. Roy's pain came with the infection that set in, and it became more intense as time passed. I will order hospital admittance and surgery. Take Roy to St. Francis Hospital right now."

The doctor turned toward me, "How are you doing, Annelee?" he asked. I shrugged and cried. "Your wife's pregnancy is advanced, and she is in shock, so we will admit her, also. She can share a room with Roy, and her doctor will order her care."

I was dazed and barely able to move, so Kenny helped me downstairs and into the car. He placed Roy, still in a deep sleep, in my lap. I stroked his face and held him tight. I didn't want to let him go. The nuns were waiting at the hospital entrance, and one of the sisters gently took Roy, and another led Kenny and me to our room and helped me to bed.

The hours slowly ticked away. While Roy was in surgery, we waited and prayed. All I wanted was Roy in my arms. I wanted him without pain, and I wanted to protect him from all the changes that would lie ahead.

It was mid-morning before the doctor came back. "The surgery went well," he assured us. "Although Roy will be blind in his injured eye, I did not remove it. We must keep him from further infections and colds. Roy will be here for about two weeks, and your wife's doctor will determine how long she will stay."

My doctor was most concerned about a premature birth, so he ordered complete bed rest. Roy's presence in my room was good for me. I held him while the doctor put drops in his eye, and I read to Roy until he knew the stories by heart.

If I skipped a line, he reminded me, "Mama, go back. You missed a part. Please read it again." His mind would be sharp, thank God.

At times he climbed on my bed so he could feel the baby kicking, and he gleefully announced to every one, "That's my little sister."

"What if you get a little brother?" the nuns asked.

"Oh, no, that's my little sister," he insisted. "I want her for my fourth birthday and her name is Sandy."

"Roy may get two wishes. But the date," the doctor pondered, "that may be pushing it a little too far. Besides, we don't expect this little one until mid-January, and it will be a Monday baby like most of the babies

I induce."

Roy and I were discharged. To the onlooker, our home and our life looked the same. But Kenny and I didn't share our innermost thoughts like we used to. We carried the hurt of our little boy within our hearts, and we were fragile.

I nagged myself, why didn't Kenny move the ice pick out of Roy's reach? Why didn't he tell Roy not ever to touch the ice pick because it could hurt him? We didn't want to hurt each other, so we tiptoed around our feelings and thoughts. We didn't talk about that horrific night, so we couldn't heal. We watched Roy closely because he ran and bumped into the edges of tables or cabinets. He had not yet learned to compensate for the blindness in his left eye. We held him when he cried, and it was so heart wrenching because we could not take away Roy's pain or really explain it to him. Every day, I was seething inside. I didn't like the doctor we were seeing.

In fact, when we entered his office, Roy cried out, "I don't want to see the doctor, I want to go home!"

The doctor invariably said, "Now Roy, don't cry. You want to grow up and be a man, and big men don't cry. Come on now. It will just hurt for a little while, and then you will be fine until tomorrow."

I wanted to scream, "Doctor, treat Roy for what he is, my little boy."

When I complained to the family, Mom, Dad, and even Reverend Fellger told me that people worshiped the doctor. People came to him from miles around.

Everyone said, "He is gruff, but he is the best."

So what did I know? Everything was so different here. I felt so alone, and didn't know where to turn. Finally, I wrote to Mama and I shared my feelings and innermost thoughts. Instead of writing, she called. Her voice sounded scratchy, but her words were a healing balm.

"Anneliese, I am with Pepp. He is paying for this call, and we can talk as long as we need. Listen to what I am telling you. I know Kenny and you will get through this, but, Anneliese, this is important. You must be strong. Don't blame Kenny, and don't allow Kenny to blame you. You hear? Don't fall into that pit because if you do, you will hurt each other, and you will destroy your chances to heal. Then you will be truly responsible for little Roy's injury because you will add to his suffering more than you can imagine. Kenny and you would take Roy's place, but you can't. Roy's accident is in the past, and no matter how much you wish it didn't happen, it still did. Your wishing will not change anything, nothing will be different. Through blame, no one will feel better. Blame only destroys."

"Another thing, and remember this, too. Allow Roy to be the boy he was before his accident. Never treat him like he is handicapped. If you do, he will feel handicapped and he won't grow into the man he can be."

I cried softly all the while she was talking. Mama went on, "You must take care of yourself. Stay well for the little one you carry. I'll give you Pepp, before he goes through the phone."

"Anneliese," Uncle Pepp's voice was gentler than I remembered, "I promised your mother that I would just say hello and let you know that I told the priest to read several masses for you and your family. Remember Archangel Raphael, the angel of good health? We hope he will bring good health to all of you. Of course, you are in our prayers, and we surely think of you more than you know. You and Kenny should be here."

I heard Mama say, *"Pepp, nun gebe mir das Telefon."* (Pepp, now give me that phone.)

"Mama," I said, my lip quivering, "It is so good to talk with you. Kenny isn't here, but we thank you and Uncle Pepp for caring enough to call."

"Anneliese," Mama urged, "Remember what I said, and let us know when you need to talk. Bye for now."

"God bless all of you!" Uncle Pepp called out, and the phone went dead.

I was glad Roy was asleep, and Kenny was working. I could sit still and reflect on what Mama had said. How did she know that within me there was that guilt ridden inner voice? I had told her about my worries and Kenny's silence, but not about that voice within me. Why didn't Kenny put the ice pick up higher like on top of the refrigerator? Or, why didn't I check what Roy and Gary were doing in the kitchen? Why did I knit on that baby blanket that I couldn't even look at now? At home we never had an ice pick, but here every household I had been in had an ice pick. Where did other families keep it? What was Gary's role in the accident? The inner voice nagged on and on. I knew that Mama was right. How I wished Mama could be here with me. She would hold me and let me cry on her shoulder.

Then she would say, "Now straighten up and take care of your family."

I waited until evening when Roy was asleep, and I told Kenny what Mama had said. He reached for me and reflected, "Your Mama is right. I felt like I carried a big stone within me. It wouldn't move, but it just got heavier all the time. Whenever I looked at Roy or you and saw how you two suffered that stone got heavier and heavier. I always thought, why didn't I put the ice pick way up into the cupboard or on the top of the refrigerator? I thought this a thousand times, and day and night all this has lived within me. If you blamed me for Roy losing sight in his eye, I could not cope with that."

I knew we had to help each other. We had to concentrate on Roy. The three of us had to heal together. It would take time, but we would talk to each other like Mama had said we should. I thought of Kenny's folks. They had retreated into their own shell and although they were there to help, they never spoke of the accident itself. They never asked how we felt and they never shared their feelings with us. We had no medical insurance because Dad and Kenny did not believe in insurance. In Germany, every family was insured by the government and Papa even carried additional health and accident insurance.

Roy's eye surgery and our combined hospital stay came to almost $1,200. We had a double room and it was $11.50 a day. Dad helped out, and he tried to still my concern.

"Kenny and I will work it out," he said.

Roy and I were home for well over a month. We lacked the Christmas spirit, but we decided to decorate a tree, bake cookies and wrap presents. I wanted Roy's upcoming birthday to be special, so I invited Gary, Mark and Dean. They had been markedly absent from our home since the accident and the hospital stay. Roy still talked about his tiny birthday present he thought he was getting.

"I get my little sister, Sandy, for my fourth birthday. It won't be a boy."

I worried about his fixation and wondered how we would deal with his reaction if the baby was a little boy who would also be a late birthday arrival at that. It was early morning December 19, I didn't feel well, and by noon I knew I was in labor. We took Roy to Grandma's, and after the doctor examined me, he shook his head and scolded, "Today is Friday! You'll do anything not to have a Monday baby. This baby is four weeks early, so get to the hospital, and I will meet you there."

After the walking routine, I was wheeled into the delivery room, and from then on I was oblivious to my surroundings until I awoke later.

Kenny was at my side. "Annelee, how are you feeling? We have a beautiful little girl."

"I want to see her, I want to hold her," I said weakly.

"You know Annelee, our little girl is premature and in an incubator doing just fine," Kenny assured me. "You can see her tomorrow. They will wheel you to the nursery."

The next morning, Kenny came and he held four roses. "Roy is giving you a yellow rose, and he wanted a pink one for his little sister." Kenny explained, "The red one is for you from me, and I have a white one to welcome our little girl."

He held me tight for a moment and went on. "About 10:00 p.m. last night Sister Mary came to me and said, 'Little Sandy is here. She only weighs four pounds ten ounces, but she will be fine.'" Kenny shook his head, "Since Roy had called her Sandy, I wasn't even asked what we would name her. Roy was ecstatic to have his birthday present, and he asked, 'When can I see Sandy?'"

Roy had gotten what he wanted. Kenny and I had decided to name our little girl Sandra Kay, but everyone called her Sandy. She had black hair, she was healthy, and she was ours. Since she couldn't come home with me, the Sisters allowed Roy to come to the nursery window and meet his birthday present, his little sister, Sandy.

He was euphoric, "You see, Sandy is nice. I love her and I want to take her home soon."

It was January 1953. Roy was happy when we learned that Sandy weighed six pounds and she could join us at home. Within days we fell into a routine caring for Roy and Sandy. Except for our $675 hospital bill, life was better than it had been for months. We chipped away at the huge bill, but we knew, someday, the stay would be paid for.

CHAPTER 14

Coping

After a long, hard winter, the spring sun finally won. The remaining snow drifts protected by trees and homes were reduced to spurts of murky water that ran along the curb. I placed Sandy in the buggy and with Roy at my side we went for walks. Gary and Mark joined these outings, but they wouldn't come in and play with Roy. It bothered Roy and me when they said good-bye as soon as we approached our home.

I remembered Mama's advice so I talked with Libby, Evelyn, and Dean's mom, Marie. I learned of their genuine concern for Roy's safety.

"Annelee," Libby said, "you have been through so much. You know how little boys are. We didn't want Gary, Mark and Dean to roughhouse with Roy. We told them to let Roy heal and wait until he feels better."

I echoed Mama's advice, "Please don't treat Roy like he is handicapped. If you do, he will believe that he is. Treat him like the little boy he was before the accident. You and I know that we can't protect Roy from everything and neither can he always protect himself. Roy needs his playmates now more than he ever did. You maybe won't think this is wise, but we will let him try sports or whatever he wants to pursue within his ability. So please, let the boys play with Roy. By the way, I too missed the boys and you."

We hugged, and from this point on, I knew our friendships could only grow. Mark and Gary came that very afternoon. At first the play was cautious, and their moms watched from a distance, but soon they were off on their own.

Roy frequently came home with Dean and his dog Rover. Everyone in the neighborhood liked Dean because he was a stabilizing factor for Mark, Gary and Roy. We, the parents, surmised that Dean's ongoing struggle with the aftereffects of polio made him wise beyond his years.

Sandy continued to thrive. She sat up, but rarely crawled, and like her brother, she walked long before her first birthday. She was curious about everything around her and she was quick. By the time she was two, she had eaten soap and she was hospitalized because she blew soap bubbles with every breath she took. She even found a mothball and ate it. Once we were at Grandpa's house and while he was counting the church offering, Sandy suddenly choked and coughed. She had swallowed a coin. When Grandpa asked her what she had swallowed, she whispered, "The one with Jesus on it."

"That must have been an Indian head penny," Grandpa muttered. "What can we do?"

Even if there were several people around, Sandy seemed to find the right moment and she ate whatever was within reach. She was hospitalized because she had swallowed ink and shoe polish.

Our pediatrician assured us, "Since Sandy was premature and such a tiny baby, her taste buds must be slow in developing. Just watch her and she will outgrow it."

During the summer of 1954, our next-door neighbors, the Bucks sold their home to a young couple, Curt and Harriet. Within days, their two-year-old boy, Paul, and Sandy shared the sandbox and the little pool we had bought. Kenny was delighted when he learned that Curt owned and operated a filling station at Lakota, North Dakota. They became fast friends and on weekends, when Curt was home, they enjoyed exchanging ideas and stories. On Sundays Kenny was free from 1:00 to 6:00 p.m. So we drove to the lakes singing the children's favorites, *Three Blind Mice, I am a Little Teapot, Davy Crockett,* and other songs that they requested. We built sand castles on the beach, took the children to the swimming area, and we enjoyed roasted wieners and marshmallows before we headed for home and sobering responsibilities.

Mama's letter overshadowed our summer contentment. As I remember, she wrote:

Dear Anneliese and Kenny,

It is with great sadness that I write today. Now it is your brother Max, who followed you to a distant land. He emigrated to Canada, and he will live and work in Kenora, Ontario. Max didn't see any future for himself in Germany. So he left, but he promised that he will be back in two years. Max hopes that he can earn enough money, come back and start anew in a small business. Pepp and Grandma blame me for the decisions my children make. If it were not for Theresa, Irmgard and Werner I could not go on. I struggle with Max's leaving, and

I asked why do my children leave? Pepp always has the answer, "You and Max were parents who always encouraged your children to be independent thinkers. Look what that got you?"

What will I tell Papa when he comes home?

I hope that you, Kenny, Roy and Sandy are well.

Love and God's blessings, Mama

My heart ached, and I felt guilty because I now understood the worries and pain I had caused Mama when I left. She had spent sleepless nights and days in despair, but I was determined to leave and follow my heart and my destiny. Would Max have left if I would have stayed at home? Now again, Mama was going through the pain of losing her first born son to a foreign land. Surely, Mama worried even more about Max than when I had left. I had Kenny waiting for me, but Max, barely nineteen, ventured out alone into a new land and an uncertain future.

I shared my feelings of guilt and my worries with Kenny and he promised that we would look for Max and visit with him as soon as we knew where he lived. I wrote Mama and hoped our promise would lessen her worries and concerns.

During late summer, Sandy cried a lot and was restless, and we again had frequent sleepless nights until our doctor diagnosed Sandy with what

Eugene Field Kindergarten - 1954-1955
(Roy is in the front row, second from left with wearing a hat.)

he called her 'weak spot' ear infections. Aspirins, penicillin, and ear drops were now staple medication in our home.

After Labor Day, we missed the tricycles and small bikes littering the sidewalks, children running in backyards or playing in sand boxes while they shouted back and forth. School had started and Roy and Gary attended kindergarten. For a while, we felt like displaced moms.

Evelyn advised, "I hate to admit it, but after Mark, my third one took off for school, I was almost glad to gain some time to think of myself. By that time you know it is okay since the boys come home around four each day. You become proud of their accomplishments and help them to cope with small failures. That is part of life."

While Roy was in school and Sandy was down for her afternoon nap, I reflected on how different my first day of school had been back in Germany. It had been hard for me to wait for the first day of school because I imagined what my school cone would be like and all the surprises it would hold.

I remembered like it was yesterday when I asked, "Mama, when can I go to school?"

"Anneliese," Mama reprimanded, "now listen. How often must I tell you that before you can go to school, you will need a health exam?"

"Why do I have a health exam when I am not sick?"

"It is the law! If you don't have Doctor Franz's booster vaccinations against diphtheria, whooping cough, scarlet fever and German measles and the dentist's certificate that your little choppers are fine, you won't be able to start first grade. Then you will have to wait until next year. Is that what you want?"

When Mama or Papa said 'that is the law', children had to do what they said. After we had seen the doctor who vaccinated me by making five little cuts on my upper right arm, we picked my new dress up at the tailor shop. At last I was ready for school.

On the first day of school, our mamas came with us to the first grade room. The room was crowded with girls. Mama said that there we were fifty-four girls for Sister Margaret's class. Inside teacher's helpers, who were in the eighth grade, led us to our assigned desks. One helper stepped forward. She said that she would teach us how to sit properly in our desks.

"All right, everybody," the helper called out. "Now watch carefully and do what I do. If you get lost, look at the drawings on the blackboard, which show you how to sit. Your mama can help you. This is what you do. First, sit up straight. Now put your feet together and lay your hands on the desk."

She looked around. "You are good. Now do you have your feet on the floor and your hands together on the top of the desk?" We nodded in silent agreement.

"Watch me. Keep your hands on top of the desk, move your two pointing fingers next to each other. Then hide your thumbs on the bottom side of the desk, like this. Good, let's do it again." The helper coaxed, "Let's show your mamas how nicely you can sit in your desks."

We sat rod-straight while the helper continued, "This is how you will sit in school. When you have a question, keep your feet together, your hands on the desk, then put your right arm up, and the inside of your hand must face Sister Margaret. I know all this is hard for you right now and you may forget. You will learn more about that tomorrow," the helper said. She went to the dunce chair and sat down.

Cousin Erna had warned me almost everyday, "Anneliese, do your lessons and you better listen when Sister Margaret explains something. If you don't, you'll have to sit close to Sister Margaret's podium until someone else takes your place. The worst thing is when you sit on the dunce chair. Everyone will tease you because you are a dunderhead, and everyone in the whole school will know that you misbehaved."

I vowed I would never sit in that chair and everyone must have thought the same because we remained silent and sat up straight in the four-seat desks and we waited for Sister Margaret. She came in with many older students, hidden partially by the tall school cones they carried. The cones were shaped like ice cream cones, two to three feet high. Some were decorated brightly with pictures of school, work and play. Others were wrapped in scraps of beautiful gift wrapping. Each cone was topped off with cellophane held together by colored ribbons.

Excited as we were, the room remained quiet. Sister climbed up four steps until she reached the podium floor. She bowed her head, and everyone in the room did likewise. "Praised be Jesus," she prayed. "Now and in Eternity."

"Amen," the mamas responded.

She was so tall and stood way up high. I noted that all the while we were in school we had to sit still and wait until someone motioned or told us what to do. We even sat down carefully because the Sister's looked down on us.

"Girls," she said, "welcome to first grade. I will be your teacher, and you will call me Sister Margaret. I do hope each of you will enjoy school this year and I know you will be good." She paused, turned to the girls by the blackboard and commented, "These girls hold a surprise for you."

She motioned and the older students stepped forward one by one. Each read the name of a tag and brought the cone to each lucky girl. Finally, I heard my name, "Anneliese Solch."

It was so hard to sit still until everyone had a cone. We waited and waited until Sister Margaret gave permission. "You may open your cone now but don't throw things on the floor. You must keep our classroom neat at all times."

I loved my cone. Right under the cellophane cover I found the *First Grade Reader* and a letter box filled with letters and a board so I could form new words and learn how to spell them. There were a lot of words I could read already because Mama had taught me so I would be quiet and not ask so many questions. I reached down into the cone and there

I am in the second row - second from front.
Note, there are 52 girls in the classroom.

were more things. A new abacus with red and blue counting beads was taped to the *First Grade Counting Book.* Along with that there were two small boxes of white and color writing chalk.

I was so happy I had made it into first grade. All fifty-four of us were always quiet and listened intently because talking out of turn earned you Sister Margaret's reprimand and the dunce desk for the day or more.

Through Roy, I had relived the joy of that first school day. I had kept my school cone in my room until Mama took it to the attic. During the war, it came in handy for my sisters and brother, Max. Even when only used books were available, Mama kept the tradition going. I was surprised that starting first grade in America wasn't celebrated like it was in Germany.[5]

Roy liked school. He was a quick learner and he questioned what he didn't understand. What a difference his classroom was from my school days. Sister Margaret kept us, her fifty-four students, working quietly at all times. No one spoke without permission nor did we leave our desks until we were told to move. Roy's cheery classroom held eighteen students. They walked around to get the things they needed and shared items and ideas. At times it seemed like a free for all, yet they learned not only from the teacher but also from each other.

During this time Kenny and I were never free of worry. The infections in Roy's injured eye became more frequent and Sandy's painful ear infections brought anxious days and nights.

Roy had just started second grade when his doctor called us for a consultation. After an exam, he showed us an X-ray which showed definite shrinkage of Roy's injured eye. The doctor explained that it was shrinking to the point where eventually the lid would close. The only option was the removal of the injured eye. After two months of healing, Roy would be fitted with an artificial eye much like his own. We needed to prepare Roy for the up-coming surgery by explaining to him that we only wanted the best for his future and for him.

Kenny held me while I cried and asked, "Just tell me, doctor, how we explain to our little boy who has been through so much, that he will need another surgery? He has adjusted much better than we could hope for and now for him it will start all over again. I don't know how we can tell him and help him through this."

"You will", the doctor answered, "because you are strong, and you want the best for little Roy. Don't talk to him today. You are too upset. Wait until you are calm and then you both must tell him. But don't wait too long because the surgery must be done soon."

We rode home shaken and hurting. I paced throughout the house not knowing what to do.

"Annelee," Kenny said, "call your mama."

Kenny had thrown me a life-line. I called Uncle Pepp and within the hour Mama was on the line. She listened quietly while I repeated what the doctor had told us.

"Anneliese," she said, "listen. You will have to be strong for Roy, so rely on Kenny and your friends. That's what friends are for. Tell your friends and they will help Kenny and you to carry your hurt. Roy may not see it as being the best option for him, but you must explain and emphasize how his eye will close. An artificial eye will be best for him. Can you find someone who had that type of surgery? Here we have several soldiers who had lost an eye during the war. They had this type of surgery. They look good and you hardly can tell that they have an artificial eye. I wish you were here so we could help you through this, but you are in our prayers. Here is Pepp."

"Anneliese, Peppi will tell me what you must face." Uncle Pepp added, "Stay strong. We keep you in our prayers. Peppi says that she will write to you as soon as she gets home. God bless you!"

As always, Mama's voice and advice brought me calm. Our dear friends were there to help. They took care of Sandy, and Libby took Roy home with her so we had time before we spoke with Roy.

Roy listened as we told him what the doctor had said and he asked, "No more infections and medicine drops?"

"It should be much better once your eye heals from the surgery," we assured him, "and you will have a new eye that looks like your own."

We told him that he could think about what we had said, and we would talk again. He went to his room, and quietly played with his fort while we couldn't shake the feeling of doom.

Roy called out to us, "I played a war game. The Indians said that I shouldn't have the surgery and the soldiers said that I should. The soldiers won. I will have the surgery."

Kenny and I were stunned and troubled. How could our little boy decide so quickly? We wondered if tomorrow a second battle would change the outcome, but he never wavered. Roy wanted to attend morning classes before we took him to the hospital. His teacher had arranged a surprise party. Cards and gifts from his classmates and their parents eased our way for what lay ahead.

We stayed at the hospital until Roy fell asleep, and we returned as dawn broke. By noon, we learned that the surgery had gone well, and the doctor advised that except for clinic visits and frequent eye patch changes, Roy should return to school immediately after his hospital release. We were concerned because we could not always protect Roy from questions of curious strangers.

Unthinking, they would ask, "Hey little boy, why are you wearing an eye patch?"

Roy would question, "Why do they have to know?"

We tried to bring back our previous pattern of family living but we didn't always succeed. We still were without health insurance. Kenney's dad paid the hospital bill, and in turn Kenny kept working for his dad noon and evening hours.

CHAPTER 15

1956-1959

July 1956. It was a lazy summer's day, a Sunday when the incessant ring of the telephone brought new changes into our lives.

"Anneliese, how are you?" Was it my sister Theresa's voice? "Theresa," I asked, "is everyone all right?"

"Yes, Anneliese, at home everyone is fine but I am not calling from home, I am calling from Rochester, New York. That's where John and I are living. Like you, we immigrated to America."

My thoughts were racing. "When did you arrive?"

"We arrived a week ago. We stayed in New York with John's friends, and then we came to Rochester where I have work. We rented a small apartment, and I hope you can come and see us."

John came to the phone. "Anneliese, I hope you can visit us soon. We will call again, bye."

Kenny looked at me. "Annelee," he asked, "bad news? You look aghast."

"I can't believe it! That was Theresa. She and John are in America."

"Wonderful!" Kenny exclaimed. "When will they visit us?"

"They won't come," I explained. "Theresa hopes that I can come to Rochester, N.Y. to meet John. They will live and work there. They will live in America."

Kenny shook his head, "What did your mama say to all this?"

"Theresa didn't say how Mama took her leaving. Mama must be beside herself. Kenny, what is going on? Theresa was always the one who stayed near Mama and now she too left to live in America. I need to call Uncle Pepp. I need to talk with Mama."

Uncle Pepp was livid when I called. "Anneliese, if they were still here, I would see to it that Theresa would never leave! John could go by himself, but I would make sure that Theresa would stay. Did you know they were leaving?"

"No, Uncle Pepp, I am telling you the truth. I surely didn't know, and I was probably more surprised and upset than you are. How is Mama?"

"Wait until she writes to you," he advised, "I will tell her you know. Her heart is broken. You don't know the details, so you can't imagine the shock it was for her and all of us. I don't know if she will ever get over this. She moved the four empty chairs, your papa's, yours, Max's and Theresa's from the kitchen table to the attic. That isn't like your mama at all, so if it weren't for Irmgard and Werner, I would worry even more than I do right now. Irmgard and Werner are the only reason she is coping and trying to go on. Just think, she had five children and ever since the war she has struggled to survive. Three of you left. Not just for another town. Oh, no, you had to fly across the ocean! What has she ever done to all of you that you had to leave?"

I was crying softly, "Uncle Pepp, what can I do? How can I help Mama?"

"Come home. That would help her. Otherwise just keep writing. A letter is a poor substitute for your being here, but it is better than nothing! Well, now you know. I know Peppi will not come to the phone because she can't talk about Theresa's leaving. She hurts too much. I will tell Peppi you know. Good-bye!"

I sobbed and I couldn't stop. If Uncle Pepp had wanted to make me feel guilty, he had achieved what he had set out to do. Did Max and Theresa leave Mama because I had followed Kenny?

Kenny came toward me, "Annelee, what was that all about? You are more upset than when Theresa called. How is Mama?"

"According to Uncle Pepp, she can hardly go on."

"I imagine that was an understatement. How could Theresa do that to Mama?"

"Was it all right for me to leave when I did? Don't tell me that was different for Mama. I am also her child."

Kenny was silent. After I wrote to Mama, I worried even more. Her letters were short and she just wouldn't address Theresa's leaving. My longing to fly home and visit with her surfaced and held me captive. When it came to Mama I hurt every day because now I felt that I had abandoned her when she needed me most and I could not ever make it right. Kenny could not help me, so he focused on his work.

Kenny was known as an expert mechanic, and as his business grew, our medical bills shrunk. To fill my hours I became the den mother for Roy's Boy Scout troop, and I worked within the local PTA organization. Life went on, through 1957-'58 but my longing to see Mama loomed over all my actions. Roy had entered fifth grade, and his teacher, Mr. Reseland, was a new experience for Roy and me. What a difference a teacher can make in a child's life.

Roy came home elated, "Mom, Mr. Reseland said that it didn't matter that I can only see out of one eye because my brain didn't shrink and he knows that I could do great things. I could even be president if I work hard."

Mr. Reseland's encouragement brought Roy's work to the top of his class.

Sandy admired her brother and he could do no wrong. We had celebrated a quiet Christmas and we hoped that 1959 would be a good year. As spring came Kenny's stomach ulcers became extremely painful, and his breathing difficulties that had bothered him ever since he had been in the Army were now of longer duration. He tired easily and soft food became his prescribed diet. Yet nothing helped more than the days he took off from work.

"Kenny," Dr. Sanders suggested, "You can not work in that garage and think that you will ever get better. The gasoline and oil fumes emitted from the cars and trucks aggravate your lungs, and your ulcers will come to the bleeding stage and never heal. It is time that you look for different work."

CHAPTER 16

1959 - Ada, Minnesota

After Dr. Sanders's prognosis, Kenny decided to quit the work he loved and the J.E. Schraeder Company immediately hired Kenny to manage their new automotive parts store located in nearby Ada, a town of 2,000 residents. We would have to move.

Roy, our eleven-year-old, was adamant, "I am not moving to Ada. I'll stay with Grandma in Crookston, go to high school and be with my friends."

I understood his feelings of utter loss and despair but I was no help to him since I was devastated also. We needed to sell our home, move, and again live in an area where I didn't know anyone. I dreaded starting anew in a community of strangers. One Sunday morning we drove to Ada to find an apartment or home we could buy. Suddenly Roy, who had sat listless in the back shouted out,

"Mom, I will not move! I will stay with Grandma. I will not move!"

"Roy," I reprimanded, "What has gotten into you? We are your family so you and Sandy will live with us in Ada."

"Just look at their water tower."

"Now what is wrong with their water tower?" I asked exasperated.

"Just look! Why did they give their town a name spelled backward and forward the same, A – D – A.   Couldn't they think of something better?"

Kenny shook his head. "Roy, one thing is for sure. You will never misspell the town's name, right?"

During the last week of April 1959, Roy stayed with Grandma and Grandpa to finish fifth grade while we moved to Ada, the county seat of

Norman County, where the residents were mainly descendants of Norwegian immigrants. We bought a new, three bedroom home on the east side. A gravel road fronted our yard, while corn and wheat fields were to the west and north of our home. Four houses down, at the bend of the road lived Gus.

It seemed everyone in town knew Gus or had heard a story about him. It was not unusual to find his cow, pigs or chickens in our yard. When that happened, Gus came running. He held a stick in his right hand, raised it high, and as his dogs came along side, he shouted, "Round up these critters! You dumb, lazy dogs, you're not worth the food I feed you. You let them get away again!"

I couldn't believe how everyone tolerated Gus's animals running loose.

I told Kenny that I had not expected to trade our city living in Crookston for Gus's love of farming. Angrily, I asked Gus to remove the cow pies and the pig and chicken messes from our front yard.

He laughed and replied, "That won't hurt. All it will do is fertilize your grass for free."

As days went by, I missed my Crookston home, my friends, and the church members who had become dear to me. Their friendliness and their caring had laid the foundation for my feeling at home in Crookston. This base had again disappeared and the few people I had met in Ada did not yet fill the void I felt. I had met Alice, who had three children. She was kind and caring, and I knew we would be friends, but friendships take time to grow. I also had met Simone, a war bride from France, and

1959 - Our home in Ada.

Marcella, a war bride from Florence, Italy. What we had most in common was our longing to visit our families in Europe again. Whenever we did visit, homesickness surfaced and took hold much stronger than I had experienced in years. I felt that if I did not get home to my family in Germany this very summer I would be here forever. I was without hope, without a plan and without interest in my new surroundings. Our home in Crookston was still unsold, and we paid the monthly mortgage and at the same time we also paid on our new home. Money was tight. We still had no health insurance, so we were billed for clinic calls and medications. Roy needed eye drops, Sandy needed penicillin for ear aches, and Kenny took ulcer medication. When the kitchen stove quit working and the electrician said it was beyond repair, I broke down and wept because the additional monthly payment, of $14.00 for the new stove, took our budget to the breaking point. While I worried every month if we could meet our bills, I learned to serve macaroni and cheese several different ways. Sunday's hamburger and tomato casseroles or various hot pies cut the cost of food. Baked potatoes were another inexpensive food because several farmers sold one hundred pounds of potatoes for one dollar. Next fall, we could pick what was left in the fields for free. I improved my sewing skills, and we managed to meet our payments due on time.

While Roy and Sandy made friends at school and in the neighborhood, I was losing it. Life seemed not worth living, and I had bouts of depression that seemed to drag on longer and stronger each time. I was guilt-laden and homesick. I sent photos of our new home to Mama, but I never shared how we lived within. Kenny was worried and when the local bank president had asked Kenny how the family was doing, Kenny said later that he couldn't understand why he confided his concern about my depression to the local banker. The man immediately invited us to visit him and his wife and share their Saturday supper. I liked them instantly. They fussed over Roy and Sandy and in their gentle way they asked me about my family in Germany.

I told them about Mama and how we all waited to hear from Papa who was still missing in Russia. I recalled how Max was living in Canada and that Theresa and her husband John were living in Rochester N.Y. I shared that Irmgard was now married and had moved to Munich, while Werner, who had been a toddler when I had left thirteen years ago, attended tech school and lived at home with Mama. The family I had left behind was no more, and I missed them like never before. Suddenly, homesickness gripped me, I wept and couldn't stop.

Kenny put his arms around me and pleaded, "Annelee, come on, I will take you home."

"No, Kenny," I lashed out, "It is thirteen years since I was home. I should be home, but I can't go home and you know that!"

Kenny looked shocked. He could not believe my sudden outburst but I felt better. Maybe, just maybe, he would finally realize just how much I hurt. I felt he took and took from me. Well, I couldn't give anymore. Roy and Sandy matched our silence on the way home and they quietly readied themselves for bed. They said good night and closed their doors.

Kenny sat at the table, and he took his medication for his ulcers. He looked at me, a beaten man. His words came slowly, "Annelee, I am trying to do the best I can but it seems it isn't good enough for you?"

"We should have stayed in Crookston," I retorted. "We wouldn't have double mortgage payments. Roy and Sandy were happier there, and I think you and I were happier also."

"As soon as we sell the house in Crookston," Kenny uttered, "I will send you home since it seems Ada isn't home to you."

I remained stubbornly silent and went past him into the bedroom, grabbed the bedspread and punched the pillow before I held it close to me.

"Good night, sleep well." I called out, "I am sleeping on the sofa."

"Oh, no, you won't," Kenny admonished. "I will sleep on the sofa!"

"Well, that's fine because I am not going to fight with you. Good night!"

I slammed the bedroom door shut and went to bed. The next morning, Kenny had left early. Roy and Sandy were silent and they held hands while they walked to school. Alone, deep shame overtook me. I had never embarrassed Kenny before and my lashing out at him in front of almost strangers troubled me deeply. It didn't help that Mr. P. was the bank president and I knew that from now on Kenny would avoid meeting him. But Mr. P. had other plans.

It was mid-morning when Mr. P. called, "Annelee, I would like to bring my wife and visit with you and the family. Would that be okay? I checked with Kenny, and he said you should set the time and day."

How could I say no? So I agreed that right after supper would be a good time. I knew I could bake a buttercream torte, one of the fanciest and most delicious German desserts.

After Kenny came home, I questioned. "Do we owe any money to the bank for house payments or for anything else?"

"No." Kenny assured me, "It has been hard, but we always made the payments on time. Matter of fact, I do try to make them a couple days early, and we are never late. Just relax."

If our guests were perplexed or bothered by my verbal onslaught last night, they surely didn't show it. They had small gifts for Roy and Sandy, and Mr. P. addressed the reason for their visit.

"Annelee," he said, "let's talk before we have dessert. We have seen how homesick you are for your family and Germany. We understand and we want to help because flights are expensive. We talked with Kenny. We want to lend you $1,500 so you and the children can visit with your mother and family. It is our private money not from the bank, and you can pay us back when you can. This is our condition before we lend you the money - this will be just between us; no one will know that we are helping out. Say yes, so we can have that beautiful dessert I see in the kitchen."

Kenny's nodded, and I was overwhelmed and filled with wonder. How could these people we had just met be so good and understanding and selflessly lend us a sum of money that would take us years to save.

"Well," Mr. P. asked, "is there a problem?"

I shook my head and reached for him and his wife. "Thank you, thank you," was all I could say.

"Please, don't address us as Mr. and Mrs. P. From now on, we are simply Lawrence and Thea."

The evening passed with delightful suggestions from our new friends. Lawrence offered, "If you need any help arranging the flight or with anything else, you only have to ask. Otherwise, we won't interfere."

I was surprised because my next door neighbors, the Schlagels whom we barely knew, expressed how happy they were for me that after thirteen years of absence I could go back to Germany. There was so much to accomplish before we left. Appointments for passport photos, health exams and shots, flight arrangements and the purchase of clothes and small gifts filled our days. When I was sure that everything was in order, I called Uncle Pepp and asked him to have Mama call me.

Uncle Pepp threatened, "Anneliese, it just better be good news or I won't get Peppi to the phone. Are you pregnant? Are you well? You know that your mama can't take any more bad news."

"Just let her call. I promise it will be good news, and I am not pregnant."

I knew it was Mama when the phone rang. "Anneliese, Pepp insisted that he stay on the phone. What is your news? Just tell me right now, I can't wait, and neither can Pepp!"

"Mama," I exclaimed, "I am coming home! I am coming home with Roy and Sandy on June 6."

"Thank you God," Mama whispered. "How I have prayed all these years that I would live to see you again. June 6 is in two weeks. Anneliese, see to it that all of you stay well so nothing will change the day of your arrival. God Bless you till then."

Uncle Pepp took over. "Where do we pick you up, in Munich or Nuremberg?"

"We will take the International Express Railroad from Amsterdam to Nuremberg, arrival time 1:00 p.m."

"We will be there." Uncle Pepp's reply was euphoric. "Finally, some news we can celebrate. We will have a lot to do before we see you and the children. Wait. Why isn't Kenny coming?"

"He just started a new job, so he feels he can't leave. His parents will stay here with him."

"That's good then he won't be alone. Will you need anything?"

"No, Uncle Pepp, I have everything I need. I am coming home to be with all of you."

"We will make your arrival a day to remember!" Uncle Pepp added, "We will call the day before you leave. Good-bye and God bless your family."

The two weeks flew by and finally it was June 5. Thea, Lawrence and the Schlagels, our neighbors, expressed their good wishes as they bid us good-bye. I, Roy and Sandy, Kenny and his parents were packed and ready for the long drive to the Airport Motel in Minneapolis where we spent the night. I was tired but the anticipation of seeing my loved ones in Germany after thirteen years kept me awake. I imagined how I would greet Mama and Uncle Pepp. I wondered how they would react to my children, and how Roy and Sandy would cope with the language barrier. All these questions kept me unsettled into the morning hours. Kenny, too, could not sleep because he was concerned how I would manage with two children and four suitcases when we changed airports in New York.

"I should have gone with you, but I thought I should not leave my new job right after I started working. Annelee, I love you, so come back to me."

"Kenny, the summer will go by quickly, and we will come back, I promise. You know I love you."

We stayed in each others arms until sleep overtook us.

It was morning when Roy called out, "Mom, Dad, Grandpa said that we need to have breakfast and get to the airport. You must get up! We can't be late or we will miss our flight. Come on!"

CHAPTER 17

June 1960 - Off to Germany

Roy's and Sandy's eyes darted back and forth as they entered the Minneapolis airport and watched the big planes land and take off. "I should have come with you," Kenny said again, "but it is too late now. Annelee, I need you and the children. I can't live without you. Just remember that."

"I love you, and we will be back," I assured him. "Stay well while you wait for our return."

After the last boarding call, we walked outside and boarded the plane.

As the plane lifted smoothly into the sky, Sandy and Roy were quietly watching the white field of clouds that lay below us. Within minutes, Roy who would be twelve on December 19, and Sandy would celebrate her eighth birthday the very same day, started what they called their sky game. The distant powder-puff shapes became their animals, snowballs, dinosaurs or whatever their imagination could see in the distance. We changed airports in New York and after I pointed out the Statue of Liberty, Sandy grew quiet and asked, "Mom, if we go down and I fall into the big ocean, will you save me?"

"Sandy, we are not going down. But if we do, I surely will save you."

She remained doubtful, "Mom how could you save me when you can't swim? What will happen to us?"

"We will hang unto each other until someone saves us."

Darkness fell. The lights dimmed and the interior of the plane became quiet while we slept. After refueling at Reykjavik, Iceland we flew into Amsterdam where a custom official waved us through and we could leave the airport. A porter, hailed us a taxi and we boarded the European Express Train to Nuremberg, Germany. It was Roy and Sandy's first train ride. They were amazed that huge windows framed the narrow walkway which led to the pleasant, roomy passenger compartments. Roy and Sandy settled down in the cushioned window seats that could be made into recliners. We watched the changing countryside, but travel weariness overtook us and we slept soundly until the conductor announced the approach of our final stop, Nuremberg. I watched in wonder because there was no trace of the 1947 Nuremberg that I remembered. The miles of bombed out homes, churches and official buildings that had been huge mountains of rubble were now rebuilt in their former architecture. New cars and bikes moved smoothly on the newly constructed roads. Nuremberg was pulsing with activities and life. My heart pounded, and I could barely breathe while I made sure our clothes were neat and our hair was combed because we wanted to look our best when we finally met Mama and Uncle Pepp.

The train came to a stop. The conductor guided three redcaps to our compartment, "Frau Woodstrom, we will take your luggage and help your children to exit safely," one redcap explained in fluent English. "You will go with Mr. Solch."

Cousin Joey, Uncle Pepp's son, who had always been my favorite cousin, stepped aboard the train and came rushing toward me. "Anneliese, you are here! Welcome home."

He hugged me until someone reminded us that that we had to move before the train would leave. Roy and Sandy were helped down the steps and into Uncle Pepp's open arms while Mama cried out,

"My Anneliese, my Anneliese! You are here! You are home!" She reached for me and hugged me until I thought my ribs would break. As she released me, tears wet her cheeks, and she looked up to the heavens.

"Thank you, God, for letting me live to see my Anneliese again. Thirteen years I have waited for this day! Now I can hold my grandchildren."

Sandy and Roy reached out to their grandma, and Mama hugged and held them tightly, "Pepp," she said, "just look at my beautiful grandchildren!"

"Yes, Peppi," Uncle responded, "Roy and Sandy's blue eyes and blond hair surely show they are Solch children!"

He reached for me and hugged me, "Anneliese, you are finally where you should have been all these years! You are home!" He went on, "I must say, you have two beautiful children. Now let's take you home."

I looked at Mama and Uncle Pepp. Of the two, Mama's physical appearance had changed the most. She was now fifty-six, she had dyed her hair to a soft ash blond, and her azure eyes and her once gaunt face were now aglow with happiness. She was not as thin as she had been the day I had said good-bye. I could see that the days of hunger and struggle for daily survival were over. She was smiling as she clasped Sandy's and Roy's hands tightly.

Except for the thinning hair, Uncle Pepp, now sixty, looked much the same. He was six feet tall, slim as a rod. His thinning auburn hair was still parted on the left side and combed back from his forehead. His deep-set, steel-blue eyes watched Roy and Sandy, and he took charge like he always had.

Cousin Joey had been fourteen when I left for America, so he had changed the most. His red hair was combed in a young man's style, back from his forehead and it ended in a blunt cut at the nape of his neck. He was slim and carried himself erect like his father, Uncle Pepp. His blue eyes, the freckles around his nose, his pearl-white teeth and his smile kept him looking much younger than twenty-seven. He and I had shared border crossings with Aunt Lisbeth. We had said even then that at barely fourteen, when it came to dependability and responsible actions, Cousin Joey acted like a man of mid-twenty. He and I had always looked out for each other. We were more than cousins' we were best friends. Cousin Joey was now a newly-wed young man and he could hardly wait to introduce me to Marianne, his wife of four months.

Uncle Pepp had rented a minibus to take us home, and he wanted Roy and me in front with him, but Mama would not have it.

"Pepp, Anneliese and Sandy sit with me, and Roy and Cousin Joey can be up front if Roy won't mind?"

Along the way I named points of interest for Roy and Sandy. Roy was fascinated by all the brick and plaster covered homes that were built into the hills and cliffs or nested in the valleys. Most towns and villages had doubled in size since I had left. Mama explained that former refugee families had settled in the area since they could not return to their homes in Czechoslovakia or the East Zone. But some things had remained the same. Neighbors still tried to outdo each other when it came to varieties of flowers, gardens and trees that beautified each home. As we left Marktredwitz, a town about eleven miles from my hometown, we encountered a change of scenery. The highway, bordered by century old evergreen and leaf trees, led also to side roads that took the traveler into the deep woods. Beautiful walkways and paved roads enticed hikers, berry pickers and people out for a leisure walk. I knew the area because I had picked blueberries, wild strawberries and raspberries during summer vacations and during our Sunday walks. The heavily scented air of the pine needle trees beckoned me to the woods, and I asked Uncle Pepp to stop at one of my favorite spots.

"Anneliese," Mama protested, "We need to get home. Everyone is waiting there."

"Mama" I pleaded, "let's stop for just a minute."

"Peppi let her be." Uncle Pepp said, and he stopped near the walkway I wanted.

The fir trees in the old grove were much taller, but the pine scent was still invigorating as I had remembered. I ran from tree to tree, touching the bark like I had done often as a child. Roy and Sandy followed and touched the trees where I had been.

"Wow!" Roy exclaimed, "These trees are so tall and there are so many."

I took my children by the hand and walked to the tree break where the wide open, hilly land bordered my hometown below. I sat down on the grass while tears welled up and clouded my sight because what I had seen so often in my dreams was right here. At long last it was here for me to touch.

Uncle Pepp and Mama stood quietly by while Cousin Joey sat near me and reflected, "Anneliese, as children, we walked through these woods, now we shall show our woods to Roy and Sandy."

He reached for me and helped me up. We remained silent while Uncle Pepp slowly drove on to the outskirts of Mitterteich where I sighted my childhood home decorated with garlands and flowers. Uncle Pepp leaned on the horn before he stopped, and people came streaming out of the house, blowing horns or shouting, "Welcome home, Anneliese. Welcome, Roy and Sandy."

Irmgard and her husband, Adolf, came toward us. I was hugged and Roy and Sandy were fussed over, and before I knew it, Sandy was lifted up onto Adolf's shoulders so everyone could see her. Uncle Pepp took Roy and lifted him atop the iron railing that surrounded the steps to our home's entrance.

"Just look at these beautiful children," he shouted. "Anneliese isn't bad-looking either."

Some locked arms, others laughed and clapped as Uncle Pepp led us into the canopy they had set up in the backyard. The music, meat and vegetables, and baked goods could only be rivaled by the good wine and conversation with neighbors, classmates and friends. I was pleased how well Roy took care of Sandy while I was detained by family and visitors who had many questions for me. After all, it had been thirteen years since I had said good-bye. So much had changed.

As the evening wore on, I told Mama that I had to take care of Roy and Sandy. They needed to have some time with me. As I readied them for bed, they eagerly jumped in, hugged the soft feather pillows and crawled under the light down covers.

Sandy asked, "Mom, did you sleep in this bed when you were a little girl?"

"No, not in this one," I said. "After the war I even slept on the floor on straw."

I lay down beside them and they told me that they liked Grandma and Uncle Pepp. We recalled the long flight over the ocean, their first train ride, the woods and the big trees. We thought of America where it was early morning and Dad most likely had gone to work. I promised that we would call him when they woke up. Tiredness overtook them, and it wasn't long before they fell asleep.

I rejoined the welcome home party and it seemed no one wanted to leave. We reminisced about old times when Kenny, the 'Gentleman Soldier', had walked eight miles to see me. They wanted to know why he wasn't here with me, and they asked, "Do you really like it in America? Did you miss us and Germany?"

"Kenny would have loved to come," I explained, "but he had just started working as manager of an automotive parts store and felt he couldn't leave." I added, "Yes, I like my life in America. I was accepted as Kenny's wife, and the people I knew never treated me as the enemy alien I was when I came to America. Even the families where a son or father was severely wounded or died fighting against Adolf Hitler's army, even these families were kind and accepted me. Some of us bonded and we now have deep, lasting friendships."

"You haven't answered my question, did you miss us?" Anni, who had been and still was our neighbor and friend, persisted.

"Did I miss you? Certainly, I will always feel a degree of homesickness. I miss that I can't meet you on the street or in our home. I miss you because with my American friends I can't reminisce about our childhood and what we experienced during the war because we are unaware of each other's past. You will always be part of my life."

It was 3:00 a.m. when people started to leave. Uncle Pepp took my arm and motioned for me to come with him. "Anneliese," he whispered, "don't spoil your mama's happiness. Don't ask or mention Theresa and John or for that matter, even Max. Wait until she brings their names into conversation. Tonight, your mama is happy. She deserves that happiness more than you will ever know. I know that you don't understand my request, but do as I ask. You will understand later," Uncle Pepp pleaded quietly. Then he raised his voice for everyone to hear. "For now, sleep well tonight, I will see you tomorrow." He hugged me and walked away.

After everyone had left, Irmgard and Adolf, Werner, Mama and I were together as a family. Irmgard had been eight years old when I had said good-bye to her. She was now an attractive twenty-year-old about 5 feet 4 inches tall. She had cut her blond braids and now loose, open waves, framed her face. Her blue eyes still had that pensive gaze that I remembered, and she seemed as friendly and trusting as she had been as a child. Her husband Adolf was almost six feet tall. He had brown eyes and light ash brown hair. From the way he treated Sandy and Roy, I knew he loved children.

Werner, fifteen, was a handsome teenager. His curly, auburn hair was combed back to the nape of his neck, exposing a high forehead and his eyelids with their long, black lashes shut at times. He tried to stay awake while listening to the sister he had heard so much about. He shifted awkwardly, but managed a smile when Adolf reminded him that he better be a good uncle to Roy and Sandy. We reluctantly went to our rooms because the night sky would soon give way to sunrise and another day.

Roy and Sandy were sound asleep next to my bed. The heavy scent of the tall evergreens penetrated the cool night air. I stood by the open window and looked at the sky while I thought of Papa and I looked at the distant woods where we had walked and parted for the last time.

Into the silence I whispered, "Papa, are you still living? I wish you were here with us." I remembered what he had told me as he bid me good bye, and I begged him not to leave me just yet. "Anneliese," he had said, "I will never leave you because you will remember and do the things I taught you."

I knew now that he was right, since I frequently taught Roy and Sandy what Papa had taught me. While I looked at my sleeping children, I thought of Uncle Pepp. Why did he request my silence? No one had spoken of Max or Theresa and John tonight. Surely, there would be answers during the days ahead? For now, it was so good to be home. I thought of Kenny. While we were still in Nuremberg, I had sent him a cable and assured him that we had arrived safely, and that Mama, Uncle Pepp, and Cousin Joey were there to meet us. Now it was after 4:00 a.m. here and past 11:00 a.m. in America. I wished Kenny could see how good it was for me to be home.

It was after 9:00 a.m. German time when I awoke. Roy and Sandy were next to me, giggling. "Mom, we are so glad you finally woke up. Grandma came in but we didn't understand what she whispered to us."

"Well, let's find out what's going on." I replied.

Mama was energetic and glowing with pride as she shook her head and said, "Werner couldn't wait. He had to go to work. Pepp has been here already. He brought a tray of various rolls for Roy and Sandy, fresh sourdough bread, honey and homemade butter. We also have peanut butter, oatmeal, milk or orange juice."

Mama and Irmgard stood near Roy and Sandy. All they had to do was point and they got what they wanted. Adolf filled my cup with strong, black coffee while I held two slices of sourdough bread. I savored the aroma of the hard, brown crust and slowly spread its grain laden insides with butter and honey.

"We have so much in America, but where we live I could never find sourdough bread." I reminisced, "The last time I tasted bread like only Uncle Pepp bakes, was the day I left. This is my favorite breakfast fare."

Adolf sipped coffee and patiently waited until we were dressed and ready to enjoy our first morning at home. They had thought of everything. There were coloring books, dolls, doll clothes and a doll buggy for Sandy. Roy got a toy army base with German and American soldiers, a German toy train, and there was a toy farm with animals, birds and tractors. I gently reminded Mama that it was only June, not Christmas, and she said,

"Not everything here is new. Roy and Sandy need to feel at home. So don't worry."

For several days aunts, uncles, cousins, and classmates stopped by, and they invited us to their homes. A ten minute walk to Uncle Pepp's bakery frequently took an hour because acquaintances and even strangers stopped and pulled me into a conversation. Everyone thought I was so lucky to live in America. The movies had done their part to bring that impression to the people. They believed that everyone in America had money, lived in a big house, employed servants, drove a big car and traveled the world. The American way of life was a dream they wished

Before we left on vacation with Adolf and Irmgard.
L to R: Adolph, I, Mama, Irmgard & Sandy

they too could live. I tried to tell them we worked and not everyone in America was rich, but it fell on deaf ears. I could fly home, I had two well-behaved, beautiful children, we wore beautiful clothes, so we surely were rich and no one would believe otherwise.

It was Irmgard's and Adolf's vacation time so Mama suggested we should spend time with them. Adolf borrowed his brother's Mercedes Benz because it was roomier than his Volkswagen and it came with the most modern feature, a sunroof. Adolf reasoned that Roy and Sandy could remain in the car and view the ever changing landscape of Southern Bavaria and the Alps. The Zugspitze with its miles of century old glaciers kept us in awe. Along the way ice and snow were melting, and Roy and Sandy announced every waterfall by keeping count and shouting, "waterfall, waterfall!" With its window boxes, and the bounty of flowers throughout the Passion Play Village, Oberammergau, brought a welcome contrast to the stark mountain ranges. We stopped at the Wieskirche, the most beautiful baroque church I had ever seen.

Roy questioned the wisdom of the architect. "Mom, why would anyone build such a beautiful church with nothing else nearby? Just look at all the marble statues, the beautiful paintings and that big organ even though the next farm or village is miles away."

The *Neuschwanstein Castle* where gold, Italian marble, and the finest wood and porcelain were used profusely to decorate each room, was a stark contrast to the *Salzburg Fortress*. There, the rooms were sparsely furnished, the floors were cold, and dark hallways led to the torture chambers where the subjects of the Barons and Princes were tortured for real or imaginary disobedience.

Whenever Roy or Sandy gave me some reprieve from their constant questions, Irmgard and I reminisced. We thought alike and we found that we still had a bond between us that had never been broken. She told me how hard my leaving had been on my family and how good it was to have me home.

The week on the road ended, and we discovered Munich while we stayed at Irmgard's and Adolf's apartment. Momentarily, I had flashbacks to the horrific bombing I had experienced at the main depot during World War II but as we walked through the newly constructed depot and the streets of Munich, I marveled at the changes that had and were still taking place. The miles of destroyed homes and the hills of bombing rubble had been removed and downtown Munich was an example of revitalization. The architects had paid close attention to details that before World War II had given the *Altenstadt* (Old Town) Munich its distinctive character. The contractors and men who worked underground Munich doubled the space of shops and the three-story U-bahn, the Munich subway, connected the distant small towns and villages to factories, businesses, offices and other workplaces in and around the metropolitan area. Munich with its baroque, gothic, and modern style churches, museums, castles and shops was once again beautiful.

Munich had ceased to be the almost pure Aryan city it had been during Nazi time. Now in 1960, refugees and foreign workers from Italy, Turkey, Yugoslavia and Hungary were employed everywhere. They worked in menial jobs that they had found more desirable than what would have been available for them in their native countries.

"Just think, 'these people' live for procreation." Adolf complained, "They have children that they can't afford. One every year is their norm. The tax payers must subsidize their apartments while our schools and health care systems are overloaded. You can go down the street and not understand a word that is said."

We heard foreign languages spoken as we neared the Munich town hall where we joined tourists from all over the world. The huge crowd became silent and watched as at the stroke of twelve, the Glockenspiel figurines danced the *Schalffertanz (*Cooper's dance) around the huge clock as it had been first done by barrel makers in the *Marienplatz* (area around the *Rathaus*, townhall) after the bubonic plague had ended in 1517.

We walked past the *Hofbrau House* where Adolf Hitler started his rise to power. We had no desire to recall Adolf Hitler's past so we selected one of the smaller restaurants known for its Bavarian specialties. As we entered, the aroma of sausages on the hot grills filled our nostrils. Momentarily the waitresses clad in Bavarian dirndls held my attention. The low-cut, white blouses with elbow length sleeves were set off by tight fitting Bavarian blue, ankle length jumpers. Light blue aprons with beautiful embroidery enhanced their tiny waists. The waitress took our orders. Within minutes we enjoyed the traditional *Munich weiss wurst* (white sausage) and sauerkraut while Roy and Sandy loved the small, hot and succulent little bratwursts on a hard roll and the fruit-flavored mineral water.

We spent afternoons visiting the zoo and the many parks where street vendors and puppeteers entertained us. Roy and Sandy had gained confidence to go on their own with Adolf while Irmgard and I browsed in small specialty shops until we got tired. Then we met them at the farmer's market where the scents of the gladiolas, roses, daisies, and other flowers competed with the yellows, reds and greens of the fruit and vegetable baskets. The days flew by all too quickly, and soon their vacation time had ended. Irmgard and Adolf reluctantly drove us back to Mitterteich.

CHAPTER 18

Return to the East-West Line

Mama, Uncle Pepp, Cousin Joey and Anni, my cousin who spoke fluent English, were waiting at home when we returned ten days later. They were happy because we were back and they shared with me what they had planned.

"Anneliese," Uncle Pepp said, "we will take you and the children along the East-West line and I will also take my granddaughter Angela with us since she has never seen the border between Bavaria and Czechoslovakia."

Mama and Cousin Erna emphatically refused joining us, but Angela, Cousin Erna's six-year-old daughter looked forward to the trip. During the short drive to the border, Anni patiently answered Roy's questions. He couldn't understand why so many German people could never return to what once had been their homes and their country. I was startled by the absence of the small villages and farms that had enhanced the area in 1946. When I asked about it, Anni recalled,

"After the borders between Czechoslovakia and West Germany were officially established, fires could be seen for days and the black, jagged remnants of small villages and isolated farms were bulldozed. Since then only tall grasses and weeds remain where families had worked, children played and life had been good."

We left the car and Uncle Pepp introduced two German border guards who cautioned us, "Stay two feet within the German border. Take one step across the line and the Czechs will arrest you."

Uncle Pepp and Cousin Joey flanked Roy while Anni and I held onto Sandy and Angela's hands. The guards walked near the border's edge constantly watching the Czech and Russian soldiers who focused their high powered binoculars on us. I shuddered as my mind drifted to 1946 and I wondered if we crossed the line with Aunt Lisbeth's possessions right here. My thoughts were interrupted as Angela said, "Why... why they look just like us!"

Momentarily, I didn't grasp what she was talking about and I asked, "Angela what did you say?"

She pointed at the soldiers across the border and again exclaimed in wonderment, "Why they look just like us."

I realized she was referring to the soldiers across the line.

"Why, yes, Angela they do look like us," I assured her and then questioned, "What did you think they would look like?"

She looked at the Russian and Czech soldiers again and uttered, "Monsters. I thought they would look like monsters!"

Uncle Pepp who had heard part of our conversation remarked, "When will it end? Now we learn what Bertha has put into Angela's head."

That evening we listened while Uncle Pepp explained, "Bertha is the sister of Katrina, my first wife, who died after Cousin Erna was born. Bertha was also ousted from Czechoslovakia during 1948. She had been married to a Czech and thought that she and her son were safe. When her husband left her, she and her son could not stay. Bertha has never adjusted to losing her son while she was crossing over. She lives with Erna, and Angela is frequently present when Bertha relives her night of horror. The Czechs shot her son after she had crossed safely over to our side. She could not save him. She could only watch while the soldiers dragged his lifeless body away. Now whenever she gets the chance Bertha vents her hate. We heard today how Angela views the Czechs and Russians. She sees them as monsters." Uncle Pepp shook his head, "I wonder how many children are hearing similar stories on either side where people live with horrific experiences and memories of war. Given that, how can we think there will be peace some day?"

CHAPTER 19

A Broken Heart

Even though Kenny and I could not erase our memories of World War II, we had slowly started to heal. However, I found that in Germany the long term consequences of World War II were still evident. In 1939, Mitterteich had 4,469 residents. By 1945, 286 young and middle aged men were casualties of the war. Fifteen years later, 126 additional men were still missing in action. In most homes, women were the head of households and also the bread winners who coped as well as they could without a man as the head of a household.

Mama was well off financially but she sighed, "I would gladly live on less if Papa came home from Russia and I had my family near me."

Uncle Pepp who had been sitting near Mama suddenly urged, "Peppi, tell Anneliese what pain you are living with to this very day."

Mama hesitated, but Uncle Pepp insisted, "Peppi, get it over with so you can enjoy Anneliese's visit."

Mama looked troubled, and I was not prepared for what she finally revealed, "After you had left for America, it was hard for everyone in the family. We missed you so. Theresa cried for days, especially during the evening hours or whenever she came to the table. No one would sit in your chair. It was like we were keeping it empty for your return. Six-year-old Irmgard thought you would come back in a few days and when you didn't, she fussed whenever I left for a few hours because she was afraid that I too would leave and not return."

Mama paused before she went on, "Max left for Canada in 1954 and he planned to be back in two years. Well, it will be six years since he left, and he still isn't home. Theresa was always close to me and I knew I could always depend on her. Before Theresa married John in 1950, she promised that she would still live at home with me. John commuted every week to and from Amberg where he worked. A year later, they moved and worked in Amberg, about seventy-five miles from here. They still came home almost every weekend and that was good."

It seemed as if Mama forgot that we were listening, as she recalled with effort, "It was July 1956. John and Theresa were home for the weekend. On Saturday John painted the window frames while Theresa and I cleaned until everything sparkled. John had purchased several varieties of cold cuts, vegetables and fruits for the Sunday evening meal, so we had a cold plate supper with breads and hard rolls. Theresa and John visited amiably with Irmgard and Werner before they left with their friends. Later that evening, I readied myself to accompany Theresa and John to the depot."

Mama paused, but Uncle Pepp urged her to go on, "I was surprised when John said, 'Mama, you worked so hard. Maybe you should skip coming to the depot with us.'"

"Now John, I am not that old," I joked. "I always stop in and visit Cousin Erna or Pepp after you leave. We were half way to the depot when John again insisted, 'Mama, you should go back before you get too tired.' I was upset at his insistence for me to leave them. So I told him, 'If you don't want me to come with you, I won't.' Theresa was a few steps ahead. She turned toward me, waved and called out, 'good-bye Mama' and then she walked on. John also said, 'good-bye, Mama,' and he hurried to catch up to Theresa. The abrupt way in which we had parted bothered me and I wondered why Theresa and John were persistent to see me leave? As I arrived home Irmgard and Werner greeted me, so I put our strange parting out of my mind.'"

Mama was pale, and she opened and closed her hands. "Mama, do you want to go on?" I asked.

Uncle Pepp coaxed, "Peppi, go on, or you will live with it all the while Anneliese is here. She needs to know."

Mama hesitated, and I knew she was reliving what she recalled, "It was the second weekend after John and Theresa had left so abruptly. I was on my way to the butcher shop and the bakery when the mailman approached me. 'Peppi,' he said, 'I have some mail for you. Do you want it, or should I take it to the house?' 'I'll take it,'" I said.

"He handed me a few envelopes and then he gave me a postcard. I put the envelopes into my purse. Since the card had a huge cruiser ship on the front, I became curious. Who is on vacation? I soon had my answer."

Mama turned and reached for a small box that lay on the round table near the sofa. She took out a postcard and as I recall laboriously read,

Dear Mama,

When you read this card John and I will be on this ship and we are on our way to America. We will first stay with friends of John's in New York, and then we will live in Rochester, New York, where I have secured employment as a seamstress. John will look for work. We will call Anneliese as soon as we are in America.

Love Theresa and John
Greet Irmgard and Werner

Mama closed her eyes and tears rolled down her cheeks as she continued, "Dizziness overtook me. I tried to steady myself and I held on to the trunk of one of the chestnut trees that border the road. No! No! No! I cried out! I sobbed, my chest ached, and I was oblivious of anything or anyone around me. After a while I steadied myself and walked on to the kiosk nearby and rested. My stomach felt queasy. Like a zombie, I ended up at the bakery."

Uncle Pepp laid his hand on Mama's and interrupted, "When Peppi came in I thought that someone had died. She looked as if life had been taken from her. She swayed. I caught her before she fell and then I saw the card in her hand. I took it from her and read what I could not believe. My fist hit the desktop with a force that matched my anger. It was good that I could not get at John because I don't know what I would have done to him." Uncle Pepp cried out, "How could they do that? How could Theresa leave her mother without telling the truth about their carefully laid plans? It wasn't as if they had to decide within a day. Getting an exit permit takes months and even years as we well know. Had I known what they were up to, John could have left, but Theresa would have stayed. It was John's fault. I know Theresa would not have left that way on her own initiative."

Uncle Pepp looked at me and said, "Anneliese, believe me, your leaving was painful for all of us, but you told us that you would not change your mind. You would follow Kenny. Max left for Canada to gain a better life. I still hope that he will return. Both of you were honest. I will never forgive Theresa and John for what they have done to your mother. Had they been parents maybe they would have understood what pain a child's long term absence inflicts."

I read the card with a heavy heart because I understood now how my leaving must have hurt Mama. I stood by her chair, and I enveloped her in my arms while she cried softly. Guilt overwhelmed me. How could I leave Mama? I should have asked Kenny to reenlist and apply to live in Germany. My guilt turned to anger because I could not understand how Theresa and John could leave Mama, Irmgard and Werner the way they did? They were married, they had work, and Mama depended on them to be with her while Irmgard and Werner were in their teens. I was hurting for Mama and I was confused.

"Mama," I asked, "has Theresa and John ever explained why they left in such secrecy?"

Mama shrugged and Uncle Pepp answered. "John had a ready made answer. His reply always was, 'I had applied twice to emigrate, but Theresa always said no. This was the third time for me to get an exit permit and it was made clear to me it would be my final and only chance to leave Germany. I knew it would be best for all concerned if we left the way we did. I made the right decision because we have done very well in America so it was right for us. Theresa did what Annelee did long ago. She married me, the man she loved and Theresa, like Annelee, knew that she needed to follow her husband wherever he would reside.'

"John never considered that it was cruel to leave Peppi that way." Uncle Pepp went on, "We heard later that John's boss in Amberg had offered him a managerial position and a raise if he stayed in Germany. But, no, John was going, and that was that."

Now I understood why Uncle Pepp had asked me to wait until Mama would tell me about John and Theresa's leaving. I saw how Mama suffered because three of her children had chosen to leave home and move to distant lands. I thought of my children, Roy and Sandy, and I wondered how I would cope if they would leave me for distant lands some day. I had grave doubts. Could I be strong like Mama and go on living if my children were gone for years? My admiration for Mama's strength grew and I loved her more than I ever had. I silently promised myself I would come home and visit Mama as often as we could afford the flight. Mama was more relaxed the next morning and as if by silent agreement, we rarely mentioned Theresa and John in Mama's presence, and it became necessary that we gave our immediate attention to Roy.

He had developed a severe eye infection. Before I could despair on how I would get the right care for Roy, Cousin Baerbl, who lived in Landshut near Munich, secured an appointment with one of the best ophthalmologists in Germany. He found that Roy needed a better fitting prosthesis because his present one caused constant friction for the inner eye socket lining. Our extended family offered their help. Cousin Anni insisted that we would stay with her whenever Roy needed an appointment. They transported us to the doctor and within three weeks Roy had a prosthesis that was an almost perfect match.

By now Roy spoke sufficient German so he could partake in conversations, and he loved the fact that he had mastered the finer points of chess. His adult opponents said that when Roy played, he won fairly. Sandy and Cousin Joey frequently took to the riding trails on Uncle Pepp's horses Max and Fritz. Uncle Pepp brought his black carriage out of storage, and he bought a black riding tuxedo for Roy. They led the horses while Sandy, Angela, Cousin Joey, Mama and I sat inside and enjoyed the scenery around us until we reached the picnic areas scattered throughout the woods and hills. We stopped at chalets where it was as if time had stood still. Although the accordion player and the singers had aged or were newly hired, the music was still the same. We shared Bavarian food specialties while Cousin Joey and I let the memories of childhood antics spring forth. Whenever I protested that Roy and Sandy and I were getting spoiled beyond belief, Mama and Uncle Pepp just laughed and told me they were making up for lost time.

Within a month, Kenny's letters concerned me greatly. He rarely touched on my family in Germany or asked how we spent our time. All he focused on was my coming home. Annelee, why do you have to stay that long? You have seen your family so cut your vacation short and come home as soon as you can. I NEED YOU HERE WITH ME! My neighbor Joyce wrote that she was concerned about Kenny's well being because he was not his usual self. He was depressed. He smoked well over a pack a day. He didn't sleep nights and he was always out of sorts. I sympathized with Kenny but I could not bring myself to shorten our time with Mama because I felt strongly that she deserved every day we had previously agreed upon. Uncle Pepp said that Mama looked ten years younger since we had come home. Relatives arranged a reunion with cousins and friends and time flew by all too quickly.

Since we didn't want a huge farewell party, our departure date of August 29 was known only to the immediate family. We had said good-bye to Irmgard and Adolf on their last weekend visit, and now Mama, Uncle Pepp, Cousin Joey and Werner took us to the depot in Wiesau. Roy and Sandy truly loved the time they had spent with my family, and their tearful good-byes made the parting for everyone difficult.

Roy rushed up to Mama and used the German he had acquired. *"Oma, danke schoen fuer alles. Du machst viel fuer mich und Sandy."* (Grandma, thank you for everything. You did so much for me and Sandy) *Sandy und ich kommen bald wieder.* (Sandy and I will come back soon.) *"Ich liebe dich. Ich liebe alle hier."* (I love you. I love all of you.)

Uncle Pepp could not stop his tears as I thanked him for all he had done for us. He turned to me, "Anneliese, you, Roy and Sandy must come back soon with Kenny. Take good care of everyone. We love you and will miss you."

Mama and I hugged and I promised, "Mama, we will stay in contact with Max and I will urge him to come back to Germany. Stay well until I come back. I hope by then we know more about Papa's whereabouts." We silently hugged once more and we boarded the train.

CHAPTER 20

The Gulf Between

On the flight from Luxemburg to New York and then on to Minneapolis we frequently reflected on our good times with my German family and Roy already asked, "Mom, when can we visit everyone in Germany again?"

We landed at forenoon in Minneapolis, and I spotted Kenny as he waved a white hanky from the observation area. We went through customs, and finally we were united with Kenny. He kissed and hugged the children, and he held me tight as he said, "I will never let you go. I just can't take living without you."

I cabled Mama that we had arrived safely and I would call her after we arrived in Ada. All this time I hid my shock at what I saw. Kenny had lost thirty pounds. His facial features were drawn and his eyes had no luster. The smile that I loved so much was absent. He politely asked about my family and relatives in Germany and then he kept silent. Roy and Sandy sensed that something was not right and they talked quietly while Kenny drove through St. Cloud, Alexandria, and on to Ada.

Kenny's parents were glad to see us, but they were packed and ready to return to Crookston.

"You are tired from all that traveling. You need your own beds and you can come to Crookston next Sunday and tell us all about your trip."

Kenny took his parents back to Crookston while we unpacked our suitcases and settled in at home. We ate the supper Ma had made for us and as tiredness soon overtook them, Roy and Sandy were ready for bed.

I could not rest. I needed to talk with Kenny. I needed to know why he was so sullen.

On his return I offered him a cup of tea. "Kenny," I asked, "what is wrong? You don't seem to be happy that we are home?"

"Well," he replied, "you were really anxious to return when I asked you to come home early, you selfishly ignored my request and stayed on and on with your mother. That showed me how much you cared."

I was taken aback by his outburst, "Kenny, I cared about how you felt, but did you really expect I would leave Mama early? If you would have seen how happy she was, how much Roy and Sandy enjoyed being there - not to mention what it did for me - maybe you would have understood why I was not ready to leave."

"Just how much did you care about me and my family? It seemed we were out of sight and out of mind, right?"

"Yes, right," I retorted. "Since we are in Ada, we visit with your parents every weekend without fail. Ever since Roy was born, we hardly ever had a free weekend just for us as a family, and throughout the week you worked for your dad noon and evening. Your mom and your dad have been with us on every vacation we have ever taken. Remember, just once we had planned a four day vacation to Mt. Rushmore and we were going as a family. When the phone rang as we were leaving, I told you not to answer - but you did! Your dad had found someone to work for him and our family vacation disappeared right then into thin air. I should have known, they would be with us. They were with us even on our honeymoon."

Kenny remained silent, but I couldn't stop, "So I get to visit with Mama for twelve weeks, which after thirteen years doesn't even come out to a week a year. Yet you want me to follow your request, which was stated more like an order, 'Annelee cut your visit short and come home, now!' Never mind that Mama was happier than she had been in years. Never mind that Roy and Sandy loved meeting their grandma and my relatives. Never mind that for once my homesickness was still. I am selfish? Well, think again!"

"I can see that trip home was not good for you because you have changed!" Kenny exclaimed. "Now you say things to me you have never said before. So I should be happy? Annelee, I am concerned."

"I am concerned too. It is your attitude that concerns me. Even Thea and Lawrence saw that I needed to go home. I felt like a drowning person who couldn't get a log to hang onto. I don't know what would have happened if I could not have gone home when I did. I needed to see my family in Germany. I needed to smell the woods. I needed to feel the earth. I needed to get back to where I was born."

Kenny shook his head, "I don't think your heart and soul have ever been here. I see now that you belong much more to Germany than you belong to me."

"I have tried my best to make this my homeland," I cried out. "You don't have a clue what it takes to leave everything you ever knew and start anew in a foreign country, in a foreign environment. Overnight I lost the ability to communicate, I changed from war to peace, from being single to being married, and I changed my faith and became a Lutheran. You are forty-four years old and you have never left your mom and dad. To this day, you still are much more tied to your family than I ever was to mine."

I could not stop the rambling, nor could I stop the flow of my tears.

"Kenny," I expounded, "sometimes I feel like an onion because you peel off one skin after another. Well, I am telling you, you had better watch it! I don't have anymore skins left to peel. When I flew home to visit Mama, I think I was down to my last skin."

I was weak inside, but I couldn't stop bringing to the surface what I had kept within me all these years. "Now I have a suggestion for you! Why don't you come to Germany and make all the changes necessary to live there? Could you survive there? I don't think so! No, I know so! Since we spent every weekend with your mom and dad, what would you do if you could not see them for thirteen years? Only after you have experienced what I lived through should you judge what you think are my failures. Now you can think about what I have said. I am going to bed, and I don't feel like celebrating because presently I am not happy that I am home with you. Good night! I will see you in the morning."

I felt drained. Kenny and I had never been so far apart, and he must have felt the same way because he slept on the sofa and went to work without waking me. I knew we loved each other, but so far nothing was resolved. Our relationship suffered and Kenny and I were cordial to each other, but the closeness we once had was lost, and we did not know how to retrieve it.

It was good that we were kept busy. Within a week Roy entered sixth grade, and Sandy could hardly contain her excitement because she now was in first grade and she finally could ride her bike to school. Ten months had passed when the Crookston real estate agent called, and told us that he had a buyer for our Crookston home. As soon as the sale was final, Kenny said, "I am going to see Lawrence today and I will pay him in full."

Lawrence told Kenny that there was no hurry we should make monthly payments, but Kenny would not hear of it and paid in full. After we paid off the mortgage on our Crookston home and made a payment on our Ada home, we barely stayed financially afloat.

CHAPTER 21

1960-1963 - The World of Work

Ever since my return I had felt guilty because the rift between Kenny and me remained. I wondered if the $1,500 I had spent on our trip was part of the cause. So I voiced a thought that had been with me for some time.

"Kenny," I said, "Roy and Sandy are in school. I think it is time that I find work."

Kenny admonished, "Wives stay at home and take care of their family. My mother always stayed home. She took care of us and was satisfied and happy."

I argued, "Times have changed. Roy and Sandy are in school. I am not your mother and I am going to work because I want to help lessen our financial struggle."

He shrugged, "Who can argue with a stubborn German? I can't believe how you have changed since you were in Germany."

Within a week I was employed part time as the secretary of our church, but working just sixteen hours a week at one dollar hourly wage was not sufficient to ease our financial commitments. I needed additional work and within a month I was employed as a sales person at the J. C. Penney Store. The pay scale was eighty-five cents an hour and the manager offered a twenty-seven hour work week. I took the job, and with a seventeen percent sales discount on purchases, I hoped we could manage. Within weeks, I was promoted to do the store windows. The mannequins were heavy, and after the first frost, freezing cold made me shiver while I displayed seasonal merchandise. I learned to print all the sale and price signs. Being around customers and other sales clerks increased my self-confidence, and I knew I could do a good job with all the new skills I had acquired. After six months on the job, I approached the manager and asked for a wage increase.

"You are still new here," he reflected, "so why should I give you a raise?"

"When you hired me, I had no idea how to do windows, make signs, or do inventory," I recounted. "You said yourself that the customers like the way I dress the mannequins and display the merchandise. I should be worth more than when I started. If you don't think I am doing an adequate job, then maybe you should let me go."

The manager looked perplexed, "I will not promise anything but I will let you know my decision. For now, get back to work on that window."

It was almost closing time when the manager approached me. "Annelee," he said, "your new pay scale will be a dollar an hour. See you tomorrow." He turned and walked on. I wasn't sure if he heard my "Thank you" and my sigh of relief.

We still spent evenings with Lawrence and Thea, and our social interaction with our neighbors, Joyce and Marvin, and their four-year-old daughter Beth, became more frequent. Marilyn's and Leo's backyard joined ours. Their son, Mike was in Sandy's grade and soon we shared leisure times and our friendships took roots.

As I had promised Mama we stayed in touch with Max, and finally in 1962, we arranged to meet in Kenora, Ontario where he worked as a wood cutter. When I had left Germany in 1947, Max was a twelve-year-old, nature loving sixth grader. When we couldn't find him at home, we knew he was roaming the woods and he would return with hurt birds, neat stones, and worms for his fishing rod. Now he was twenty-seven, and he and I were elated as we met at the Kenora Motel. Max spoke English without an accent and we recalled old times in Germany. Roy and Sandy were fascinated by the stories their Uncle Max told about cutting huge trees in the deep woods of Canada. Wide-eyed, they listened as he told them about lying still barely breathing while the bears stole the food that the workers had hung on tree branches near their work area. It became evident to us that Max still loved the woods and he hoped to become a foreman of a cutter group. Max briefly mentioned Theresa and said that John had offered him a job in Rochester, but the offer was tied to several conditions. He could live with them if he promised to work in the factory where John was employed. However, when Max explained that he detested factory work, the offer to live in Rochester was withdrawn. We exchanged recent photos I had taken of our family in Germany, and we took photos of Max and our visit. As time came for us to leave, we promised each other that we would soon meet again.

During spring of 1963, Theresa called. "Anneliese," she said, "John has purchased a tourist ticket from the Rochester German Club, and he has booked a July split flight for Mama to visit us. If you drive to Rochester, Mama can return with you to Ada and stay for at least ten days. Then she could use her split return flight from Fargo to Rochester."

Roy, Sandy and I were euphoric and even Kenny was happy that he could see Mama again. I worked double shifts because our 1951 Ford needed major repairs before we could attempt such a long trip. Kenny bought a reconditioned motor and his friends helped with the installation. The bottom floor on the front passenger side of our car had broken through and while Kenny drove I could watch the paved highway and gravel roads go by. I covered the hole with my best, large size cookie sheet. The inside door covers showed wear and tear, so I purchased blue upholstery material and recovered the inside doors and seats. Before we left, Joyce told me that she could not believe it was the same car she had seen before.

Finally, we were on our way. After an overnight stop at Kenny's sister at Rochelle and another in Cleveland, we drove on to Rochester where Mama was waiting. We had barely stopped when Roy was out of the car and threw himself into Mama's open arms.

"Grandma, Grandma," he shouted, "come home with us!"

Mama smiled, ruffled his hair, and reached for Sandy. Wordlessly, Mama hugged Kenny as he rushed up to her and held onto her.

"Mama," he said, "good to have you here."

I joined them and I hoped that with Mama here, Kenny and I would have a chance sorting out our differences that kept us apart. After sixteen years I finally met Theresa's husband. He was highly focused on becoming financially secure and successful. John liked Rochester because it had numerous beautiful parks, several authentic German grocery stores, butcher shops, bakeries, and small department stores where people still spoke German. All these factors made the transition for Theresa and John less difficult.

One evening we walked through a park, and we were accosted by a severely inebriated young man. "Mee e steer," he cried out, "do you have a dime?"

John threw several coins as far from us as he could and the man waddled after them.

Disgusted, John recalled, "Several weeks ago Theresa and I saw a drunk, young man sitting near a building out here. He muttered Polish phrases, so I knew he was a landsman and I thought I would help him. He slurred, "Do you have a dime? I need a dime for coffee!"

I walked up to him and reprimanded in Polish. "Listen, you are a landsman of mine, and I don't like seeing you drunk and giving our country a bad name. Promise that you will quit drinking and I'll tell you what I will do for you." That got his attention so I offered, "I will put you up in a hotel and pay for a week's stay. We will have to get you clean clothes. Then you must find a job, and no more drinking. I set all that up for you right now if you promise to follow my rules."

John shook his head, "Can you believe it? All I wanted for him was to better himself. I was going to give him a start."

"You know what that drunk said to me?" he sneered, "All I want is a dime for a cup of coffee."

John related, "Did he take me for stupid or something? If I gave him any money, he would just drink it up, so I let him sit there and for all I care he can die a drunk. I only threw money to the guy tonight, so he wouldn't bother Roy and Sandy."

John and Kenny had tried to contact Max. But his lumber company manager had told them that the wood cutters moved deeper into the woods every day and they would not be back in Kenora before Mama's return flight.

We stayed the weekend before we took Mama on the long trip home to Ada. I recalled my first trip from New York to Crookston, and Mama too could not envision the largeness and diversity of each state. After we had been traveling for three days, she asked, "Anneliese, when will we get to your home?"

"Remember when we left St. Paul this morning, I told you we would be home in about five hours. Now, we have about an hour's drive left, and we will be home."

Mama liked our home and she quickly adjusted to our daily routine. We shopped so she could bake and serve German apple strudel, strong coffee with whipped cream, a dash of cinnamon and sugar and two teaspoonfuls of rum. Supper guests were introduced to steaming hot potato dumplings or Spaetzle with Sauerbraten, gravy and salads. Her buttercream torte served with ice coffee became the favorite of our guests. I was happy because everyone liked Mama and Kenny loved having Mama with us. She still called him her 'Gentleman Soldier.'

I treasured my private time with Mama because we could talk about what was important to us. One day, she remarked, "Anneliese, now that you have children of your own and I see that you and Kenny are good parents, I want you to think back. Were Papa and I good parents or should we have done things differently?"

I didn't have to think, "Mama," I answered, "of course you were good parents. There are many things I pass on to Roy and Sandy because you and Papa taught me what was right."

"We tried," she said. "You know people still mention how well behaved Roy and Sandy were when they were in Germany."

I interrupted, "Mama, I think that there is one thing that could have been handled better."

"Tell me, what was that?"

"Do you remember when we lived in the Stingl house and Papa bought Elsa's piano so I could take piano lessons from the nuns? I was barely six. I went for several lessons. I didn't like the nun, and I wouldn't practice unless you sat right beside me so I couldn't leave."

Mama nodded and said, "I surely remember. I finally told Papa, 'Theresa is going on two and she needs my attention. I don't have time to sit with Anneliese while she plays and complains. I am not going to fight with her. If she won't practice, she doesn't need a piano.' But Papa cajoled, 'Peppi, don't be so hasty. Try her for two more weeks.' I did," Mama recalled, "and we had the same scenario every day. When Papa came home I told him that I was through forcing you to sit and play. Papa talked with you, but you told him that you didn't want to play the piano.

He had a chance to sell it and you were happy, no more lessons."

"I know." I reflected. "Mama, do you remember when I was in third grade, Cousin Erna got an accordion. I loved the music and I wanted one too. I begged, I pleaded, I pouted and I cried. All I wanted was an accordion for Christmas. I promised I would go to lessons, I would practice, and I would be the best player ever. But you didn't relent." I continued, "I think you and Papa were wrong. You should have given me a second chance because I know I would have been good. I learned to play the flute on my own, but I never really enjoyed it as much as I would have enjoyed an accordion."

Mama couldn't hide her surprise. Pensively she looked at me, "Anneliese," she softly scolded, "I don't feel that Papa and I failed you, and I will tell you why. As you grew up, whenever you wanted something you usually went after it until you got it or you mastered it. So my dear, if you wanted an accordion that badly, you would have had one by now!"

I was taken aback by her words, and before I could respond she said, "Remember this, sometimes we pine for years for what we missed out on or couldn't have. But then when we finally get it we find it wasn't worth all the energy and thought we had wasted on it. I hope you either get that accordion and become a good player or forget it."

Astounded I looked at Mama. She was right! If I wanted an accordion that badly I could see to it that some day I would get one.

My friends invited Mama to their homes. She couldn't believe that children ran back and forth across open front lawns and that we didn't lock our doors when we drove to Itasca Park with Joyce and Marvin. Mama was amazed at the acreage the farmers worked with their modern machinery. She attended the Lutheran Church service with me and she enjoyed the church member's picnic where games, music and contests entertained the children. While we were on our way home, Mama took my hand and shared her feelings with me.

"Anneliese, the people I have met in America are truly caring and friendly. Now I will feel better since I have seen where and how you live. You and Kenny have good friends, and Roy and Sandy are safe within this community. Personally, I would miss my hills, the woods and the streams. Although your lakes and parks are beautiful, they are far away from Ada where you live. I could not acclimate to the miles of flat land, which is often devoid of trees. I am older and the century old wisdom is right, '*Verpflanze den alten Baum nicht, denn seine Wurzeln sterben im neuen Ground.*' *(*Don't transplant an old tree, the roots will die in new soil.) Yet, for you, I can see that you are where you should be. I will always miss you. It seems you made the right decision when you came to America."

Mama's acceptance of where and how I lived was her gift to me. Seven vacation days had gone by and Mama wanted to purchase several special gifts for her family and her friends back home. I marveled at how quickly she came to a decision on what was right for each person while I could not decide on the appropriate birthday gift for Cousin Erna's daughter Angela. Finally, I knew that I had the perfect gift for her for her tenth birthday. I bought a Barbie Doll with several outfits because I was certain she did not have a Barbie.

We were wrapping the gifts when Mama suddenly stopped, "Anneliese", she asked, "is that a Barbie doll you are wrapping?"

"Yes, Mama" I answered. "I know Angela doesn't have one. Won't she be happy to get that gift?"

"I know she would be ecstatic, but I will not take that kind of gift to her."

Taken aback, I asked, "What is wrong with that Barbie doll?"

"Anneliese, I can't understand it. What you are thinking?" Mama shook her head and explained, "Little girls shouldn't have a Barbie. That doll is endowed with a fully developed body, she is dressed like a model and she has a boy friend named Ken. From what I have observed here, even four-year-olds cry because their Barbie doesn't have as many clothes as the Barbies of their playmates."

"Why do you in America rush growing up? Let children be children. Little girls need playtime. They should play with baby dolls, hold them and take them for walks in their buggy. One must start early to teach nurturing and loving. Some day, when you wonder where Sandy and her friends get the idea that they have to look like Barbie, wear designer's clothes and date good-looking, young men, maybe you could find the answer right here. I expect that we will see these dolls in Germany. I know with each generation values change, but I will not be the one who introduces Angela to that kind of doll."

I knew Mama was serious with her refusal so we settled on a summer dress with a "Made in USA" label. Mama said that Angela surely would show off that label whenever she had the chance.

We missed Mama after she left. I was encouraged because Kenny had promised Mama, "As soon as we can we will see you again."

I knew then that Kenny understood why I needed Mama and my homeland in my life. He realized that it was a bond that I could not or would not break.

CHAPTER 22

1963 - 1967- Turbulent Times

Mama called after she had arrived safely at the Frankfurt Airport where Adolf was waiting. She told me that she hoped that it would not take another thirteen years before we would visit her again.

As I reflected on the past decade, I knew that since we had lived with almost daily concerns that involved Roy or Sandy's health, their progress in school, our struggle to survive financially and getting our own relationship sorted out, neither Kenny nor I were active in politics. We were concerned when in 1961 the Russians closed off East Germany by building a ten foot high wall along its border. Yet, from 1961-1963 our youthful, charismatic President, John F. Kennedy, had inspired and united the nation, and he was loved and admired not only in America but Europe as well. He proved that he had nerves of steel when during 1962 he blocked the installation of Russian missiles on Cuban soil only ninety miles from our shores. The Cuban missile crisis had passed, and America was at peace. Rows of new homes extended the borders of towns and villages. Everyone who sought work could find employment. Young couples drove up to the drive-in theaters and watched family oriented movies while their small children were bedded down on the backseat. Life was good.

Friday, November 22, 1963, remains vividly in my mind. While I watched the local noon news, Walter Cronkite announced that President Kennedy had been shot. Unbelieving we watched the replay. As the motorcade approached the Dealey Plaza, in an instant the President's hands were around his throat, blood spurted out onto Jackie's suit while she crawled up onto the car trunk seeking help. We watched mesmerized as a Secret Service agent pushed her back down. The limousine sped to the hospital where the bullet was removed and the President was pronounced dead. A grieving nation watched as Vice-President Lyndon Johnson was sworn in as the President of the United States. Lee Harvey Oswald was arrested and he was shot before the Secret Service could arraign him for trial. Jackie Kennedy made the funeral arrangements. She observed traditions, and she addressed the wishes of the family. As his father's flag draped casket went by, Little John saluted. Now, decades later, Little John's salute still touches readers and viewers everywhere.

During 1964 America became enmeshed in the Vietnam War. We listened and read about North Vietnam's effort to enforce communism throughout South Vietnam. America supported South Vietnam's struggle to remain free. As early as 1961, 2,000 military advisers were sent to South Vietnam. By June 1965, our involvement of 23,000 escalated by November 1965, to 184,000 U.S. troops. They were now fighting in a country foreign to them in location, culture, and religion. I was against the war in Vietnam and mourned every soldier who died on foreign soil. Kenny and I walked on different paths again.

Emphatically, he said, "If your country calls you, you go and serve. If it means going to war, you go."

"Yes," I retorted. "That is exactly what Germany did under Adolf Hitler.   Kenny, I know that Roy's injured eye will keep him from being drafted, and I am glad. Most mothers, anywhere, don't rear their sons up to go to war, to fight, to get horribly maimed or die on a battlefield in a foreign land. The soldiers who do come home will be scarred for life you should know that! Look, your health has deteriorated ever since the war. No one can see that you suffer from ulcers and that your lungs are not functioning the way they once did. Yet, you are one of the lucky ones you came home in one piece."

When the nightly news reported the body count of the enemy soldiers our troops had killed that day, I could not listen. They were the sons of mothers who had hoped for a future for their sons just like I did. Antiwar protests broke out and paralyzed commerce in the metropolitan areas of our nation. I mourned the loss of the America I had known.

The civil rights movement gained strength and under the non-violent leadership of Dr. Martin Luther King, who won the Nobel Peace Price in 1964, the Civil Rights Act and the Voting Rights Act became law. Malcolm X, a strong voice within the Black communities, opposed Martin Luther King and he called for Black Power to gain dramatic change for his people. Riots erupted in Los Angeles, Chicago, Philadelphia and other cities. During 1965, Malcolm X was assassinated. In Vietnam, our soldiers fought bitter battles even though they knew the support of the American public was waning. Soldiers came home to a country that had forsaken them.

During August 1965, the owner of the locally owned Sears store offered me a job as his assistant sales person with periodic salary increases. After two months of training, I managed the store while my boss made sales trips out of town. Although my responsibilities were much greater than they had been at the J.C. Penney Store, a salary advance was never mentioned again. It seemed the hourly wages for women were frozen at one dollar. After Christmas 1965, the owner told me that his wife would take my position and I was laid off.

I told Kenny that I would never work for such hourly wages again. Theresa's husband John lent me three hundred dollars and during January 1966, I enrolled in basic accounting classes at the Dakota Business College in Fargo. I could ride with Marianne, an acquaintance who took classes at the Joseph's School of Hair Design. We left at 8:00 a.m. and we were home by 4:00 p.m. so our families hardly noticed our absence. I loved learning new skills, meeting people who aspired to have a better future and I experienced another world.

It was spring and the 1966 school year was in its final quarter. Sandy was in seventh grade, and she loved being in Junior high school. She was a sought after piano accompanist at music contests, and she also was considered a tough competitor for first chair flute in the junior high band. Her popularity became evident when she was voted in as Junior High Queen of 1966. On the other hand, Roy, a senior in high school was confronted by conflicting attitudes. He liked the Beatles because many of their songs dealt with social issues of our time. During 1964–1966, the school administration considered front bangs and sideburns similar to the Beatles' hair styles a bad example for the student body. I was upset by the negative reaction of otherwise sensible adults when Roy adapted his hair cut to the Beatles's style. Suddenly, he was viewed as someone who was different. Some parents, wary of the Beatles' influence, voiced their opposition whenever they found someone who would listen.

Several heated discussion erupted at home because Kenny listened to his store customers as they said, "Kenny, if Roy were my son, I would tell him as long as he has his feet under my table, he will cut his hair the way I say."

Kenny and I were active in church and we were Sunday school teachers, but even in our congregation we could feel the disapproval and hear demeaning remarks. "Why don't they tell Roy he better do what he is told" others would say, "I would tell Roy you will have your hair cut, today! Well, that shows you who runs that family!"

One Sunday after church Roy asked, "Mom, Dad, I don't understand it. When people go to church they worship Jesus. He had long hair - much longer than mine. Would people say it was all right if I said that I want to follow Jesus and like Jesus I want to have long hair?"

Kenny answered, "Roy, Jesus lived in a different country and he lived hundreds of years ago. You can't use that as an excuse for your long hair."

I told Roy that I focused on the importance of his behavior. As long as he didn't drink, concentrated on doing his best in school, and kept his hair clean, his hair style would not be on my priority list. Kenny, however, stayed angry. He took Roy's hairstyle as an affront of his parental authority and lack of respect. Roy's hairstyle created two camps within our family. Kenny and Roy's grandparents, they wanted the hair cut, but Sandy and I said that the length of Roy's hair should be his decision.

Graduation from high school loomed ahead. Roy had been accepted for his freshman year at Moorhead State College so during September he would move to his dorm room. We had spent the weekend of May 21 with Kenny's parents in Crookston. Roy and Kenny mowed the lawn, and Sandy and I readied Grandma's vegetable garden and cleaned the windows. We felt good because Grandpa and Grandma's home was ready for summer. We left late Saturday evening. On Sunday, I completed all remaining details for the open house celebration on Roy's Graduation Day, June 3, 1966. I felt good because everything was ready. But life changes loomed ahead. It was Monday, May 23, when Dr. Sanders called from Crookston,

"Annelee," he said "I am so sorry to be the bearer of bad news. Will you tell Kenny that his mother died at home, at 12:30 p.m. Can you both come right now to be with Andrew?"

"What happened?" I inquired. "How did Ma die?"

"Until we get specific confirmation, I assume that it was a heart attack or massive stroke. Tell Kenny and come as soon as you can."

I couldn't understand the sudden death of Ma because we had a good visit with her just two days ago. How could I tell Kenny?

Several customers were in the store and Kenny was not pleased when I asked him to come to the back because we needed to talk "Annelee, I have customers here. They don't have time to waste. We can discuss whatever it is tonight!"

"Kenny, it is important." I urged, "Come to the back, now!"

The customers watched and were silent wondering what was going on.

He shrugged his shoulders, "Women," he muttered and joined me.

"Kenny," I said, "Dr. Sanders called me," and before I could go on, Kenny interrupted, "What's wrong, with Ma or Dad?"

"Kenny, everything is terribly wrong because Ma died this noon."

Kenny paled and he was breathing rapidly. "We just saw her. She was fine. How is Dad?" he asked.

"I don't know, Dr. Sanders asks us to come immediately. I can pick Roy and Sandy up at school and then we can leave for Crookston."

"Annelee, these guys are working in the fields. I must give them what they need for their machinery. You can pick up the children and then leave for Crookston. I will get a ride and come up as soon as I can lock the store."

"Kenny, your mother died. You need to come with me. Your customers can get what they need tomorrow!"

"No, Annelee, just go without me and I will be there as soon as I can."

I knew Kenny would not change his mind, so I drove to Crookston with Sandra and Roy close to me. They wondered why Grandma had died.

I replied, "We will never know how much time we have to share with our loved ones. Death comes like a thief in the night."

I knew my answer wasn't the help my children needed, but at the time I, too, didn't understand what happened. As we approached Dad's home, we found that several friends, neighbors and relatives had already gathered there. Ma had already been moved to the funeral home.

Roy rushed up to his Grandpa and asked, "What happened to Grandma? Why did she die?"

Haltingly he recalled, "Your grandma was listening to her favorite soap opera, *Ma Perkins.* I asked her if she wanted her coffee refilled, and she nodded. I came back with a full cup. She took it from me, took a sip then she suddenly dropped the cup and fell forward. I put her head back. She closed her eyes, and she was gone. I called Dr. Sanders, but I knew he couldn't bring her back. She was dead." He held on to Roy and Sandy as he wept. They would not leave his side.

"Annelee," Dad said, "Agnes must be somewhere with Reverend, I couldn't get a hold of her. Helen needs to be called."

I called Helen and she offered to call her sister, Irene, and they would leave shortly. Finally, Kenny came just before supper time and his dad repeated what he had told us, Kenny talked with his sisters and assured them he would spend the night with his dad. Roy and Sandy and I returned to Ada.

On Wednesday after the funeral, family and relatives returned to Dad's home. It was then that Cousin Louis spoke up.

"Andrew, are you staying here in your home? If you do, we can look after you since we are just a block from here."

Our eyes were on Dad while he replied, "Thanks, Louis, but I am not staying in my home. I couldn't live here without Caroline. I am going home with Kenny tonight and I will live with him."

I was dumbstruck while all eyes were on me. How could I deny an eighty-two-year-old man who had just lost his partner of fifty-four years a night's sleep at our home? I looked at Kenny and hoped he would suggest that we should take it a day at the time. Kenny remained silent, and it seemed that Dad took the silence as an agreement to his plan and he stood up.

"Kenny, help me pack a suitcase. We will come back later for what I will need."

Kenny's sisters and their families cleared the table and Kenny and his dad emerged from the bedroom.

"I have what I need for now. We can leave anytime you are ready." Dad turned and said, "I will see you girls tomorrow."

The men sat in front, and Roy, Sandy and I took the backseat. As we left Crookston, I feared that Ma's death was also the death of the family life we had known. The changes became reality that very night. As we entered our home, Kenny directed,

"For the next few nights, Dad will sleep with me. We know it will be probably the hardest time he ever had to face, so he will need me and I will be by his side. Annelee, since there are two twin beds in Roy's room, why don't you and Sandy sleep there. Roy can sleep in Sandy's bed for now until we figure out what we will do."

I felt uneasy and overwhelmed by the circumstances thrown at me. I watched as the two strong-willed men who had an iron-clad bond between them entered our bedroom. I felt sorry for Roy and Sandy. Why should they have to give up their rooms that were decorated to fit their personality and had been their private sanctuary for the past seven years?

Suddenly, I decided, "Roy, Sandy, you will stay in your rooms. I will sleep on the sofa in the living room."

"But Mom," Roy said, "Dad said that we should change rooms."

"No, that won't happen," I determined, "I will not change your sheets, clothes closets or your dressers from one room to the other and that is final. Good night, try to get some sleep."

Roy and Sandy were relieved that they could stay in their own rooms, but I spent a restless night on the sofa and wondered what the future would hold for my family. I hoped that Kenny's sisters would come up with a solution. Silently, I lamented, "If it were my dad, I would never expect a sister-in-law to take care of him."

However, the changes I hoped for did not happen. As we met in Crookston the next morning, Helen brought up her dad's determination to live with Kenny and me.

"Annelee," Helen said, "it should not be your responsibility to have Dad living with you. I wonder if he would come to Rochelle."

Before I could say anything, Irene interrupted, "Hans and I would take Dad, but I know he will never live in California. He wants to be here with Kenny. We thought maybe we should find a nursing home for Dad. We could split the cost between us, and Dad could be in the same nursing home as his brother Charlie."

Agnes agreed. At noon, Kenny and his dad came back from the funeral home. His sisters shared their concerns with him. I knew Kenny would never hear of his dad living in a nursing home and I knew his answer.

"Don't worry," he said to his sisters and their husbands, "Annelee and I will take care of Dad. He will live with us. Dad told me that without Ma, he didn't want to live here any longer so we put the house on the market this morning."

My head was spinning. I had no control over any decisions. As a matter of fact, I wasn't even asked. I respected Kenny for caring for his dad's well-being and not move him to a nursing home right after Ma had died. I wondered, is that what happens when we get old? Do children just ship their parents off to a nursing home? I could see Kenny's struggle and decision. I thought of Mama. Even when we were children, we were told that we must honor people who were older, and we were expected to be courteous when we were in the presence of Grandmas and Grandpas. On a train or in public places, young adults always offered their seats to the elderly and asked if they could be of help. The elderly were never sent off to nursing homes. In Germany, it was the law to provide a stipend and living quarters until their death. I was scared. What changes would Dad bring to our lives? It was late when I finally had a chance to talk with Kenny and I asked,

"Kenny, we have three bedrooms in our home, one for Roy, one for Sandy and our bedroom. Tell me, where will your dad sleep?"

"He can sleep in Roy's room there is an extra bed in his room."

"Kenny, what are you thinking? You will put an eighteen-year-old and an eighty-two-year-old man who just lost his wife of fifty-four years in the same room? Whose room will it be, Dad's or Roy's? I can think of several reasons why that won't work. Roy loves the Beatles. I know for a fact that Dad abhors their music."

"Annelee, it is not an ideal situation, but I know one thing for sure, my dad is not going to a nursing home. I have seen what life in the nursing home is like for Uncle Charlie. He has become just another ninety-three-year-old guy to take care off. Uncle Charlie has changed. He hardly ever smiles and he has little to say about things that used to interest him. He just exists ... waiting to die. That won't happen to my dad because he will be living with us! That is the way it will have to be. Besides, Roy will only be home for three more months and then he is off to college so that should work out."

"Tell me Kenny, at what cost? Roy loses his room. He comes home and he is lucky that he can sleep in his grandpa's room. Did you ever think of asking Roy or me how we felt about the changes?"

"Roy said it was okay with him."

"Kenny, what do you expect he would say? After all, your dad is his grandpa. Roy still must give up his privacy and his room. No matter what you say, it won't work."

Kenny remained adamant. He took charge while changes were snowballing. Ma had been buried on May 26, and Roy's graduation from high school was scheduled for June 3· I would not postpone the open house because I felt Roy deserved his day of celebration as we had planned.

The day of graduation, friends and acquaintances met Dad and they admired the well-dressed, stately man who stood erect and had beautiful manners. His silver-gray hair neatly combed, his blue eyes alert, and his youthful facial features belied his age. Everyone guessed that he was approaching seventy, and no one guessed that he was almost eighty-three.

Roy and his classmate Linda Bjorge who had been his senior prom date, spent a great deal of time together during the summer of 1966. Roy took a summer job flagging for a crop sprayer that kept him away from home into early afternoon. He hardly ever had breakfast or dinner with us. Dad had moved into Roy's room. I worried because Roy just withdrew and took the changes in stride. Sandy seemed the least affected. She baby-sat at a neighbor's home while the mother worked, and in the evenings she brought her friends home as always. They closed the door to her room, took turns at the piano, sang and laughed until they tired.

I was frustrated but tried to adjust. We knew that Dad in his present state of mourning could not be left alone, so I didn't return to the Dakota Business College. It was good that Roy would start college in September because now Kenny had reinforcement when it came to the issue of Roy's long hair.

One Saturday morning Roy said, "Mom, I could have earned one hundred dollars this morning."

"To earn that kind of money," I pondered, "what would you have to do?"

"Grandpa offered me one hundred dollars if I went for a hair cut, and the other condition was that I couldn't tell you about the money."

"Roy," I asked, "did you take the money?"

"No, Mom, I told Grandpa that I didn't grow my hair long to earn money. I told him that I like my hair the way it is and I just wish he would let me be. He offered me more money, and when I told him that I wouldn't cut it for any amount, Grandpa got angry and told me that I was an ungrateful, spoiled rotten kid."

I confronted Dad who was in Roy's room. "Dad, what were you thinking off when you bribed Roy to get his hair cut, and then you asked him not to tell me? You may not know it, but we don't teach Roy or Sandy to keep secrets and take bribes."

"Annelee," he retorted, "I am a lot older than you. If you were smart, you would know that I am trying to save Roy and us a lot of trouble caused by his long hair. Most of the problems we have around here are your fault because you okay whatever Roy does."

Kenny's reaction to Dad's bribery attempt was, "Annelee, Dad is right, look at all the talk and all the problems Roy's long hair has caused."

I never expected that I would be glad Roy was in college, but I was because his absence kept him away from the changes that took place within our family. As the months passed, I realized when Kenny was with his dad, he was not the man I had married because he reverted to the dutiful son who honored and respected his parent. He even made it clear that we would do well to heed his dad's advice. Now I heard about decisions just before finalization set in and I realized that Kenny and I were no longer a team like we once had been.

Roy's first year in college became a time of great romance. He and Linda were in love. We realized that it had blossomed into a serious relationship, when Roy painted "I love you" in ten foot high, red letters on the street in front of Linda's home. He worked diligently on a dusty, old immigrant trunk that he had found in the basement of Dad's home.

Roy filled it with poetry and red roses and gave it to Linda. After Linda's dad died, they talked of the future and marriage. For Linda's mother, Hilda, and for us it became a time of great concerns. We felt there were so many issues that could influence their decisions. Linda had lost her dad; Roy had lost his grandma, his room, and the support of part of his family. But Roy and Linda were sure that they wanted to spend the rest of their life together and they planned to marry within a year.

Summer 1967 was past, and we expected Roy would return to Moorhead State but he told us, "I am going to leave college, for a year. I will find a job, save money, and then Linda and I plan to get married in December."

Upset, I interrupted, "Roy, statistics show that once you leave college, you most likely will not return. Think about it! You will be nineteen. You will need a college education especially if you are married."

"Linda and I won't be statistics. We will return to college because we know the importance of higher education."

Linda's mother, Kenny and I insisted that they should wait until they had graduated from college but whatever we said fell on deaf ears. They told us that they were determined to get married even if they had to drive to South Dakota and elope. Reluctantly we agreed to their chosen wedding date December 26, 1967. I needed time to cope because my dreams for him were not his dreams, and I feared what the future would hold for them.

While Kenny and I tried to adjust, Dad was disappointed in the choices of his grandson and frequently voiced his disapproval of letting that young one run the show.

After one such outburst, I said that it was best Roy and Linda were getting married in church rather than elope, Dad retorted, "Annelee, in my family, I was the boss and Kenny never went against anything I asked him to do. For everyone's good, I ruled our family. But here in this family, Roy, who isn't even nineteen, can do as he pleases without consideration for anyone else. It is mainly your fault and it goes all back to your family because your mother let you leave and fly across the ocean when you were barely twenty. That would have never happened in my family. You would have stayed where you belonged!"

Shock penetrated through me and I stood frozen to the spot. He blamed me and my family in Germany for Roy's long hair, for Roy getting married? I needed to get away before I would return in kind, "Dad, times have changed since you dictated to your family."

I kept silent. Kenny came home and when I served dinner without a word, Kenny asked, "What is wrong?"

Dad responded, "I guess Annelee is angry with me because I told her if she would have been in my family, she would never have left for America, she would have stayed in Germany where she belonged."

Kenny looked at me, I left the table and went into our bedroom. Kenny came after me and tried to console me, "Annelee, Dad still suffers from the loss of Ma so you shouldn't take everything he says literally. I am sure he didn't mean it."

"Oh, yah! This is the second time he throws my leaving Germany up to me. I wash his clothes, clean his room and cook his food. I take him to the doctors in Crookston. What am I? A maid he can kick around, telling me what I do wrong, and then he really tells me what he thinks of me? I think he wishes I would still be in Germany where I belong!"

I hurt to the core of my being and tears rolled down my cheeks while I went on "Another thing, I never can call him Dad again. I know for sure, my papa, after he lived in my home and changed our life like your dad has, would never have told me that I should go back where I came from, never! Another thing, he pays you fifty dollars a month for being here. Who is home and takes care of him all day?"

"Annelee", Kenny pleaded, "Remember, I have offered you the checks but you would never take them. You told me if they weren't made out to you, they weren't meant for you to cash. I do what I can under the circumstances. Believe me. It isn't easy for me either."

I interrupted, "Kenny, it isn't the money, it is his attitude toward me! I need to get away, I am going out for fresh air and coffee, I am going to visit with Judy."

I was still fuming when I arrived at her home. To an onlooker our friendship would have seemed highly unlikely. Even though this beautiful, young woman was barely twenty-four and I was going on forty-one, we loved to visit together. We frequently differed on ideas and beliefs yet our friendship grew steadily. She listened quietly while I voiced my frustration about my inability to bring life back to what it was before

Ken's dad had moved in with us.

"Judy, I know that Kenny's dad has a most difficult time accepting the loss of his wife. But neither Kenny nor his dad consider what they ask of the rest of the family. Roy gave up his room, I quit taking classes at the business college, and Sandy frequently spends more time with her friends. Our family life changed and will never be the same. I need to get some footing if we are to survive as a family."

Judy interjected, "Annelee, you always told me that you wished you could go to college, I am going back to Moorhead State College this fall so why don't you enroll and take classes? I already have one student riding with me. She pays me two dollars a week for gasoline. Enroll and you can ride with me too. Same deal."

"That would be wonderful," I said dreamily. "But I have no money. Kenny would never agree to it and his dad would nix it from the start."

"I'll drive in tomorrow to set up my schedule," Judy explained. "Why don't you come with me, meet with the financial aid director and find out if you could get a student loan. If you can secure a loan and you have a ride, Kenny could hardly forbid you to attend college."

That evening while Kenny was playing cards with his dad I told them that I planned to go into Moorhead the next day.

"Go Annelee," Kenny said. "It will do you good to have a break. I will check on Dad at noon and I will tell Sandy she must come home right after school."

It seemed fitting for Judy to strive for a college education, but what reaction could a forty-one-year-old expect from the financial aid director? Roy had been a freshman and I, his mother, was trying to become a college freshman. The enormity of what I was about to attempt hit me, and I hoped that the director would not be in for the day and I could go home telling myself that I tried but it just didn't work out.

But after the secretary had listened to my reason to seek an appointment, she said, "You came at the right time. Dir. A. is free for the next thirty minutes. He will see you."

As I entered his office, Dir. A. extended his hand, smiled and asked, "What can I do for you?"

"I want to find out if I can go to college," I answered. "I emigrated from Germany and married an American soldier. Roy Woodstrom, my son, attended college here. I would like to enroll this fall, but I don't know if it will be possible."

"Why don't you answer a few questions and we will see. First, I need to know your financial situation."

"I will be honest." Reassuring myself, I recounted. "Hardly ever, is there any money left after we pay our monthly bills, like the mortgage on our home, insurance, and living expenses. I truly need a loan to finance my college costs."

"Obviously, you have a family. May I ask your age?"

"I will be forty-one next month."

"How much education did you have in Germany?"

"That will probably keep me out of college." I uttered. "I was thirteen in 1939. Before World War II, I attended the Catholic Witness School, and after Adolf Hitler closed it in 1937, I attended the German People's School. Papa arranged for additional classes at the Catholic school in Waldsassen where I took short hand and typing. Before I could take English, we were pulled out of school right after eighth grade. Education was quite different in Germany. Monday through Friday our school day started at 8:00 a.m. and ended at 4:00 p.m. Except for recess and noon lunch, every hour of the school day was strictly for academic learning and there was daily homework for each subject. The teachers were extremely strict. If a student didn't master a subject within the given time, he/she was held back until a passing grade was achieved. After eighth grade, Adolf Hitler had decreed that we had to work either in a home, on a farm, or in a factory. I worked in a home and I was allowed to attend school every Monday afternoon. At barely sixteen, I was sent ninety miles from home, to the telegraph office in Regensburg. After six weeks of intensive training, I worked as a telegrapher until the war ended.

"Did you speak English when you came?'

"No," this situation can't get any worse, I thought, but I explained, "I knew, 'yes', 'no', 'hot', 'cold', and 'Crookston, Minnesota'. Since Kenny didn't speak German, we conversed using a dictionary at all times."

The director smiled, "Your English would be fine for college, you have a charming accent and you express yourself quite well. You need to complete a lengthy questionnaire this morning because I must see what you can do. Two more questions? Why do you want to go to college, and what do you want to study?"

I didn't hesitate to answer. "I always wanted to be a teacher, and that is what I want to do for the rest of my life. I also would be able to earn a better salary than a dollar an hour and I could help with the family expenses."

He advised, "As it happens, the board is meeting tonight, so I will bring your case to their attention. They may want to meet you and ask questions. If they agree to your admission and my proposal of a financial aid package, you will be starting college next month. By the way, leave your German graduation date open. Just write in 'no graduation because of war'. That is the truth, and it should be acceptable. I will call you tomorrow morning."

We shook hands. I knew I had a mentor in my corner and with his help I would work hard to succeed. Yet, I felt apprehensive while I completed the questionnaire and somberly handed it to the secretary. Trembling, I left the room, and I thought about the changes that could await me after my future would be decided tonight in this very building.

Judy listened carefully as I recalled my endeavor and she broke in, "You most likely will make it since the director is extremely truthful. If he thought you were a lost cause, he would have told you that there is no way that you could go to college. So how will you break all this to Kenny?"

Reality hit me, but I decided to put off the inevitable confrontation until I knew that the board had approved my application. I slept fitfully. I wondered what changes the telephone call would hold for me and my family. It was shortly after nine the next morning.

"Mrs. Woodstrom," Dir. A. explained, "several board members would like to meet with you about seven this evening. Can you be here?"

I didn't know how, but I promised him that I would be there. Panic overtook me. I told Grandpa (I had started to call him Grandpa) that I needed to talk with Judy. I ran to her home and as soon as she opened the door, I babbled,

"Judy what can I do? Several board members want to meet me tonight at seven. I need to be there. I need to get to the college."

"Slow down, Annelee," Judy said. "This is so exciting! Tonight can change your whole life! I'll take you. We will leave after five. Tell Kenny you need to go in with me and that's no lie."

Kenny was not pleased with my leaving for Moorhead again, but since he knew I was still angry with Grandpa he didn't object.

We arrived early. Dir. A. was waiting. "Don't be inhibited by these four gentlemen," he cautioned. "They may look forbidding, but they are actually very nice people. Judy may come in with us if that will make you feel better. We are in your corner."

Their questions were lengthy and more in depth. "Why did I want to attend college now?"

"Since Roy is going on nineteen and Sandra, fifteen," I explained, "I am free to attend college without worrying who would take care of my children."

"Your daily round trip will be a hundred miles can you manage that?" They asked, "Will you give up when winter driving gets difficult?"

"I have never given up on anything I really wanted to accomplish." I assured them, "Being a teacher is the priority on my list."

"Why do you want to major in English when it is not your native language?" One board member asked, "Would it not be easier for you to major in German?"

"I did not come here to take classes that are easy." I explained, "I want to achieve fluency in the English language, lose my accent if possible, and then teach English in high school."

"We understand," another board member said, "you will need a fully funded student loan. Have you thought of how you will pay it back?"

"I will make monthly payments taken from my teacher's salary, and if possible I will make double payments whenever I can."

"Can you start on September 27 when the fall quarter starts?"

"I surely would like to start soon." I interjected, "I plan to attend summer sessions because I hope to teach within three years not four."

The board members told us that they would take a fifteen minute break and then they would give me their decision.

Dir. A. brought us coffee, and Judy said, "I don't know why my hands are shaking." She looked at me, "You must be jelly inside, but I think you will be accepted as a student."

"I may get in because I will probably be the oldest student here, and I have an accent to boot." I reasoned.

Then we sat, sipping coffee until the board members finally entered the room and one of them spoke, "Mrs. Woodstrom, we voted to accept you as a special student for the fall quarter. If you do well, we will extend your loan each quarter as needed. Dir. A. will give you a $250 check. That amount should be sufficient for credits, books, gasoline and some snacks. Good luck to you. Dir. A. will keep us posted on your progress. Good night and have a safe trip home."

Dir. A. extended his hands, "Congratulations!" He said, "I knew you would make it after I interviewed you, and I know you won't disappoint me."

Judy put her arms around me, "Come on college kid," she coaxed, "I will drive you home."

Seated in the car, I said, "Judy, I may not have a home after Kenny hears what I have been up to."

"Annelee, don't worry. There are always the dorm rooms."

The 10:00 o'clock evening news was on when I entered our home. Kenny and his dad were playing cards. Kenny turned toward me and asked, "What was so important that you had to go with Judy tonight?"

I wanted to give Kenny my life-changing news so I asked, "I suppose Sandy is sleeping, and Roy is out with Linda?"

"That boy stays out way too late," Kenny's dad grumbled.

"Kenny," I suggested, "It is such a lovely night. Let's go for a short drive before we turn in for the night."

"That's a good idea, Kenny, grab my cap and jacket, while you are getting yours," his dad said.

So much for telling Kenny right now I thought. Well, it will have to wait. We made small talk while we drove around. When we were home again Grandpa said, "It's time we go to bed."

I had decided, "Why don't you wait a few minutes, I have to say something and I don't want to repeat it again in the morning." The men looked at me, startled. I knew I had their attention.

"You may not like what I will share with you, but it is done and I will not change my mind."

"What are you talking about?" Kenny interjected.

"Just listen." Anxiously I continued, "For the past two days I have been at Moorhead State College. I tried to find out if I could go to college and work toward a teacher's certification. I hope I can get a degree to teach English. I have been accepted, and I will start going to college on September 27."

"Now wait a minute," Kenny interrupted. "Have you wondered how you will get there? Our car has such high mileage."

"That is taken care of, I can ride with Judy everyday."

"The ride isn't even as important as the fact that we just can't afford college for you."

"That is taken care of too. I secured an approved student loan in my name. I hope to complete a teacher's degree in English within three years, and then I can pay back what I owe."

His dad broke in, "Why do you think that with your accent anyone will hire you to teach English? A German teaching English...that will be the day!"

Anger rose within me, "Grandpa, nothing you say tonight will change my mind. I know I can not get a job teaching without being certified, so I will achieve that first and then worry about getting a position and paying back what I owe."

Kenny looked at me, "Annelee, you won't be home all day. How will that affect Sandy and your housework?"

"I think Sandy will be proud of me, and we have almost three weeks to work out the changes that will take place. Let's go to bed now, and we can work on all the changes tomorrow."

In our bedroom, Kenny turned away from me and said, "Annelee, I don't know you anymore. You do things behind my back, and I am not told what you plan until it is a fact."

"Kenny, be honest. If I would have told you would you have agreed to my attempt to go to college?"

"Not by a long shot, because we need you at home. Women should be home for their husband and children."

"Now you know why I didn't tell you!"

"What will be your next plan that you will keep from me?"

The gulf between us had widened. I knew I had caused this particular rift, but I would not back away from what I had gained so miraculously because I needed to know what I could achieve.

Sandy and Roy were surprised when they heard about my endeavor.

They were excited and pleased. "Just wait Mom," Sandy exclaimed, "until I tell my friends that my mom will be a freshman in college. Wow!"

"Just think, after I am married and return to college, Linda and I will be in college with Mom. When my professors find out, they will say, 'Roy, you may be married, but if you skip a class we can always tell your mom.' Oh, man.'"

Kenny and his dad reluctantly went along with the changes. I told them that we would have casserole meals for supper, and they could heat up leftovers for noon the next day. Thursday would be washday, Friday evenings Sandy could go to games, but I would stay home, clean and iron. Saturday we would concentrate on grocery shopping and school work and plan for the week ahead. Sunday we would decide what we would do.

I needed new clothes, but that was easily solved when two acquaintances had a rummage sale. I bought two skirts, two blouses and a dress, all for fifteen dollars, and one black and one brown pair of shoes for five dollars completed my college wardrobe. I planed to interchange skirts and blouses and the dress would do fine with cardigan and a scarf.

Finally, it was September 27. Judy was at my home at 8:00 a.m. Harriet, had already taken the backseat, so I joined Judy and we took off. My classes were all 101 freshman classes: American History, English, psychology and biology made sixteen credits. I had purchased mainly second-hand books, and as I searched through the indexes and chapters my euphoric feeling of attending college was replaced by fearful apprehension. The contents were completely foreign to me, and I knew I needed hours of study.

At 9:00 a.m. as I stepped into the huge auditorium for Psychology 101, my courage dwindled. How could I compete against all these young people? Their eyes sparkled; they were in a jovial mood, and they called out and waved to friends who joined them. The energy of youth was all around me. These students were Roy's age and I wondered if they were thinking she reminds me of my mother. What is she doing here? I felt even worse when I realized that because I was hearing impaired since the war, I needed to secure a front row seat. As Dr. Solso entered, the noise in the assembly hall abated, and the 140-150 students applauded Dr. Solso's greeting. He reviewed the syllabus and told us that we were expected to use the terminology of the first chapter. I glanced at the list and again, I felt the onslaught of doom. How could I learn and remember the English terms for the German terms? brain or hypothalamus *(Gehirn)*, or Gestalt psychology (the body, personal build, mental and physical*)*, behavior or behaviorism *(das Verhalten, das Benehmen)*. Every chapter had terminology foreign to me which made taking notes as Dr. Solso lectured a frustrating, frightening experience.

Throughout the morning my experiences in each class were much the same. History 101 and Biology 101 made me question my decision to attend college, but English 101 gave me hope. The twenty-six students smiled as I entered. Several extended a friendly greeting and motioned for me to join them. The professor was a young attractive woman we learned to call Mrs. G. She told us she expected our best efforts then advancing to English 102 would be no problem. After the class ended, I waited.

She looked at her attendance record, "Mrs. Woodstrom, what can I do for you?"

"I thought I could manage college," I explained, "but now I am not so sure. I haven't been in school in twenty-five years, and I find that my education in Germany was much different than what is taught here. Maybe I should just drop out before I even start, but I want to become a teacher and I can't achieve that without a college education."

"I understand that you showed courage and determination when you applied for admission so don't give up your dream. With hard work you can reach your goal. If you have any concern or problems, my door is always open during office hours."

I could not believe it. This young, beautiful woman, a professor yet, took an interest in me and told me that she would be there when I needed help? I learned soon that she never wavered from her promise.

No one made a comment when I started to call Kenny's dad 'Grandpa.' Since my classes demanded hours of study time, I had to learn to organize my work load at home to precise hours and details. I rose at 6:00 am, prepared breakfast and lunch for Roy who had left college but lived at home while he worked for a construction company. Then Kenny, Sandy, Grandpa and I had breakfast. We cleared the table, made beds and readied ourselves for work and school. Grandpa stayed at home while shortly before 8:00 a.m. Kenny, Sandy, and I left for our respective day. Judy, Harriet and I attended classes, and we were on our fifty mile return trip by 2:30 p.m. I usually made an oven dinner, meat, vegetables and potato dishes so there would be leftovers for Grandpa's and Kenny's noon meal. We had supper at 5:30 p.m. Since we had no dishwasher, Sandy and I washed and dried dishes, shared our daily experiences and concerns, and every other night we took care of clothing. Kenny and Grandpa competed fiercely in whist and cribbage while Sandy and I started on our homework. I worked late into the night because I needed to look up unfamiliar English terms and then translate them into German before I could gain understanding of the chapter's content. Sometimes it took several hours before I could retire for the night. But with each passing week my confidence rose I expected to at least pass all my classes and I did.

CHAPTER 23

1967 – Wedding Vows

Christmas vacation started and Roy and Linda were busy with preparations for their wedding day, December 26.

Theresa's husband, John, called. "Annelee, we received an invitation to Roy's wedding. What is going on? I thought Roy was in college? He will be nineteen so why is he getting married?"

"John, we are not pushing that marriage. They promised that they would complete their education. Are you planning to come to the wedding?"

"No, we can't. You remember, we longed for sixteen years to have children. Now we have Heidi, two-and-a-half, and little John celebrated his first birthday this October. With two little ones we just can't travel that far."

"We understand. Hopefully, we will be able to meet soon."

Linda and her newly widowed mother had planned the wedding Linda wanted. Family, friends, several neighbors, classmates and teachers celebrated with them and wished them a blessed future. After a one day honeymoon in Fargo, they came home. Their youthful dreams were to drive to New York, find work, save money and tour Europe. On their way, they stopped at their Aunt Helen's home, in Rochelle, Illinois. While they were there, John, Theresa's husband called us,

"Annelee, why don't Roy and Linda come to Rochester and work for our company. Should Roy decide to pursue a law degree, our company will loan him money for his schooling. He will have to agree to repay us and become our company lawyer. Linda could find employment elsewhere. We'll provide a house on the property and in return for the lodging they are required to mow the yard, feed the swans, birds and deer and keep the small lake clean. Roy is my nephew and I think it would be wise for him to take the offer. Tell him to let me know if he will come."

We called Roy and Linda and they were on their way to Rochester, NY, while for us at home, life had fallen into a rigid routine. Sandy was back in school, and I had started the winter quarter. My classes at college were not easy, but like a dry sponge, I soaked up new knowledge because it filled the gaps that I knew had been there ever since the war. I understood now how right Papa had been. When I complained as a child that I didn't need to learn English because we would win the war and everyone would have to speak German, Papa advised,

"Anneliese, learn all you can and then some more. You'll see that if you stay physically and mentally fit, whatever skills you acquire and all the knowledge you gain will be yours forever. The more you know the more control you will have over what successes you have in life because no one can take your knowledge away. So, as I said, 'Learn, and learn some more.'"

I wished Papa could be here and see that I now wanted to learn not because he told me to. Now I wanted to learn and learn some more because it was important to me. We had heard from Roy on the sixth of January that they had safely arrived in Rochester, and he and John were talking about the offer. However, things would quickly change. It was Sunday. The temperatures were thirty degrees below throughout the Midwest and no warm-up was in sight. The phone rang, and I answered.

It was Helen, my sister-in-law in Rochelle, Illinois. "Annelee," she said, "Roy and Linda are here with us. They have taken warm baths and right now they are eating hot soup and drinking tea."

"Helen, what happened? Why aren't they in Rochester?" I stammered.

Helen explained, "They can stay here with us as long as they want. Roy can tell you what went on in Rochester. Right now, I just want you to know they are okay."

"Helen," I pleaded, "please let me speak with Roy".

"Mom," Roy said, "As you now know, obviously, things didn't work out. After we had learned about all the details Uncle John had in mind for his job offer, we found it was much more confining then we had expected."

"What happened?" I anxiously interjected.

"Linda already had a job to start next Monday. Uncle John told me that I would work in the factory during the day and attend law school at night. After I had my law degree, I would agree to be their company lawyer, like forever. John told me that I needed to cut my hair short just like I would do if I joined the Army. I wasn't going to do that! Mom, we are not even twenty! Linda and I couldn't see that we should commit ourselves to work for years for a company we knew very little about. What if we didn't like living under these conditions? So we told Uncle John that we were no longer interested in his offer."

The next morning Theresa said, "Roy, John wants you out of the house before he comes home tonight. So you will have to leave now."

"We were stunned. We packed our few belongings and drove away. We drove through Rochester, investigated the possibility of other housing and checked our limited amount of money. While we were exploring Rochester our car stalled so we locked the doors and spent the night in our car. By morning it had turned freezing cold, a station owner did minor repairs before we could leave for Minnesota. We made it to Illinois and decided to stop at Aunt Helen's who welcomed us with open arms. We will stay here for a while, and we will let you know in a few days what we will do. Don't worry, Linda and I are in good hands, and we are now warm and comfortable. I'll let you talk with Aunt Helen."

I thanked Helen for taking them in and hung up.

I shared the disturbing news with Kenny. I wanted to call Theresa but Kenny took the phone from me and said, "Wait a minute. We need to talk."

"What's there to talk about? My sister sends our son and his wife out into a city that is unfamiliar to them. Their car stalls and they sleep in it all night. Kenny, they could have been robbed or even killed."

"Annelee," Kenny cut in, "you know John just wanted for Roy to get a good start and have a chance at a better life. So Roy would have to cut his hair and give up his ideas. Everything we do in life has a price, but it would have been worth it. Now what will he and Linda do? He has a wife now, so he should think of his responsibility toward her, shouldn't he?"

"I knew you would side with John. Why don't you call him and thank him for all he did for our family. While you are at it, ask John how he would react, if we kicked one of his children out of our home? For me nothing is resolved. Let's wait and see what the newlyweds will do."

Roy and Linda had decided to stay and work in Rochelle and within a week they found a place of their own. They planned to travel to Europe, so they took temporary jobs. Linda worked at Del Monte as a receptionist, and Roy worked as shipping clerk at the Rochelle Wool Factory.

Kenny and Grandpa grumbled, "For that, Roy traded law school? Well, I hope he is satisfied."

"Kenny, it is not what you had expected of Roy or Linda," I admitted, I have to realize that they have plans of their own.

We learned months later, after they had returned to Ada, that the newlyweds had dreams they wanted to make reality. For almost a year they scrimped until they had saved two thousand dollars. We were elated until they told us that they were going to travel.

Roy and Linda spent time with us and in conversation one night, Roy said, "I always wanted to return to Europe. I want to show Linda the places of art and history I had visited and I want her to meet my grandma in Germany. When we return, we will go back to the university."

I was deeply disappointed, but Kenny thundered, "How can you do that? Put a down payment on a small house, get your education, work for awhile, and then make plans for travel or whatever you want to do, but secure your future!" Kenny's anger rose, "That's what John wanted to do, give you a future, but you just threw that away. Now, you make another mistake and throw the start you could have out the window so you can travel. There is a war going on, you travel while young men your age die in Vietnam."

"I never was or will be for that war. Dad, we are taking several months of our life to do what we want to experience while we are young and healthy. During our travel, we will be frugal. We plan to climb mountains and walk in the Bavarian woods while we visit with Grandma. We will make the most of our time and money, believe me."

Kenny and I realized that they had set their plans in motion. As the day for their departure came, we took them to the Fargo Airport. We hugged, assured them of our love and waved good-bye. For five months we pinned the European map, England, Germany where they spent time with Mama, Adolf and Irmgard, then they traveled to Austria, Switzerland, Greece and Turkey.

Kenny was disappointed and worried, "Are Roy and Linda seriously thinking of their future? What will they do when they return?"

They returned during February, and within days they were enrolled in classes at Moorhead State College, had part-time work in the library, and found an apartment within a five minute walk to their classes. It was good to have them home. At times we would meet between classes. Roy and Linda excelled in their studies and they planned their future.

CHAPTER 24

1970 - Finally Teaching

I loved my college classes because every day became a new, invigorating experience. My favorite classes were English and psychology. My happiness knew no end when as a sophomore during the spring quarter I made the dean's list. During April 1970, sadness gripped me when Mama called and told me that Uncle Pepp had died of bone cancer. He had suffered, but his mind was sharp as ever until morphine destroyed his alertness in payment for numbing his pain.

Mama wrote that people came from far distances to pay their respects, many spoke, "You may not have liked what he told you, but you could be assured that Pepp always told the unvarnished truth, and he always was a man of his word." That was the re-occurring tribute.

Mama told that he was missed by the family and she still looked out the window hoping to spot Pepp on his way to our home. Even the customers still missed him. They entered the store at the bakery and it was not unusual to hear, "It doesn't seem right, Pepp should be here!"

I, too, missed his calls. Whenever Uncle Pepp scolded me, I knew it was because he loved me and wanted for me to be the best I could be. I knew he would be proud if he could hear that I soon would be a teacher. I imagined him looking down from heaven urging me on, "Go, Anneliese! Go for it and do your best!"

During the summer sessions I purchased tickets for myself, Sandy and Kenny and we attended the Straw Hat Players performances. Kenny and Sandy loved the musicals and Westerns. But when I asked Kenny to join me for the play <u>Virginia Woolf</u>, he walked out after the first act and grumbled, "I have had enough of that kind of garbage, I am driving home. You can come with me or you can come home with Judy."

I was angry with Kenny, but Judy was philosophical, "Annelee, Kenny has his good traits I am sure, but when it comes to women's lib and the fact that women can think for themselves it seems more than he can presently handle. After all, he is fifty-three and probably set in his ways."

One day Kenny approached me about a rumor he had heard. "Annelee, you have changed," he complained. "Things are not good between us since you started college. I even heard that you are interested in a professor. You and he eat lunch together frequently."

"Kenny," I said, "should I ever be interested in another man, you will be first to know because I am not in the habit of sneaking around. Yes, I have had lunch with the professor at the Comstock. He answers my questions about humanities and religion and that is the end of our meetings. Why would I want to get involved with another man? Living here with two men is difficult enough. All I want is to finish college and get a job."

"Annelee," Kenny said, "I admire what you are accomplishing, but I will be glad when you are done with college. Maybe then we can find common ground again."

I was surprised. This was truly the first time that Kenny expressed a positive opinion toward my endeavor. The 1970 winter quarter had brought me close to my goal. I was assigned to student teach junior high English at the Ada High School. This time period gave me hands-on experience, and I realized that each student came with different skills. To some learning came easy. Others worked hard and struggled. Yet all were contained in a one room setting and I needed to adjust to their individual needs. The three months flew by and I knew spring and summer quarter would fulfill my requirements for teaching certification.

Spring quarter brought many changes. The principal and superintendent for the Twin Valley school system were interviewing prospective English teachers. I was one of the many applicants for the high school English position, and we were required to express our philosophy of living. I wrote the following:

MY PHILOSOPHY OF LIVING

It took me a long time to sort out what I consider most important to reach the capability of living a successful life. As I reflect, I find that there have been three decisive periods in my life.

The first was a pleasant, happy childhood, during the second period of my life I survived World War II, and the third period demanded the double role of wife and mother. During that time, I had the mistaken idea that it was my job to make my husband, my children, and possibly everyone close to me happy.

However, I learned that I can only contribute to the well-being of others if there is give-and-take on both sides. Now I am able to withhold judgment on other people's actions and opinions. Although at times I falter, on the whole I like myself better and I feel content.

Soon I will start on the fourth probably most important period of my life. It will begin with my first teaching position. Since my major is English, I will listen to my students because I want to know what the spoken word means to them. I believe that only then will I have an atmosphere in which the students and I can begin to learn.

I am not a romantic, thinking this will happen over night and maybe it will not take place this way at all. Some students may be too pre-conditioned and not think for themselves. But that, for me, will not be a sufficient reason to give up before I try.

Within two weeks I learned that I had been hired by the Twin Valley School District as of September 1970. I was jubilant. Kenny and his father said that they could hardly believe it, but Sandy, Roy and Linda told me that they always knew I would achieve my dream.

Since Judy's and Harriet's hourly spring schedules conflicted with mine, Kenny, who was a master mechanic, assured me that our 1964 Chevy Impala that showed 120,000 miles would get me safely to classes until graduation. I drove the county roads because they were almost my domain, and so was the land that I had not seen so clearly before. While I drove on Highway 9 and County Road 11, I started to love the early morning hours when the sun rose and the long, yellow sunbeams warmed the earth. It was then that the sky colors became vibrant and changed from red to a soft gold or clear blue interspersed with white puffy clouds. Birds flew above and twittered. Since I was a regular traveler on the road, the farmers waved to me while they guided their huge machines over the black fertile soil that swallowed grain and sugar beet seeds. The seeds lay dormant for some time until a gentle spring rain moistened the ground, broke open the top crust and suddenly, the earth was covered with the awakening seedlings. The new greens stretched for miles that were dotted by trees and broken into by far apart farmsteads. During spring storms grayish-black clouds shrouded the land in darkness and the wind pelted the heavy rain onto the fields and roads. As the storm moved out, everything around me looked washed clean and free of winter grime. The spring air had a smell so clean, that I wished I could breathe it in forever.

As the summer quarter started, the scenery around me changed. The green stems of grain turned every day until they reached a rich gold. How beautiful it was when during the morning drive the land was silent until a soft wind swayed the golden miles of grain back and forth. The crowns of the sunflowers turned their faces toward the sun, and the sugar beet fields hid the rich black earth under a thick, lush green carpet. Now I saw a beauty that was not present in the German landscape. In Bavaria, trees covered the hills. Snow-capped mountains hid the glorious sunrise and sunset and the cities and villages that lay beyond. A traveler had to be patient until each valley would reveal its own surrounding beauty. But now, every day, the land of the Red River Valley before me beckoned for appreciation of the open prairie that shared its fruitful bounty with other states and nations and fed them. Finally, I understood what in 1947 Kenny had tried to show me when I was homesick for my native land and was blind to the beauty around me. I wondered how the woods and hills of Bavaria could keep me in their grip for years, so I couldn't feel what I felt now. Every day I was struck by the massive beauty of the valley, when at twilight time the setting sun flooded the land with shades of red or gold and gave the land a glow of its own. The golden globe of the sun got smaller and smaller, and finally it receded into a dot that the earth took in. Nature's daily show came full circle as the night clouds slowly, ever so slowly, covered the sky and gave way to the moon's brightness or on a moonless night covered the land with darkness.

It was during late spring and early fall when in the early morning- or late evening hours mother nature hid the changing seasons under a blanket of fog that anxious travelers didn't dare to penetrate until the moist, dewy blanket fell or was lifted.

It was during fall when the rich bounty of grains and the fields bare of sugar beets ended the crop season. The leaves of century old trees that flanked the lakes and country roads and the newly planted small trees and bushes that plotted gardens and yards broke out in kaleidoscopes of dull green, yellow, brown and red, and painted the valley like a glorious canvas. Then, the November wind gusts and the first frost denuded trees and bushes. Now I understood that the seasons of spring, summer and fall gave the residents of the Midwest the resilient attitude to marvel at the bare tree branches and needles of evergreens as the raindrops changed into ice crystals that glistened like diamonds in the winter sun. When heavy snow closed roads and kept everyone prisoner in their home, the frigid, often Siberian-like winter temperatures stayed for days. Then everyone waited longingly for the ice to thaw, so nature's cycle could start anew.

I felt free, I felt good, because now I realized how fortunate I was. I lived and had come to know and appreciate the beauty of two different countries. I loved each for its own bounty and beauty, for its own people, and the richness and appreciation of life they had given me. Now I knew. . . I was home! Now I could say, "Germany is my native land, but America is my home!"

I was happy with my newly found peace, and I also was happy that I was mastering the summer quarter classes with ease. Bittersweet sadness gripped me at times because I realized that the past three years had been a learning experience that may not be repeated in its power and richness. My heart burst with joy as on Friday, August 26, 1970 I crossed the stage, and while my family watched, I received my teacher's certification.

Minutes later Dir. A. rushed up to me, "Congratulations, Annelee!" he said. "After our first meeting I knew you would stand here one day, and I am so glad that I could help you become what you always wanted to be - a teacher. I wish you the best."

Kenny gently tapped my shoulder, "Annelee, your going to college was the best idea we ever had!"

So many changes lay ahead. Sandy was a senior and she would graduate during May 1971. She rarely dated, but one weekend she was asked by the most popular athlete of the senior class for a supper and movie date. We were impressed when the young man arrived promptly at 5:30 p.m., came in to meet us, spent time visiting with Kenny and promised, "I'll have Sandy back at 10:30 p.m. like you said."

"Nice young man," Kenny observed as they left.

It was after seven when Sandy returned, walked past us without a word and into her room.

"She must have forgotten something," I concluded.

But instead, Beethoven's Fifth reverberated throughout the home. I knew then that something was wrong. My knocking was either not heard or ignored, so I walked in and asked,

"Sandy I thought you were going to the movie? Aren't you?"

"No, I am not going as you can see," she retorted.

"Do you want to tell me what happened?" I urged.

"Not really," she responded.

"Maybe you will feel better if we talk about it?"

"Mom," she said, "If you want to go out with octopus hands, you can go out with him. I am staying home." She shook her head, "I am surely not getting involved with a guy who has octopus hands. His hands were all over me. I told him to stop it and take me home, or I would be walking. I never want to see him again."

I hugged Sandy, and thanked her for coming home when she did.

I recalled my promise to Mama that after my first year of teaching, I would fly home during the summer. My monthly salary was $375.00, and I planned to save seventy-five dollars every month. But for now my first year of teaching lay ahead. I soon found that for students to gain from my instructions, teaching demanded flexibility every day. I was assigned to junior high seventh, eighth, and ninth grade and senior high tenth grade English. The average class consisted of twenty-five to thirty-one students. We had no workbooks, so typing worksheets and correcting homework kept me up late into the night. But I loved teaching because I knew I could make a difference in the lives of my students. As the school year ended, four students who had been trouble makers at the beginning of the year spoke to me.

"Mrs. Woodstrom, when we heard that we were going to have a teacher from Germany we were so scared because we had heard so many rumors about how mean the Germans were. So we acted up at first, but we learned that you are not like that! You are strict and you give a lot of homework, but you are just like some of the other teachers we like. Now you are one of us."

I tried to encircle them with my arms, "Thank you for telling me how you felt. If you learned what you have told me, you learned a great deal."

Sandy graduated as an honor student, and she and her friend Barbara J. were already enrolled at the University Morris, MN, for the 1971 fall semester. When I talked about going back to Germany during summer vacation, Sandy assured me, "Don't worry, Mom. Fly home and have a good time. I still can keep my summer job taking care of little Casey while her mom works, and Dad and I can read cookbooks."

June days in Germany flew by all too quickly. Mama, Irmgard and I reconnected, and even twenty-six-year-old Werner enjoyed taking me places.

He voiced his disappointment, "The next time you come, you better have Kenny by your side."

I missed Uncle Pepp, and as it was customary, I had a mass said for my dear Uncle and I decorated his grave with his favorite flowers. During the hastily arranged reunion of the Classes of 1940-1942, we reminisced about the past and shared the present. I learned that many of my classmates had never left town. They were content to work in the same factories their parents had worked in, and they attended church like they always had. Their lives revolved around their families, their friends and what took place within the county. The Vietnam War that caused ever growing protests and turmoil was seen as America's problem. So far the changes that took place in America had not yet invaded their lives. After they finished their education, young people still stayed close to their roots. Cousin Joey told me that ever since childhood, he loved working with trees, plants and flowers and he wanted nothing more then to own a nursery someday. Yet because of family obligations and tradition he had given up his dream, became a master baker and since Uncle Pepp's death, he owned the Solch bakery.

"It's not a bad life," he reflected, "but it is not what it could have been. I have a small green house where I grow orchids and exotic flowers. I have a hot bed for vegetables and I cross fruit trees with other varieties. It is my hobby, at least I have that. Being the first-born or the only son in the family isn't always easy because you surely are destined to take over the family business or the farm and hold it in trust for future generations."

My family and childhood friends were happy that I had achieved my dream and became a teacher. By the end of June my vacation ended. I promised Mama that I would be back for her seventieth birthday in 1974, and she affirmed, "Kenny better be with you."

I couldn't tell her that my marriage to Kenny had changed, and I didn't know how to fix it. My family had decreased in size. Sandy attended the University at Morris, and Roy and Linda were back completing their studies at Moorhead State. They had plans to finish their graduate work and move to Minneapolis. Kenny and I went to work every morning, and Grandpa was home alone. He refused to join senior organizations. He just stayed home and became depressed and more demanding as the days passed.

I felt sorry that he felt 'abandoned' and life in our home was not to his liking anymore. Kenny, too, felt guilty and he gave Grandpa all the attention he craved. When I complained, Kenny responded,

"Annelee, you have your work. You come home and correct your students' papers until late into the night. What do you expect of us? We have to have a life too, so that's the way it will have to be."

By spring of 1972, my second year of teaching was in the final quarter. Our financial concerns lessened, but I couldn't take the stalemate of our marriage any longer. On a spring weekend, I drove to Crookston and spoke with an attorney.

"I want a divorce," I announced, "I cannot go on for who knows how many more years the way we are living now!"

The attorney listened and he advised that I should inform Kenny immediately of my decision. That very evening I told Kenny where and how I had spent the afternoon.

He was devastated, "Annelee, please don't leave me. I will go to counseling. I will do anything, but please don't divorce me."

The next day Kenny found a counselor in Crookston, who advised us that there would be weeks or months of work ahead before our differences could be addressed. Kenny kept several appointments, but when he saw no immediate improvement, he discontinued his sessions while I kept going. I couldn't understand myself, why couldn't I just break away from Kenny? I didn't want to hurt my children, but if there was a way out of the routine we were in, I needed to find it.

In his own way Kenny was trying. One morning he said, "Annelee, I talked with Helen, and she will ask Dad to come and live in her home because you and I need time to sort out our differences."

I tried to still the guilt within me because I felt that Grandpa's leaving was my fault. Yet I couldn't go on with two men trying to control the way we should live. Roy, Linda, and Sandy were devastated. They did not want to hear that Mom and Dad would not be together as always.

Sandy, who was Daddy's girl, pleaded. "Mom, don't leave Dad. What will he do without you? He loves you and we love you too. You can't do that to Dad!"

Roy took his own approach, "Mom, Linda and I don't always agree either, but that doesn't mean you should divorce. Marriage is forever!"

I wondered. Had he forgotten how Grandpa treated him because of his hair style? Did he have no resentment that he had to give up his room? Are children that selfish that they just think of what is good for them? Never mind how I had lived through all the changes.

Sandy found that the physical therapy classes she needed in college were filled for one year, so Roy and Linda invited her to come to Minneapolis and seek employment. Within weeks she was hired by the Northwestern Bell Telephone Company.

We were happy when Roy and Linda lived in an apartment in Minneapolis, Roy had found work, and they told us that we would be grandparents during January 1974.

Mama called, and she told us that Erna had died. I knew that she had battled kidney failures for sometime but Erna could not survive when cancer spread throughout her body. I mourned the passing of Erna she had been my friend as long as I could remember. Erna and Uncle Pepp had always been there for me and I knew that from now on my visits to Germany would never be the same.

CHAPTER 25

1974 - Truth Has Two Sides

Ever since my 1970 trip to Germany I had planned and saved for Mama's Seventieth Birthday celebration. Kenny grumbled about the high cost of the flight, but he knew that Mama, my family, relatives and friends expected that he would celebrate Christmas and Mama's seventieth birthday in Mitterteich.

During the first day that school closed for Christmas vacation and a brief leave of absence in hand, we flew to Germany and landed in Munich. Irmgard, Adolf and their daughter Manuela met us at the airport where Kenny and his 'Second Lady ran toward each other and embraced repeatedly. Irmgard had been six when Kenny had left, but now twenty-nine-years later, she clearly remembered how Kenny had saved her from unsightly impetigo scars. I was translating for Kenny and my family, when Kenny announced, "No dictionary this time, I brought my own translator, she is an English, German translator and she doesn't charge."

They drove us to Mitterteich where Mama, relatives and friends waited to hug the 'Gentleman Soldier' they had not seen since 1945. Kenny walked up to Werner who had been one month old when he left, but now he matched Kenny's height.

He tried to ease the strangeness between them so he said, "Werner, we both grew, I grew wider and you grew taller."

"No, Kenny" Werner said, "you look good!"

These few phrases were a start ... I felt Baby Werner had grown up, and Kenny and he could probably bridge the huge gap the years of absence had caused between them.

I sorely missed Uncle Pepp and Erna during these joyous moments.

They would have loved to meet Kenny, not as the American soldier but as part of the Solch family. The next day Kenny and I went to the nursery where we purchased evergreen branches, two little Christmas trees and Christmas lanterns. Mama said that the families had left spaces on Uncle Pepp's and Erna's grave bare for us. They knew that I would want to decorate the grave sites and while Kenny and I lit the Christmas candles, we talked to Uncle Pepp and then Erna in our own way.

On Christmas Eve, we were showered with gifts. As midnight neared, Werner, Kenny and I sat by the window and looked out at the star-studded sky. I reminisced how as a child I had looked toward the hills and waited for the first flicker of a villager's Christmas lantern. Kenny watched in awe as after that first flicker a river of lanterns wound its way down from the hills and the villagers came into town singing Christmas carols. The procession and the singing swelled as we with families from the neighborhood joined in. Minutes before midnight, the church bells reminded the congregation to celebrate the birth of the Christ Child. Kenny was deeply moved by the spirit of the Midnight Mass, and he was introduced to the traditional German Christmas customs he had not known. On December 25, the temperature was fifty-five above so we went for walks through the nearby woods and greeted other walkers. It had been our tradition to spend the evening at Uncle Pepp's home, but now Cousin Joey stood in his dad's place. Relatives and friends fondly recalled good times we had spent with Uncle Pepp and Erna. We tasted hors d'oeuvres', cheeses and wine, played charades and gathered around the small organ and sang favorite carols and melodies. Suddenly, talking abated. Werner solo'ed Uncle Pepp's and Erna's favorite Christmas hymns. It seemed that their spirit was with us and Christmas was truly here.

On December 26, the second Christmas holiday, we celebrated Mama's seventieth birthday at the *Alm Gasthaus* (Alpine chalet). The guests enjoyed a typical German dinner: baked goose, potato dumplings and gravy or bratwurst and sauerkraut. Everyone mingled and lively discussions were shared over afternoon coffee, tortes and Christmas baking. We listened to speeches that honored Mama, we enjoyed a cold plate supper with choices of vegetables and fruit, and everyone partook in the evening dance. I couldn't believe it! Kenny, who had been brought up to believe that dancing and drinking alcohol was evil was dancing with Cousin Anni, and he enjoyed the wine and the dancing. In appreciation for their wishes and birthday gifts for Mama, every guest received a bottle of 1974 red or white wine. The next day, we returned to the chalet where we were served at noon what was left over from the meals that had been prepared for over one hundred guests.

We spent the days before New Years Eve hiking in the hills, skiing, skating, visiting and playing games with family and friends. We walked to Kenny's former Army base in Waldsassen, but it had been replaced with a new school. In Tirschenreuth, the old depot where Kenny and I had said good-bye had been torn down and we faced an empty lot.

Kenny pondered, "If you didn't live through it or read a history book, you now could walk through this town and never know that good men on both sides died right here."

On the evening before our final good-byes, we had retired early. I was sleeping when Mama softly touched my shoulder and motioned for me to follow her. I wanted to wake Kenny who slept beside me, but she shook her head and whispered, "No."

She led me to the kitchen where hot coffee was perking. Mama handed me a freshly brewed cup and explained, "Anneliese, yesterday while you were visiting with Cousin Joey, I went to your bedroom to add clean towels. I was surprised because Kenny sat by the window and he quickly tried to wipe tears from his cheeks. I reached for him and asked, 'Kenny, you okay?' He wept and said, 'Kenny, no good for Anneliese.'"

"I stayed by his side until he stopped crying and said, 'Okay now. Nix say to Anneliese.' "I took it he didn't want for me to tell you. But I am concerned. What is going on? I noticed you don't seem to be in love with Kenny like you once were. What is wrong?"

"Mama," I said, "so many changes have taken place since you were in Ada. During that time, Kenny and I were a team. But when his father came to live with us, he took over and I felt like a fifth wheel in our relationship. Decisions were made and I heard about them when they were a fact. His father's remarks toward me frequently hurt me deeply."

Mama interrupted, "Since I am not taking sides, I don't want to know all that happened, but you are married to one special man. There are not many like him. If you feel you can't live with him, set him free!"

She shook her right index finger at me like she used to when I was a naughty child and admonished, "What you are doing right now is keeping score of what, in your opinion, Kenny did wrong. Think about it, and when you get back to America make a decision. I can see that Kenny is suffering from the way you treat him. You are polite but you are not a loving wife like you should be. You must also think of Roy and Sandy. Yes, they are away from home, but all their life they will have just one set of parents, you and Kenny. Don't make them choose and take sides!"

I interjected, "Kenny's father sold his home two days after his wife had died. He never even tried living by himself. He moved in with us the day after she died, and as Papa always said, 'and that was that!'"

Mama recalled, "I was not happy when you married Kenny, but I have changed my mind. Wherever Kenny goes, he is well-liked. As a matter of fact, Cousin Hans said, 'Kenny is as good as any Bavarian.' So think about that. I am getting older and I have learned a great deal. It is easy to take your partner for granted. When was the last time you told Kenny what he means to you? I want you to remember that marriage is for better or worse, and I don't think yours is that bad. Anneliese, Papa and I didn't rear you to be vindictive. Don't be. It doesn't become you.'"

She looked sternly at me, "Just for once, think! Every truth has two sides. There is your side. That is what you see as the truth, but do you ever consider the other side, namely Kenny's? You say that his father should not have lived with you. On the other hand when I look at Kenny, I admire him for not abandoning his father when he needed Kenny most. His father may have realized too late that he made a mistake when he moved out of his house and sold it. He had lost his wife, and then he realized that his son's wife wished he wouldn't be in her home. So he got cranky and short with you. He advised his son because he knew that his son respected and loved him. Well, maybe it was his way to save a shred of his dignity. Why don't you sit down with Kenny and talk it all out?"

"But Mama," I interjected, "Kenny's father never listened to me. I told him once that my Italian friend from Florence was often homesick for Florence. He answered, 'If you are so homesick, why don't you pack your suitcase and go home.' It took me a long time to get over that remark because I felt it showed how he felt about me.'"

Mama refilled our cups with steaming hot coffee. She gently took my hand and responded softly, "Anneliese, I realize more each day that getting old is not easy. Remember, some day you too will be old. Read Ecclesiastes 12:1-7. That will make you think!" She paused and looked at me, "Do you remember the story of the woman and her elderly father? Her father was frail and his hands shook all the time, so his daughter served his meals in a wooden bowl instead of her fine china. She was surprised when her six-year old son who sat on the floor was carving a piece of wood. When she asked him what he was carving, he said, 'I am carving a bowl for you and dad, so I will have wooden bowls for you when you get old.' I think you know that you are the example your children will follow, and so far, you have done a good job. Now don't start to set an example that you could reap some day. When you are back in your home, I surely hope to hear from you. Don't throw your marriage away so lightly. Believe me, Kenny and you can have wonderful years ahead. Just give yourself a chance." Mama hugged me and said, "We will always miss you, so stay in touch.'"

Before we left, Mama, Kenny and I went to the cemetery and said our good-bye to Uncle Pepp and Erna. Then we bid everyone good-bye and I planned to return for my Fifty Year class reunion in 1977. During the long flight home, I thought frequently about what Mama had told me.

The night after we arrived home Roy and Linda called, on January 4, 1974, our first grandchild Freya had joined our family. When we saw her we were sure that our little granddaughter was the most beautiful baby since Roy and Sandy were born.

Kenny and I were now grandparents and we settled into a new routine. Since Grandpa was now living with Helen, we had the evenings to ourselves. One evening I asked Kenny, "Why were you crying when Mama came to our bedroom? Mama scolded me. She said that I didn't treat you like a wife should treat her husband."

Kenny looked at me, surprised, "Oh, no! That is not what I wanted to tell Mama. I sat by the window and thought about what a wonderful family you have in Germany. I learned that you had so much more than my family or I could ever give you. Your home, your family, the cousins and relatives you have a bond of friendship with each. Christmas and the birthday celebrations were something I had never experienced. I realized you grew up with that, and after the war you would have had all that again. I had to come back to Germany to understand why you were so homesick for so long. Now I know what you had given up for me. Annelee, your family life and your style of living was so different from mine. I should have come to Germany with you in 1960. I think life would have been different for us because I would have gained insight to the way you had lived before you met me. I watched you as you danced with Cousin Joey. You looked good together. Your cousin Anni told me that you attended the opera and concerts. You learned to dance at the children's ball. You were a good dancer. You skied and skated, and you were not afraid to try new challenges. I never took you to a dance because I grew up believing that dancing was a sin."

Kenny took my hand and went on, "I realize now that we have wasted years because we had traveled different roads before we met. That's why I cried. I cried for what we had lost. I hope we can start over because I will always love you and I know now that deep down you must love me too." He sighed, "Oh what I dummkopf I was!"

As the weeks went by, anger and frustration were slowly seeping away. We were still cautious, but we treated each other with true kindness. We talked openly, and shared our differences and sought solutions. During the week, we devoted much time to our jobs. We wanted to be good at what we were doing. Saturday afternoon and Sunday were now our time together. We frequently drove to Minneapolis. We took Linda's mother with us, and we spent time with Sandy, Roy, Linda, and our grandchild Freya.

Kenny finally shared what shaped him. He was always told that he was a good little man. Even as a child, he worked in the fields of their small farm until during the Depression years, his family joined the many farmers whose farms were foreclosed.

He recalled, "I loved living in the country on our farm. I had my dog. We had a pony that always threw me off on the way home. We rarely saw anyone but our relatives. I was happy. When our farm was auctioned off, even my dog and the pony were given to other farmers because we couldn't take them to town. I cried for days. But Dad told me to be a good little man and be brave. I didn't like living in town and I didn't like school. In the country school we were less then twenty students for all grades. We were closely knit and we helped each other".

"When I came to town, the students called us 'dumb farm kids', and after school some would shout, 'Hey, dumb farm kid, want to fight a town kid?'

"It always ended with the farm kid losing because others would join the fight. Dad told me not to fight, 'Kenny, just avoid them.' How was I supposed to do that? I learned to hate school and after eighth grade, like many of my peers, I quit school and never went back. Instead, I helped support my family doing day labor cutting wood. As times got better, I wanted to venture out and try something new. But I was often told, 'Don't do it. You could lose what you have!' I know now that all my adult life I could never rid myself of the fear of losing all I had worked for."

Kenny's reflections brought me more understanding than my one-sided counseling did. Now I understood his compulsions, paying the mortgage before it was due, buying only what we could pay for, rarely spending money on something we didn't need. We agreed to work together on financial matters because I wanted to remodel our home. I would be responsible for securing a bank loan, but Kenny would see that all the bills were paid on time. Marvin, our neighbor who built or remodeled homes agreed to take the project on during summer vacation. We planned to change one of our bedrooms into a dining room, enlarge the kitchen and build new kitchen cupboards. I wanted to change all the woodwork, doors, windows, and mopboards throughout from blond to pecan stain. When we found that the professional cost would be prohibitive, Joyce, Marvin's wife, made the project possible. She volunteered and while the men shook their heads, she and I made the garage our workshop. Marvin removed the doors and window frames as needed, and Joyce shared her expertise freely. We removed the old varnish, sanded and bleached the wood, re-stained and applied three coats of oil base varnish. The huge project took weeks. While we worked, Joyce and I listened to talk radio. We exchanged ideas and our friendship deepened. Kenny's grumbling could be managed,

"I will never do that, again," he would threaten. "Nothing is where it supposed to be. It takes me half a day to find what I need. My garage is a mess."

Fall came. Marvin and Joyce returned to teaching, and Kenny admitted that the inconveniences had been minor in comparison to the benefits we had gained. The eight foot patio window opened the outside world to us. We watched as the seasons changed and we laughed at the acrobatics of the squirrels. During the winter before Saturday morning coffee, my friend Marilyn started her snowmobile, guided it through the backyards and parked it by the window. We, too, had bonded and we knew whatever we were discussing stayed between us. Arlene, my co-worker whose children were the seven J's, was also Marilyn's sister-in-law. We shared our daily work experiences as we drove to and from work, and we often remarked that besides our families the Twin Valley High School was our second home. I loved my work because our staff was special. The administration, the secretaries and all the teachers focused on giving the best education possible to our student body.

One day during prep hour, one of the teachers asked, "Annelee, is it true? You worked in Regensburg during World War II?"

I said, "Yes, I did."

"Life holds the strangest twists," he declared. "You were in Regensburg in the bomb shelters and hoped you would make it out alive. At the same time, I was in a fighter plane protecting our bombers while they released their bombs over the Messerschmitt plant and Regensburg. Who ever thought then, that some day we would be teaching in the same school and eat in the same room?" He shook his head. "Now you teach English and civics to my children. Can I ask you how you felt when you were in the bomb shelters?"

For a brief time, I had flashbacks to the shelter and I recalled. "I was scared. The noise was unbearable, it damaged my hearing, my head ached, and the stale air made my chest hurt until the pain was excruciating, and I thought I couldn't take it for another minute. No one can imagine what it was like being in an underground shelter when the bombs came down. The walls of the shelter shook and the ground heaved up with every explosion close by. The worst for me was the little children crying while their mothers protected them with their bodies. Those little ones were so scared, they wanted to go home and they could never understand why they were punished. All this time I felt like I was in a tomb. Yet, would you believe it? During every air raid alarm, I ran for the shelter and I was glad when I made it . . . and then all I ever wanted was to get out in one piece . . .'alive!'"

I got up, walked up to him and said, "I haven't mentioned this before because as far as I was concerned there was no need to do so. But now maybe you should know. You were not the only one who bombed Regensburg or Munich while I was below in the shelter. After we moved to Ada in 1959, Sandy became best friend with little Barbara J. Kenny and I met the family, and after we knew each other for some time, we became friends. One day, while we were discussing World War II, Barbara's dad told me that he was a gunner and radio operator on a B-17 bomber. His unit also bombed Regensburg, Munich, Schweinfurt and other cities where I, at the same time, had sought safety in the shelters below. I will tell you how I feel toward you and little Barbara's dad."

"That was the war. It is over now and I am glad we are friends. Now I hope that we and our children will never again live they way we once did."

He nodded, and we never spoke of it again. I taught his children. We were fellow teachers and we worked side by side.

CHAPTER 26

1977- 1978
Briefly Together — then Broken Forever

The years had gone by swiftly, and it was now December 1977. My relationship with Kenny was growing into what it once had been. Two weeks before Christmas, we planned to go Christmas shopping and if we needed to, we would take Friday night and all day Saturday selecting gifts.

"No last minute rush, this year," Kenny said.

Driving conditions were good, so on Friday night, after school we drove to Fargo, North Dakota, to shop at West Acres. As we approached, the parking lot was filled so Kenny suggested, "I'll drop you off and park the car. Let's meet at the fountain, and then we face the crowds."

We met, and we had shopped for quite some time, when I looked through sweaters that were piled high on a table. By now, I was tired and hot and I needed to get out of that store. Kenny had been standing beside me, patiently waiting.

I pulled on his jacket sleeve "Kenny," I said, "I have to get out of here. I am so hot! I can hardly wait until we get to the car."

Since there was no response, I held on to Kenny's jacket sleeve, walked up to the exit door and said, "Kenny, I am so hot, where did you park?"

He said, "I haven't got the slightest idea. Should we find your car or go to mine?"

I wished to floor would have opened up below me because I looked at the smiling face of a stranger. I turned ... Kenny was right behind us, laughing, he shook his head and softly scolded, "Annelee, can't you wait for me?"

I rushed out of West Acres, into the dark night with Kenny laughing and following me. I didn't find it funny, and I told him that by now I had cooled off.

It was Christmas 1977 when Sandy was home, and she said, "Mom, I am so fortunate. I have a family that is back together. I know you love me, but what is also important to me is my relationship with friends and co-workers. Just read what they gave me at my twenty-fifth birthday party. I will keep this as long as I live."

She handed me a card. On the front was a squirrel resting on a tree branch. I turned the card over and read what her friends had composed as a tribute to Sandy.

HAPPY BIRTHDAY!

Each day is full of tediousness, except when you're near.
For you have the gift of laughter, love, you spread your
soul for the world to see, if they wish and we do.
For in you we see ourselves as we want to be seen.
 ... Because we love you, for in your eyes we have seen
your love for us, and never has a human being felt more
welcomed than to find someone like you to love them.

Your birthday should be a holiday. For how many others
come into this world and do not know the prize of love.
They do not know how to teach this gift among us, as
you have.

Life is something to love, and you have taken people's
soul sickness and made it bloom into joy. You are a rich
person.
You have made us rich by knowing you.

To you, Woody, to present times, and absent friends, love...

The card was signed by twenty-four friends. I wept because I was so thankful and proud because my daughter was loved and appreciated by so many.

The 1978 spring weather was beautiful. Roy, Linda, Freya, Linda's mother Hilda and Sandy were home for Easter. We celebrated and we looked ahead. Two weeks later, I returned home from an individual learning workshop and I was eager to present my new knowledge to the surrounding schools. But Kenny had even better news for me.

Sandy had called. She had been promoted to supervisor at the Northwestern Bell Telephone Company.

'Dad,' she had said, 'I wish Mom could hear this too, but you have to tell her that I was promoted and, just think, I will get a company car to drive and a six hundred dollar raise.'

Kenny related their conversation. "I remarked to Sandy that fifty dollars a month was a wonderful raise, but I got the biggest surprise ever as she explained, 'Dad, listen, not fifty dollars a month, it is six hundred dollars a month, and you know what I am going to do first? I am going to buy you and Mom a new car. My promotion is effective as of May.'"

Kenny said that he told Sandy to save her money and maybe buy a condominium, or a small home, or invest some money. He shook his head and recalled, "Sandy surely was determined," She said, 'No, Dad I have made up my mind. I will see that you and Mom can finally enjoy a new car. It will be sooner not later and it will be my gift. I look forward to a good visit with the family when we are home for Mother's Day.'"

I called the florist and ordered a dozen long stemmed red roses for early morning delivery and signed it, Congratulations Sandy! We are so proud and we love you, Mom and Dad.

I was happy for Sandy but I was troubled. For the past week while I had been at a workshop, suddenly, and without reason, the death skeleton that depicted the *Totentanz* (Death Dance) in the cemetery chapel in my hometown became a vision that floated through my mind. I couldn't talk to anyone either because they would think that I had lost my mind. The death dance painted on the chapel ceiling was depicted with the skeleton carrying a scythe hovering over a baby lying in a cradle. In another painting Death was walking alongside a rifleman. However, the painting that bothered me most was death watching over humans of all ages as they entered or were already suffering in hell. While I was in second grade, four of my classmates had died of diphtheria. After we had visited their graves, Grandma took me inside the chapel to pray for my classmates souls. The paintings frightened me, but Grandma said that they were there to warn us.

"Death could come anytime and to anyone. The Death Dance painting was there to remind us that hell was waiting for us, the sinners."

I was scared because I knew I was a sinner, and I had nightmares about being pushed by Death into hell. The church and its teachings, the cruelties of the world were almost always associated with sin, ours and others. One night while I was crying and scared, Papa told me that I would get older than Grandma so I wouldn't die for a long, long time.

I asked him how he knew, and he said, "Anneliese, I know, and that is that!"

I felt better because when he said that phrase, I knew it was so. Even Cousin Hans tried to make me feel better, "I know you won't die," he announced with certainty. "You are always in trouble, and you need two

Paintings in Cemetery Chapel

Ausschnitt aus dem
Totentanz in der
Friedhofskapelle.

Death and marksman

Tod und Schütze

Ewige Verdammnis

Eternal Damnation

Tod und Säugling

Death and baby

Death Dance paintings on the cemetery chapel ceiling - 1930.

guardian angels to guard you. Death can never get near you until you grow up and do not sin so much."

After that, I avoided the chapel, and death had been still. Yet, especially during World War II, I questioned frequently why would God allow his innocent children to suffer and die? Would he plunge them into hell or purgatory because of sin? The depiction on the chapel ceiling suggested this and it fostered within me a very cruel impression that lay in my subconscious. But why would the death skeleton reappear now and float through my mind several times a day? I tried to shake the uneasy feeling, but these visions left me apprehensive. I no longer believed in such a cruel God? Now I believed in a God of love.

I looked forward to my children's visit for Mothers Day, so I tried to clear my mind and feel good. My family came home and yet the death skeleton would not leave me. Sleep evaded me. How could I tell Kenny or my children? Kenny would think I lost my mind and needed professional help. Sandy was happy about her promotion. Roy, Linda, Hilda and little Freya were content.

They would ask? "What's wrong?"

I would have to admit I did not know. I will always remember Mothers Day, 1978. The family was home. Roy and Kenny were working on Roy's car, Linda and Freya were with her mother. The dinner was cooking, and Sandy and I were in the dining room sitting across from each other. I looked at my daughter. Her blond hair was shiny clean, cut short in a new becoming style. Shaped brows set off her deep-blue eyes. Except for a soft red lipstick, she wore no makeup. She sat rod-straight and a new, light blue designer's business suit enhanced her slim figure. She shared news about the new position and the constant learning. I asked her about her friend Gary, but she said, "Mom, just relax. Whatever the future brings will happen when the time is right."

"Well, Sandy," I offered, "You are twenty-six, I hope I don't have to wait for your wedding day until I am ninety. But now I am going to take a photo of my beautiful daughter, right there on the patio under the blossoms of the apple tree."

The camera was out of film, and the drugstore closed at noon. "I will get your photo on Memorial Day." I promised.

We continued where we had left off, "Sandy, you are successful. You love your job, and you seem so happy and content."

She looked at me, "Mom, I have never been as happy in my life as I am right now. Everything seems to be going my way. It is almost too good to be true." She laughed, "If we want to stay happy, we must set the table. We eat at one, don't we?"

After dinner, we played croquet, and after a light supper, our children took off for Minneapolis. They waved good-bye. "See you in two weeks at Bonnie's wedding," Sandy called out as they drove away.

"What a busy life our girl has," I remarked to Kenny. "Next weekend she will be with LB and Pumpkin at their annual get-together at LB's parent's cottage at White Earth. Then Bonnie's wedding and she will be home to see her newly completed room. She told me that she couldn't wait to sleep in her new bed."

It was May 15. The death skeleton had become bolder. One day I awoke. The skeleton vision was near me. The scent of flowers permeated the room, and I couldn't rid myself of a feeling of doom and urgency. On Thursday, May 18, Sandy's room was not ready because the local furniture store could not supply the type of carpet she wanted. I asked Kenny to drive with me to Fargo that very night.

"Annelee, come on," he pleaded "can't we wait until the weekend?"

"No, Kenny," I said. "I want the room done, so let's go tonight."

I couldn't tell him that the smell of flowers and the skeleton made me fearful! Somebody was going to die, I thought, but I know it isn't Grandpa, it isn't Kenny, and it isn't me. Then I would abruptly stop and not go on guessing who it could be.

Within an hour, I had selected the carpet. As we arrived at home, I left the pickup and called out to Kenny, "I am going to ask Marvin if he won't lay the carpet tonight."

"Annelee, for God's sake, the man just came home from work," Kenny reasoned. "The carpet won't run away. Wait until tomorrow."

I didn't answer and I ran across the yard before Kenny could stop me.

Joyce opened the door. Marvin was sitting at the kitchen table and I addressed him, "Marvin, I have the carpet for Sandy's room. Will you come over and lay the carpet tonight?"

Marvin and Joyce looked at each other, "Tonight?" Marvin asked unbelieving.

"Yes, tonight." I looked at the clock. "I know it is 8:30, but I know you can get it done."

"Well, okay, we better get started." Marvin concluded.

We moved the furniture, and brought the carpet in. Marvin measured, fit the pad and laid the carpet. We helped where we could.

Kenny was not happy with me, and he told Marvin, "That wife of mine is really asking a lot of you two."

Joyce asked, "Annelee, why is it so important to have the carpet in tonight? Are you planning a party?"

All the while, the scent of flowers was all around me and I saw the skeleton floating by. I knew that if I told Joyce what was taking place within me, she would throw the hammer she was working with, and she would be out of the room, out of the house faster than I could think.

I answered, "No, it isn't for a party. I just want the room finished."

"We should have painted the walls before we laid the carpet," Kenny grumbled. "That's the way it is usually done. But you just couldn't wait."

"Kenny, we can paint the room some day. That isn't such a big deal, not like laying carpet, anyway."

It was after midnight, the furniture was back in place, and the room looked lovely. I imagined how Sandy's eyes would light up, and the hug I would get for a job well done.

As suddenly as it had appeared, the skeleton left . . . and darkness came.

I felt driven. On Friday night after the final teaching day for the school year, I computed all grades for the fourth quarter and the year, cleaned the house and went to bed late.

Kenny remarked, "Annelee, you don't have to have your work done in one evening. There is always another day. What do you have planned for tomorrow?"

"Tomorrow I will get the final tests ready for all my classes."

Kenny sighed, "I guess you won't rest until the school year is over."

It was now Saturday, May 20. Kenny worked until noon, so I drove to Twin Valley and worked on final tests. I numbered every test, brought them to the assigned rooms, securely locked them in the cupboards and took the keys to the office. It was after four and everything was completed. At Kenny's suggestion we drove to Fargo, shopped, had supper at our favorite restaurant, spent time with a friend at the VA hospital, and arrived at home before eleven. Tired, we fell asleep.

Kenny was shaking me gently, "Annelee, wake up," he said, "Pastor Wallace is here and he wants to talk to us."

"What does he want?" I looked at the clock. It was 2:00 a.m. "Oh, dear God, what is it?"

I grabbed my robe and rushed out, "Who is it, Pastor? Who is it?" I called out. He took my hands and led me to the sofa.

"Annelee, Kenny, I have such terrible news. Sandy was killed tonight."

I screamed, "No, no, no! She is with LB and Pumpkin at White

Earth Lake."

"Annelee, they were with Sandy."

"Where are the girls? I want to talk with them."

"They were with Sandy," the pastor affirmed. "The girls died together."

Time stood still. That couldn't be...How could the pastor tell me that Sandy and her friends were killed? My mind refused to comprehend.

"How could that happen?" Kenny asked. "Did they drown at the lake? They were good swimmers. How could they die? What happened?"

"They didn't drown. They were hit by a car." the pastor explained. "It is under investigation. The three girls were walking, not driving, and they were dead when they were found."

Kenny came toward me. We clung to each other and sobbed while our bodies were riddled by unbearable pain.

I couldn't comprehend! We would never see Sandy's smile, never hear her call us Mom and Dad. We could never hug her again. It just couldn't be... and yet, just two words ... 'Sandy died' had shattered the life we knew and nothing, nothing, could ever be the same again. I wanted to deny what we were told. Kenny swayed and he struggled for breath. The pastor pounded on his chest, steadied him and gently guided Kenny toward the sofa. He told me to make strong coffee, and he directed Kenny to breathe deeply and slowly.

"Annelee," the pastor said, "you need your friends near you. I will call Joyce and Marvin. Then we need to call Roy."

Roy too, was awakened from a deep sleep and it was the hardest call I ever made to give my son the news that our Sandy had died.

"No, Mom, no, no," he screamed. Linda took the phone said, "Please, what has happened to Sandy? Roy is beside himself."

The pastor gave Linda the horrific details and cautioned them to drive carefully when they took to the road. Joyce and Marvin came over. They too, were devastated because they loved Sandy. As always, on Mother's Day Sandy had left a note telling Joyce that she would visit with her the next time she came home.

Joyce said, "We just laid the carpet Thursday night so her room would be finished when she came home."

We cried in each others arms and while tears streamed down her cheeks, Joyce turned toward the pastor, "How can God be so cruel and let that happen?"

The pastor responded, "No, Joyce, it wasn't God's doing. This is Satan at work."

I called Betty, LB's mom. Betty said, "Annelee, remember, they were five years old when they said that they would be friends forever. They were, weren't they?"

The police stopped by and reaffirmed the horrific truth. The girls had been fatally injured by a drunk driver and they had died instantly. Roy arrived early Sunday morning. He walked in, up to the closet door and hit it angrily with his fists.

"Why, why?" he cried out, "Sandy of all people. Everyone who knew her always said that she was the kindest, most loving person. Mom, why did she have to die? Why? Why?"

We held our son, and we wished we could make this unbearable pain go away. But grief rendered us helpless, especially to the needs of our own loved ones, and there was no cure. We learned quickly that our suffering had just begun.

The pastors had announced during the Sunday morning church services that the girls had died. We learned later that the town came together as one. Friends, neighbors and strangers stopped in and shared their sorrow because sometimes, unknown to us, the girls in their own way had touched their lives. People brought food and they opened their homes as co-workers, classmates, and friends arrived.

We learned that the girls had been walking near a field and they were struck down by a twenty-six-year-old drunk driver whose alcohol level was 0.28 when he was found still unconscious from the impact. His driver's license had been suspended for previous DUI convictions, but despite the suspensions he was still driving every day. Since we had learned of the untimely and horrific death of Sandy, Barbara, and Cheryl, we were immersed in grief. I can't remember much of Sunday and Monday. We, the three families, had decided that the three girls should be buried in adjoining plots and we selected the site. I only remember the longing I had to see my daughter and hug her again. Even though, from what I saw and heard around me, I knew that when we would see her again she would be in a casket lying still.

I heard it said that viewing your loved one in the casket is necessary so one can gain closure by saying the final good-bye. That may be so, but when parents bury a child it is, as parents who lost children understand, this is incomprehensible and painful beyond belief.   It goes against all natural order.

Nothing is as inappropriate as the death of a child.   This inappropriateness is unbearable and yet it must be borne. Children usually bury their parents because that is the way of life. When a child dies after a long illness, parents will grieve, and they will miss their child as long as they live, but when the young die a death that could have been avoided, closure evades and the wish that they should still be alive is always there. Roy and Sandy had been brother and sister, but they were also friends, and we could not console Roy. Kenny and I felt so guilty and helpless because we were not there for him like we should have been...but we could hardly bear our own pain.

As we, the families, met with the pastors to plan the joint service and lay out the funeral program. Roy, Clare and Linda selected the poetry they wanted included. Clare, Barbara's sister, suggested Gibran's *DESIDERATA,* Roy had written a poem.

> If life is but a moment stolen from eternity,
> let us spend our moment in love.
> Let us destroy cruel time with love.
> All moments exist as one in God's love.
> The moment spans across the ocean-time:
> By God's love, death itself turns . . . put to flight.
> God's love the only way the soul survives:
> A nourishment, a release.
> Love the only answer known for life

>   Roy

Linda, Cheryl's sister, selected Gibran

Life has many seasons
Some we understand
Some we do not
Making "why"
A senseless question

My sister, Theresa, arrived from Rochester, New York after a three day bus trip. What had kept us apart after Roy had been in Rochester didn't matter now. We clung to each other and wept. Tuesday night we could view the girls. Anyone who has gone to view their loved ones at the funeral home knows what it is to confront the reality of death. Sandy's injuries and marks of the accident were not visible. She looked so young, so beautiful, yet so still, sleeping the eternal sleep. How could we leave her here? Here is where the shock turns to numbness -- the protective gift given us so that we can endure the pain. Her death was so wrong, so cruel, and final. Family and friends stayed with us until late into the night because we walked and moved without purpose and without a sense of time. It was good that someone had made plans and gently led us where we were supposed to be.

Wednesday, May 23. The town closed stores and businesses because it would bury three of their young daughters. We, the families, were asked to come early, long before the funeral service at 10:00 a.m. The church sanctuary and where the three caskets would be placed was a garden of flowers. Suddenly I remembered. This was the scent of flowers I had smelled for three weeks. Now the Death Dance vision caused me to question. Why did I experience it without realizing what it tried to tell me? Why didn't I tell anyone? What would have happened if I had told someone? The pastor brought me back to the present. He pointed out that Mama and Irmgard had sent twenty-six long stemmed roses in memory of Sandy.

We went downstairs where we heard final instructions. Our walk to the front of the church was broken as each family followed the casket of their daughter until the caskets were placed before us in a half circle. Momentarily I felt the soothing words of the pastors and the hymns of

The three monuments of the girls are <u>one</u> block since they were friends.
We take care of the flowers (roses) at all times.

the combined choirs. People had come in numbers that overflowed into the downstairs rooms of the church, but they too were part of the love and care the community extended to us. Then the final walk behind the caskets on to the procession to the adjoining cemetery plots where the three girls were buried. All this took place in a nebulous haze. I was there, numb with pain. Yet I was concerned because Kenny's breathing was frequently irregular. All of this I could bear only because I was in shock for my own good, so I could survive. This, I firmly believe. The body, unable to handle this indescribable pain, goes into shock and slowly brings one back when we have hours, days and weeks to get a footing to handle each hour, each day, and the long, dark, sleepless nights the best we can.

It was good that family, friends and acquaintances helped as we sorted through Sandy's belongings. She had planned to return to her apartment in Minneapolis and go to work after her weekend at the lake. Only parents, who have faced the finality of closing out a child's lifetime possessions, can understand the heart rendering pain that brought back the finality of death again.

And then suddenly, everyone had to return to their responsibilities. Kenny went back to work, and I was at home alone. Dreams and memories crept in. A word, an action of someone, or just out of nowhere tears took over, and frequently I had no control over my actions. I had to let the tears flow and cope with the sudden unexplainable tiredness. I could not explain the frequent loss of memory when I was not able to remember what was I doing or where should I be today? All that made me unable to function as I would have liked, but I learned this is part of grieving.

People told me, "It is so hard letting the one we love go."

I found that as the survivors we never really let go. We learn to survive because we remember the good times we shared with our loved one. I learned a great deal when Mama and Irmgard came.

I complained to Mama, "Frequently when I try to share a memory of Sandy's life with someone, instantly the subject is changed. I want to tell these people, let me talk about my daughter! She is dead, but once she was a living, breathing child. All I have left are the memories of her so let me share them with you."

"Anneliese," Mama suggested, "Your friends mean well. They don't want you to hurt. They think if you aren't reminded of Sandy, you won't hurt so much. So just tell them, 'please, let me talk about Sandy, it hurts, I always hurt, she was part of my life.'"

"Mama," I said, "Sometimes Sandy is so near me I can feel her spirit. I talk with her. I can't see her. She doesn't answer, but I talk to her and I know she is right there."

"Papa has been gone for years," Mama reflected. "We don't even know if he is still living in Russia or if he died a long time ago. I still talk to him and when I talk something out with him, I feel better and often his spirit helps me make the right decision. So call me crazy. That's okay as long as it helps me, I will keep on doing it."

After they returned to Germany, Mama called frequently and as always, her words eased my pain. Sandy's death never left us, but we learned to live day by day. As time went by even through the first Christmas, we realized that we had taken the first baby steps toward healing as we shared and lived with the good memories of Sandy and that sustained us.

The trial of the drunken driver took place in Detroit Lakes during Spring 1979, and it was hard to believe that 'justice was done.' The driver wore a jean jacket that displayed a colorful beer can on the backside. During the court proceedings, his six previous DUI fines could not be introduced since they didn't relate to the girl's deaths. Even though three girls were recklessly killed, the driver was sentenced to five years for each death, yet served concurrently. We felt the sentence was absurd when at the same time a hunter was sentenced to prison and a heavy monetary fine for shooting one bald eagle. We knew that we would survive the legal injustice only by not letting bitterness add to our sorrow. We could not bring Sandy back. To honor her memory we needed to go on as best we could.

Our Chevy Impala was still running smoothly, but Kenny suggested that we fulfill Sandy's wish and take part of the $25,000 insurance money we had received and buy our first new car - just like Sandy had planned. We bought a 1979 blue Bonneville right out of the show room and drove it home. At first it was hard for me to drive the car to school, but when I thought of Sandy's wish it was what we needed to do.

We missed Sandy everyday, but Irmgard's call made us momentarily focus on my family in Germany because there, changes for Mama and the family were taking shape.

Irmgard was elated, "Can you believe it? Our baby brother, Werner, is thirty-four and he is finally leaving Mama. He is getting married. He met the lady of his choice. She is from Mitterteich. Her husband died of a diabetic reaction. They had two children so Werner is getting a ready-made family"

"Do you and Mama feel good about it?"

"Yes, Werner has known Christa all his life, so it should be fine. They will just have the family present when they get married and then have a reception later."

"Will you select a wedding gift for them?" I asked, "We will settle with you later. I will write and wish them happiness and blessings."

Kenny and I were glad that Werner would have a family because Mama always thought marriage and family were the best way of life. I thought of Sandy. Would she have been thinking of marriage? I knew that now it would never be.

Grandpa, Kenny's dad, had lamented the fact that he was still living at ninety-three and Sandy had been taken to heaven so young.

"I want to be with my wife Caroline up there," he said. He got his wish when he died on November 11, 1978. He was buried in Crookston beside his beloved Caroline who had been his partner for fifty-four years.

CHAPTER 27

Titus - Irmgard - Stefan - Liv

During the early summer months of 1979, Roy and Linda had bought a home in Edina and they told us that by February 1980, Freya would have a little brother or sister. We drove to Edina for Thanksgiving and Christmas and on February 5, the day after Linda's birthday, little Titus joined our extended family. He was blond and blue-eyed, so I claimed him for Bavaria while the rest of the family thought he was truly of Norwegian decent. We decided to share him and rejoice in his good health and strong lungs. Between our jobs, Kenny and I spent as many weekends as we could with our family.

Kenny was sixty-five, and he retired on July 1, 1981. During the retirement banquet, his company rewarded Kenny's good work with two airline tickets to Germany. We spent four weeks in Germany and Kenny said, "Annelee, every time I visit your family it gets better because wherever we go, you and I are at home. I love the woods and hills, but for me they are steeper and higher and more difficult to climb than the last time I was here."

During Christmas, Roy and Linda gave us a wonderful Christmas present when they told us that by August 1982, a little girl would join toddler Titus and Freya. We still missed Sandy everyday, but the new family members made our pain easier to bear.

For Mother's Day 1982, Roy and Linda gave me a sixty minute long distance telephone card. I put it to immediate use and called Mama. We shared our mutual Mothers' Day wishes, and then I asked to speak with

Irmgard. She always came home on Mother's Day.

But Mama hesitated, "Annelee, Irmgard is not here, she called on Friday and said that she was not feeling well and she didn't want to give us what she had."

"What does she suffer from?" I asked.

"She said she had a terrible cold and she also had an upset stomach."

I was troubled, and I called Irmgard. "I hear you are not feeling well," I inquired, "Are you getting over whatever it is?"

"Anneliese, I didn't tell Mama, and please don't tell her either," Irmgard pleaded, "I was diagnosed with advanced stomach cancer, and I will be hospitalized tomorrow for treatment and surgery."

I thought of summer vacation. "Irmgard, would it help if I came home?"

"Yes, yes, come as soon as you and Kenny can arrange a flight," she urged, "I need your support and I need support for my family and Mama."

"Irmgard, I will be in touch as soon as we know the detail of our arrival." I reassured her.

"Good," she sighed and the line went dead.

Roy had understood much of the conversation, and I related what Irmgard had to face. Although we had been in Germany barely a year ago, Kenny insisted that we needed to be by his *second lady's* side.

"We brought her through impetigo. Let's hope we can help her get through the cancer surgery. She will get better. Don't worry, Annelee."

Adolf, Irmgard's husband called and advised, "Annelee, come in July, Irmgard will be hospitalized for treatments and surgery on and off until then. She will need your support when she is at home."

Since we had until July, I completed graduate work at St. Cloud to become the certified elementary and high school librarian for our school after August 1. 1981. Despite the heavy work load, my mind was on the health status of Irmgard. We stayed in almost daily phone contact and we arrived at her home as July ended. Irmgard had been released from the hospital after lengthy, painful chemo treatments. She had lost weight and her hair. Her slim figure was now skeleton-like. Pale-faced and weak, she had limited her food intake to lessen the nausea that the side affects of her medications caused. Adolf went back to work, and during Irmgard's good times we sat in the large veranda, played games or talked until she tired. She never complained. Yet, one day, she allowed me to glimpse briefly her deep true feelings.

I had just told Irmgard, "I truly admire your new home. It is beautifully decorated inside, and the landscaping is picture perfect. You deserve all of it."

She looked at me and said, "Anneliese, I will be forty-three on October 31. I wonder if I will be around for 'All Saints or All Souls Day', on November 1." I tried to interrupt, but she shook her head and I knew I could not stop her reflections. "Adolf and I have worked hard to achieve what we own. We have no financial worries. We could travel. Instead, I am skirting the edge of death. Tell me, where is God? He has forsaken our family. Where was he when Papa was taken by the Russians and Mama was left with five children? Where was he when three of you left? Where was he when Sandy and her two friends were killed? Where is he now? Hasn't our family suffered enough?"

She didn't touch the tears that were flowing down her cheeks, and I sat still as she went on. "Ever since she was born, we spoiled Manuela. Because of the war, I never had anything new until I was eight years old and you sent clothes from America. We can afford to give Manuela what I never had. She married too young. Stefan is a baby who needs me because Manuela tries, but she needs my help as much as the baby. I have wonder how she will cope with a stepmother if Adolf wants to remarry. He is young. It doesn't feel so good to think that some day a woman I probably have never met will walk in here and enjoy without lifting a finger all I have worked so hard for. Doesn't God consider that? I don't think he cares." Her eyes mirrored the pain and hopelessness she felt as she recalled.

"While I was in the hospital, during sleepless nights I had a lot of time to think. All these questions were going through my mind. When I was taking the chemo treatments they were the closest thing to living in hell. I would have the treatment, and for three days I would be so sick. I would lie on the rug in the hospital bathroom because I couldn't make it to the toilet from my bed. I never believed I could vomit that much. Then for three days I would feel better, and then the same round would start again. I prayed to die because I didn't want to live like that. I smelled my own vomit on me and I needed someone to clean me up. I was dependent on everyone for everything. I couldn't take care of my own bathroom functions. Where was God then? He wasn't listening? He didn't seem to care. I was taught that I was God's child. Why does God treat his children like that?"

"I tell you. Right now I feel better, now I don't want to die! I might, and if I do all that we have accumulated and worked for is reduced to shit!"

Sobs jolted her body I held her in my arms while I cried with her. I had no comforting words because as I looked at my frail sister, I wondered what lay ahead. All I knew for sure was that there was nothing but hope that we could cling to, and there was not much of that – just tattered threads.

"Please don't tell Adolf or Mama how I feel," she pleaded. "Just keep it between us."

I could just nod to her request, but she knew I would never tell. Irmgard and I had a sister bond between us that spanned distance and years, and it just had gotten stronger than ever. On August 15, Adolf handed me the telephone, and Roy called out, "Mom, Dad, you are grandparents to a beautiful blond, little girl we named Liv. She is waiting for your return."

After congratulations, I told Roy that we were waiting for Mama, Werner and Theresa to join us, and after we were together as a family for

At home with Irmgard - 1982
L to R: Annelee, Theresa, Mama, Irmgard, Werner

a few days, Kenny and I would return home. Irmgard seemed to rally, and we could see how having the family near gave her peace. Kenny and I dreaded our day of leaving, but Irmgard assured us that she wouldn't give up. She would be here for our next visit.

We flew home and met our ten day old granddaughter Liv who was in our eyes the most beautiful child, just like Titus and Freya had been when they were born. Reluctantly we returned home to Ada because a new school year was starting and I had to ready my classroom and check out the libraries.

Between my new duties as a librarian, I was teaching English 7, psychology and German, grades eleven and twelve, and I also became media coordinator for our school. Throughout the school year, Irmgard's health was our main concern, and we were relieved when Adolf and Irmgard wrote that the cancer was in remission, and they were looking forward to celebrate their Silver Wedding Anniversary on July 11, 1984. We were elated and we planned to fly to Germany and celebrate with them, but Irmgard suggested,

"We would love to have you here with us, but remember Mama will be eighty on December 23, and I am planning the biggest and best celebration, ever! I have secured the band and the catering. The invitations are being designed and I plan for 125 guests. You will be able to touch base with family and friends so be sure to get your tickets. We will pick you up at the airport."

As I shared Irmgard's plans with Kenny, he was euphoric that Irmgard had recovered and he said, "Well, it seems 1984 will be a good year."

Annelee and Irmgard
Kenny's Second Lady -
1975

CHAPTER 28

1984 - A Battle Lost

It was March. Winter was giving its last sigh, the snow was melting. Lilies of the valley, crocuses and tulips were coming up in various gardens. I was at our local Minnesota Education Association meeting when the members voted and I was chosen as the candidate to represent our school for the 1984 Minnesota Teacher of the Year search. The school board, the community and the students wrote letters of recommendation while I was required to assemble a slide presentation of my daily teaching and additional activities, and it was stressed as most important, that every candidate needed to state their philosophy of teaching.

I stated:

MY PHILOSOPHY OF TEACHING

My philosophy of teaching consists of two main concepts that overshadow all other factors necessary for a successful teacher-student relationship. First, a teacher must love our young people,accept them at their level of academic achievement and maturity, then encourage and help them to grow intellectually and emotionally.

I also feel that a teacher must respect our young people, accept their ideas, their likes and dislikes, in short, accept their individuality within the bounds set by society for our protection and safety.

To attain the highest level of academic learning and achievement, the second concept of student-teacher relationship   must   also   include   parent-teacher communication. I found repeatedly that a teacher-student-parent conference enabled us to work together as a team, helped establish good rapport and laid the foundation built on trust.

The above stated concepts are reinforced by the following factors which are also an important part of my teaching philosophy. To maintain a good classroom atmosphere, fair and uniform discipline rules should be initiated by the school administration, shared with the parents, and then consistently enforced by every teacher.

To enhance the learning atmosphere within the classroom, I found that the motto, 'Praise in public; admonish in private,' can work wonders. To establish trust and rapport with the students, it should be understood that to err is human. The final judgment of growth depends on what the offender has learned from a mistake.

I have learned that in order to be effective and successful within the classroom, I must be flexible and adapt my methods of teaching to the needs of the students. Since learning takes place in three particular forms or combination of the same, I try to use visual, auditory, and tactile exercises to instill love of discovering, adaptation, learning and retention of the subject. I feel the adage 'You get what you expect,' certainly holds true in regard to student performance. It is my contention that the student must be challenged and must understand from the beginning that performance must match the quality and quantity of work within her/his ability.

I firmly believe that it is our responsibility as teachers to set an example for our students, and that our attitude must teach them to treat their peers and every other individual that they encounter with respect, even if they are different and pursue another way of life than we do.

Our students must have the opportunity to learn effective research techniques because it is becoming more apparent with each day that our young people must be able to seek solutions for the complex problems and challenges that will face them, our nation and the world.

The final analysis is that teaching demands a great deal of dedication from each teacher. I am sure, though, that my fellow teachers would agree with the following statement: When the gifted, the slow learner, or the average students display that split-second glint of understanding, or the 'I got it' smile, I for one feel great! I rejoice with the student in his/her and my accomplishment because we, together, reaped the fruits of our labor.

Being part of the formative years of our young people, teaching the basics, and taking each student as far as he or she will want to go is not only a grave responsibility but also a privilege. I am sure that I not only speak for myself, but that I speak for all teachers who work toward the same goals when I say, "I AM PROUD TO BE A TEACHER!"

The slides and the book were mailed before the April 1984 deadline. Vacation started and I was pleased when I learned that I was selected by the State Committee as one of the Fourteen Teachers of Excellence who taught in the State of Minnesota.

On July 11, we called Irmgard and Adolf and wished them many more years together. Adolf said, "The way Irmgard has organized this party and the way she is working on Mama's birthday party I can't keep up with her. As soon as the celebration is over, I will take her on a two week rest and relaxation vacation. I rented a chalet in the mountains."

Kenny and I were thankful because our marriage had survived difficult times. We had been married thirty-seven years. Our children were happy. The grandchildren came to spend time with us during the summer and we felt blessed.

I wondered if Irmgard had changed her mind about God. Did she still think he didn't listen, or did she still believe that he never was present when she longed to have him near? I thought I would ask her when we were together in December.

One day Adolf called, "Anneliese, Irmgard is back in the cancer hospital in Munich. She had a complete relapse while we were on our way home from the vacation. I have been told that the cancer is now growing throughout her system. She is on heavy chemo and radiation treatments and very ill at all times. We hope she pulls through. I will stay in touch."

"Adolf, give her our love. I can't get away from school right now but as soon as we can, we will be with you."

"The one who will need you most is Mama, I just don't know how she will survive if Irmgard doesn't beat this."

For two weeks Irmgard fought, and then she told the doctors and Adolf that she couldn't go on.

"No more chemo, no more surgery," she advised, "Just make me comfortable. That's all I want."

On September 29, Adolf called, "Irmgard died this morning. She has suffered so much. Now she is at peace. We will get through this with the help of family and friends that are here with us. But please, come for Christmas. Mama, Manuela and I will need you here."

Suddenly, nothing seemed important. My little sister whom I loved very much had been taken from our midst. I thought life is just not fair, is it?

On October 16, I was honored by the Minnesota Education Association in Minneapolis and later by our school district. I expressed that the recognition and honors that I had received belonged to all the teachers who made a difference in the lives of their students, and I was proud that I could represent them.

My work in school went smoothly, but I was apprehensive because the Christmas season loomed before me. I remembered the pain and deep despair, the days when I could hardly function and nothing had made sense because Sandy had been killed. Mama and Irmgard had tried to console me, but even today pain still surfaced and frequently held me in its grip. Kenny and I had promised we would spend Christmas with Mama and the family, and I hoped we could help them.

As Adolf picked us up at the airport, he told me of his hope that I could help Manuela and he shared her outbursts of anger.

"Mama should have gone for a checkup months ago. She would still be here with us if she would have gone for her yearly checkups, but oh, no, she just didn't?" Manuela raged, "And you, Papa, you just had to build the best and biggest house around. Mama had to help all the time so she didn't go to a doctor. We have the house, but where is Mama? Stefan will barely remember his grandma, and I have to live without Mama. I hope you are happy!"

"How is Mama?" I asked Adolf.

"She has been with us for several weeks and she tries to put on a good front for Manuela and me," Adolf declared, "but I hear her crying during the night and I can't be the help I should be because I miss my love every minute of the day. Anneliese, how did you and Kenny ever manage when Sandy was killed?"

"You can't manage the pain and the helplessness you feel when a loved one dies because the pain and helplessness hold you in a vice," I recalled, "but you do learn to go on day by day. All too often we go three steps forward, then someone will say or do something, and you are back to square one in your grieving process."

"Does it ever end?" Adolf asked.

"It doesn't end, but it gets easier as time goes on." I comforted.

Adolf interrupted, "I can't tell you and Kenny how glad we are that you are with us."

When we arrived at the house, Mama opened the door and fell into Kenny's arms. "Kenny, Kenny, what are we going to do without our Irmgard?"

Mama, dressed in black according to custom, clung to Kenny, and he gently led her to the sofa. She rested her head on his shoulder and cried softly while he spoke words she couldn't understand but found soothing.

She looked at me, "I am so glad you are here. Now it will be easier for us to face the holidays."

Before Christmas Eve, we went to the cemetery and decorated Irmgard's grave with a little Christmas tree, lit the flame in the lantern and covered the earth with evergreen branches and flowers. Every grave in the cemetery was beautifully decorated.

Kenny remarked. "I don't mind visiting a cemetery here because each cemetery shows so much evidence of love. Look at this grave. This person died twenty years ago, yet, the grave is decorated and a lantern is

Cemetery in my hometown. Cemeteries are taken care of throughout Bavaria. Each family takes care of own graves. They are beautiful all year long.

lit. What does the inscription on this drawing say?"

I read, 'May your Spirit shine in the glory of God.' I pondered, "I think a little child did the drawing. From fourth grade on the nuns stipulated that we had to decorate a grave where no one was left to care for it. We usually were three in a group. We cleaned the stone and planted flowers during spring. Then we cared for them during summer and fall, and for winter we used evergreens to keep the grave neat. The nuns graded us on how well we did and told us that we had to learn to do something for someone who couldn't say thank you. I hope that custom still exists because I am glad we did that."

During the Christmas season Irmgard had always decorated the home inside and out. But no one wanted the huge tree, the hand-carved creche, lights and garlands, music, and special foods, so we down-sized to a small tree and gifts. Mama insisted on making a traditional Christmas dinner. We left after dinner and drove to Mitterteich to celebrate Mama's eightieth birthday at the *Alpen Gasthaus*. (Alpine Restaurant).

I shared my concern with Kenny and Adolf, "I wish Mama would have canceled that party. I just wonder how she can get through tomorrow without crying her heart out."

"We considered canceling," Adolf said, "but we decided Irmgard worked so hard to arrange the party, and we said that we would celebrate Mama's birthday and think of Irmgard's spirit at the same time. Don't worry. So many people knew and loved Irmgard. Most likely, we won't be the only ones crying. You don't know, but Mama even secured a local band to play after supper so the guests will have a chance to dance after we leave."

Father Neidl, who was a guest, honored Irmgard's memory at the party's onset. While friends and acquaintances shared memories of good times with Irmgard, there were tears and hugs. But then Adolf and Werner, my brother, said that we were here to celebrate and honor the lady who was born eighty years ago. Guests recalled memories they had assembled in a photo album for Mama to keep. We could feel the love, the respect and caring that surrounded her and remained as we left.

Adolf and Kenny went for a walk, and Manuela went to her room, and Werner and his wife, Christa, went to their home. I complimented Mama and told her that I could not have attended a party three months after Sandy had been killed.

Mama looked at me for a long time before she spoke, "Anneliese, I am aware of the criticism that my decision caused. Even Father Neidl stopped by and asked me if I thought it was wise to have a big party before the official year of mourning is up. I told him that I would wear black for the year like the custom still demands, but I would not ask Kenny or you to observe that custom. When Sandy died, Irmgard and I learned a great deal being with you and your friends. I learned grief is not determined by the apparel one wears, and I surely knew that grief has no time limit, so let the people talk."

Mama smiled and went on, "While the people talk about me, someone else will get a rest from their busy tongues. Don't get me wrong, I thought a great deal about canceling the party but, there were several reasons why not. First, Irmgard had arranged the party and she wanted me to have it. Secondly, I miss Irmgard terribly and I grieve her loss everyday, but I also learned that my days of life are dwindling as each day passes so I live each day as best I can. Frequently, there is time for tears, but life is a gift so I must live it well. Beside the bittersweet moments, think of the joy the party brought to so many. Irmgard would have liked that. Yes, it was a good plan. It was a good day. You and Kenny are with me. For all that, I am thankful. I just wish Manuela would refrain from blaming everyone for Irmgard's death. I suppose that is her way of getting rid of her anger. Things always went her way. All Manuela had to do was point and smile, and whatever she asked for Irmgard would give her. Now she must learn to adjust to a life that is not the fun time she thought it would be."

Mama got up and came back holding a small frame with a verse under glass. She explained. "I had this framed for you and I will have one framed for Manuela. It is a good way to live and you can take yours with you. I will give it to Manuela when she is more receptive to advice. A friend gave it to me. I don't know who wrote it, but it surely tells us how to live."

I read:
Ein bischen mehr Frieden, und weniger Streit.
    A little more peace, and less fighting.

Ein bischen mehr Guete, und weniger Neid.
    A little more compassion, and less jealousy.

Ein bischen mehr Wahrheit, immerdar
    und viel mehr Hilfe in Gefahr.
    A little more truth, always,
    And extend more help during danger.

Ein bischen mehr 'Wir' und weniger 'Ich'
A little more 'Us' and less 'I'.

Ein bischen mehr Mut, und nicht so zimperlich
A little more courage and not so fearful.

    Und viel mehr Blumen waehrend des Lebens,
    Denn auf den Graebern since sie vergebens!!
And many more flowers during a lifetime
    Because on graves, they are useless!

Mama never ceased to amaze me. Was aging really the factor that molded her and others into acceptance of birth, successes and failure, sickness and death of loved ones because the remaining days became a treasure that should be lived with dignity and grace?

Kenny and I returned home and our days fell into routine matters. I started my fifteenth year of teaching in the fall 1985, and I still looked forward anew each day to the challenges and rewards teaching brings. Kenny took on volunteer work for the social services. He delivered senior meals, drove patients to hospital appointments, joined a weekly bowling

Christmas 1984
Mama in customary black for one year after Irmgard died, 9-29-84.

group, enjoyed card games with his fellow American Legion members, and if someone needed a helping hand he was available. We enjoyed visits with our neighbors and friends, and we always looked forward to holidays and vacations Roy, Linda and the grandchildren could spend with us. Roy's family was growing up, the grandchildren were attending school, Roy and Linda both had jobs. They. Like most young parents struggled at times to keep the family finances solvent. I remembered the days when Kenny and I had struggled. Roy and Linda were good parents and they always wanted the best for their children. Kenny and I were proud grandparents and we enjoyed Titus when he spent weeks of his summer vacation time with us.

CHAPTER 29

1987 - Mama Couldn't Wait

Theresa and John called during January and told us that they were planning to visit Mama from April 13th through May 3rd. John had not been in Germany since 1963, and Theresa had not returned since 1982. During my weekly call to Mama, she revealed her thoughts,

"I will see that we have good days. Three decades have gone by since they left for America without telling me of their intentions. I learned a long time ago that we can't change how we lived the past, but we can shape the future. Theresa and John had my forgiveness a long time ago. I can hardly wait for their arrival since there will be so much to talk about and we will have good days."

"Mama, I am glad to hear that. Are you well?"

"Anneliese," she said, "At my age I could be better or I could be worse. Almost everyone my age has aches and days that could be better. At times my knees are giving me lots of problems. I wish Werner would come to visit me more often, but Christa does most of my shopping, and I have someone come in to do my hair. The young have their family and jobs. I am better off than a lot of people my age. So don't you worry. Just come when you can."

I felt that Mama was holding back on how she truly felt and I was glad that Theresa would see how Mama was coping with being alone. My suspicions were confirmed when during the first week of March. Christa, Werner's wife, called.

"Anneliese, your Mama's bleeding stomach ulcers are the cause of her hospitalization. She has a good doctor, and she should be recuperating quickly."

I was deeply troubled. Neither Mama nor anyone else had ever mentioned that she suffered from ulcers. To alleviate my concerns while Mama was hospitalized, I called her every night. She was weak, but she assured me that by the time Theresa and John arrived she would be back at home waiting for their arrival. Mama's doctor and nurse also said that it would take time, but she would be fine.

But suddenly on March 24, Mama complained of being extremely tired and weak, and before the doctor could get there, a massive heart attack took her life. She was eighty-two. For me it was hard to imagine life without Mama. Although the distance between us spanned an ocean, she had been just a telephone call away and she was always there when I needed her.

Theresa and John decided not to cancel their trip. They hoped to assist Werner with whatever help he needed and they surely planned to stay in touch with us. Within a few days of their arrival in Germany, we learned that our family was not exempt from the inheritance squabble that can destroy for life what once had been a family. The ring of the telephone awoke me at 6:00 a.m. It was Theresa.

"Annelee," she cried out, "if I could get a ticket to fly home right now, I would be on that plane and never come back to Germany again. We should have stayed in Rochester!"

"Theresa, slow down. What is going on?" I asked.

"We rented a car at the airport and we arrived here yesterday. As Werner had said, the key was at the house for us. We bathed and unpacked and waited for Werner to come, but he just called and said that he would see us early in the morning. For this evening we should rest and get over the jet lag. Werner came while we had breakfast. He walked in and said that he was glad that we were here. Then he opened his arms wide and said, 'All this is mine. The house, the two lots behind the house, the furniture, everything you see here is mine. If you want a painting or anything in this house, you have to ask me because Mama wrote out a will and she gave me everything. Should Max come back from Canada, he can't enter what will now be my home unless I invite him. You can stay here during your visit. There will be some money for the grandchildren because Mama had set up a bank account, and our attorney will send the money to them. Sandra's money will go back to our general account since she died in 1978. We sent a copy of the will to Anneliese and Kenny so that should take care of everything.'"

Theresa was sobbing as she went on. "John talked to an attorney here. You should see this will. It is hand-written in ink. It has several lines crossed out and they can't be deciphered by us or the attorney. The will is signed by Mama.   In Germany you need only two witnesses present for the will to be legal. You can guess who the two witnesses were. It was Christa and Werner. As long as the will has Mama's signature, it is valid in Germany."

"We overheard the remark one of Werner's friends made to a co-worker, 'Those Americans,' he chided, 'they come here and want to take from Werner what should and will be his. Besides, I hear these two are loaded. They weren't here for Peppi, but now they want her money.'"

Theresa sobbed but then went on, "You know, Annelee, it surely is not the money. We don't need it. I wanted something sentimental from my childhood, but everything, even all the photos in the home are under lock and key. The Hummel figurines and the jewelry are removed from their locations and nowhere to be seen. Does Werner think I will steal something? Oh, he told me, 'Theresa, you can have Mama's fur coat.'"

"Theresa," I said, "I can't believe Mama would write such a will without discussing it with us. She said that she, you and John would have a lot to talk about. Now I wonder what she had in mind, but we will never know. Mama was never vindictive, and she would never forbid Max to enter his childhood home. Until he left for Canada I always thought that Max would inherit the home. After we get the will, I will talk with Cousin Baerbl and her husband and see what they suggest. For now, visit your friends and the relatives you want to see before you come home."

"Annelee, isn't it strange," Theresa reflected, "All of a sudden we don't have access to the home where we were born. Although it stands, it isn't ours to visit."

"From what you tell me," I answered, "with her last breath, Mama took our home with her. From now on, I guess our home in Germany ceases to exist for us and our children. Now, our home is in America."

And that's the way it turned out to be because within the month

Christa's parents moved into what once had been our home.

Cousin Baerbl and her husband, who was also named Werner, suggested that we come. We flew to Germany during June. Baerbl's husband advised Kenny and me, "You always had a good relationship with your Mama and your brother. See what he will say to you. Legally, my lawyer advised me, too, that there is nothing you can do. You could contest the legality of the will because so much is crossed out, but the outcome would still be the same. You would make a lawyer rich and you gain nothing but heartache."

We stayed with Cousin Joey in Mitterteich. He was not happy with Werner's actions. "Even while Werner was courting Christa and before they were married, Werner rarely went home to check on your mama. She didn't want to tell you how she was living after Werner got married because Peppi never complained to anyone. I did visit her as often as I could because she was so alone. Her knees had given out on her and she took strong medication for pain. I thought it was way too much."

"The will - Werner justifies it by saying that he lived with your mother for almost forty years. But where were you girls? You came for visits and went back home. That's all you ever did for Mama. To him and Christa their actions are justifiable."

I anguished over meeting with my brother. He said we could stay in the upstairs rooms in his house. I wanted to see if Theresa's assessment had been correct. It was. While we stayed, whatever had a lock was locked up tight.

We also saw Werner's anger surface when he said,

"Like everyone else who is after my inheritance, Manuela, Irmgard's daughter, asked me for Mama's red cherry wood bedroom set with the black Italian marble tops. It is stored in the attic. I understand it is an antique set, but I will hack it to pieces before I would give it to her."

I just didn't understand how Mama's will was accepted as a legal document when much of the wording was crossed out and Werner and Christa were the only witnesses. Nor could I understand Werner's actions because Kenny and I had not ever asked for anything, not of Mama and never of him.

Cousin Joey explained, "Werner was eighteen when he was drafted for his one year, compulsory military service. He was away from Mama and on his own for the first time. He loved the military and a very high official took an interest in Werner because he looked much like his son. When Werner was asked to re-enlist, he was really serious and wanted to go on for officers' training, but your mama discouraged that from the very beginning. I guess she actually pressured him because then she would be alone. Werner, against the advice of his officers, came home and went back to his work in the glass factory. Werner's job there is high paying but also very dangerous. The section he works in is closed to the general public because they produce the glass for the space ships. Despite the asbestos suits and masks that the workers are wearing, the heat in that area is almost unbearable. They have a twenty minute break every hour before they go back into the oven. That's what they call the room. Werner has started to drink beer. I don't know how long he can take that kind of work. He will never be laid off. He can work somewhere else in the factory, but it certainly doesn't compare to what he could have achieved in the military. I don't know if that's the reason for his anger, but he shouldn't blame you girls because it was his decision."

Kenny and I had visited Mama's grave. "Kenny," I sobbed, "now that we have said good-bye to Mama I also said good–bye to my home. I thought I knew my little brother, but only now do I understand why he so often stayed late at the pub while we were here. I guess he couldn't stomach our visits. I loved him, but maybe he never knew that because he is not the brother I thought I knew. I wonder what Mama would say to this mess. There is nothing left for me here. Everything is gone!"

"No, Annelee," Kenny consoled, "you have memories that Werner or no one can take from you, and you still have what your papa and mama instilled in you. Remember what your papa told you as you said good-bye to him in Wiesau? He told you that he will never leave you because what he taught you, you would pass on to your children and they to theirs. So your mama, too, will always be with you. Someday, we too, will live on in our children. That is your heritage and worth much more than the money and land Werner now owns. How much happiness will he gain from what he calls his rightful heritage? Think about that."

I shared with Cousin Joey what Kenny had said, "I hope you know," he answered, "that Kenny is right. You have a lot more than Werner will ever have."

Sadness overtook me while we flew home, but I knew that Kenny and Cousin Joey were right. I was glad that I had come and stood at Mama's grave because she was the one who, with Papa, had given me life and by example taught me what was important in life.

CHAPTER 30

1988 – Max, Who Couldn't Be

From the day of his birth, Papa determined that our little baby boy Max, who was the miniature image of Papa, would follow in Papa's footstep and be an engineer or an architect.

Even as a toddler, little Max worshiped Papa. We would watch as he followed Papa and tried to step into Papa's footprints on the soft grass or moss. As he entered school, he was loved by his teachers because of his thirst for learning, his agility in soccer and hockey, and he always was good natured and peace loving. From the time he was allowed to venture out on his own, Max took to the woods where he would spend hours watching deer and other little creatures while he filled his jars with butterflies or frogs. Mama's scolding was always gentle when his shoes and socks crunched with sand and water or smelled of rotten grass. If his shirt, face and hair looked like they hadn't been washed for days, he gleefully explained, "I had to jump the creek, but it was too wide so I got a little wet. I will take everything off and then it can dry outside."

On Sunday outings Max always walked beside Papa. Little Max wore a *Leder Hose* (leather pants) while Papa wore knickerbockers. They wore short-sleeved shirts, green felt hats with a plume, and little Max tried to copy Papa's movements as he twirled his walking stick. Their voices joined as they sang Bavarian marching songs that made us laugh.

The war changed all that. Max was eight-years-old when Papa said his final good-bye in 1943. The war intensified, and Papa never came home. Max never saw the American soldiers that occupied our town as the enemy, as a matter of fact, he was constantly underfoot while they fixed their trucks and Jeeps. It was because of Max that I had met Kenny.

In 1956, Max immigrated to Canada and he had high hopes that he could make a better life for himself. When we met in Kenora during 1962, he had been a wood cutter but now it was 1972 and we thought he was working for the railroad. We hadn't heard from him nor had we been able to locate him for years when we received a letter. He pleaded with us to bail him out of the Winnipeg jail. He had been arrested in Reddit, Ontario for being drunk and unruly. Max was a changed man when we saw him.

We talked with the head jailer who revealed more about Max's past than we knew. "Max is a steady here, he goes out, gets stinking drunk and unruly, and then he ends up back here."

I asked, "Sir, why don't you put him in rehab? What does he ever learn in jail?"

"Ma'am" the jailer explained, "Max has been in rehab more often than I can recall. It doesn't seem to help him, so he ends back up here. After we sober him up, he goes to the jail library and reads every history book he can get his hands on. He speaks English without an accent, and when he is sober, he has very good manners. We like him because he is no trouble here. He is so personable and bright, he could be a businessman if he stayed sober but that is not the case. We feel that he will die as an alcoholic and will be buried at the cost of the taxpayers."

We took Max to the motel and Kenny asked him, "Max, why do you need alcohol to get through the day or night?"

Max put his hands up and hid his face as he shared with us, "All my life, everyone I ever loved left me. First, it was Papa. Oh God, how I missed Papa while I grew up. Anneliese, I loved being with you while you were home after the war. Kenny, I really liked you. You both left for America. I, too, felt that I needed a new life because I couldn't stand factory work, so I immigrated and settled in Canada. You know what homesickness is. I was not happy until I lived with the railroad foreman and his family. Mr. G., his wife and their three daughters were good to me. They soon became my second home and my second family. It was on a Saturday, I shall never forget. The family planned to spend the day in Kenora shopping and eating out. They asked me to join them, but I decided to stay home and I promised to have a fresh fish supper waiting when they returned. The girls were so excited. Finally, they would have a day in the big city. As they drove away I stood outside and waved. The whole family waved. Mr. G. had crossed that railroad crossing a hundred times before. He waved and never saw the oncoming freight train loaded with timber. The engine hit them and the car was pummeled for two hundred feet before the train could stop. I ran to the scene . . . I still see it in my dreams. The car was crushed. They were dismembered and I could hardly identify them." He paused, closed his eyes and his voice barely audible, he said, "If I hadn't waved, they would not have waved. They would have seen the train and would still be alive. I still would have someone who cares about me. Everyone told me that it was not my fault, but after what I had caused, I couldn't work on the railroad any longer so I quit that day. Now I am on public assistance. I can't wait to get my money so I can go and drink and forget what I saw." He shook his head. Trance-like he mumbled, "Any one I ever loved always left me and never came back. Over here, you and Kenny are the only ones who care about me. I quit writing to Mama a long time ago because I don't want her to know what I have become."

Kenny walked toward him and held him in his arms. They talked quietly and Kenny stayed by his side until he fell asleep.

"Annelee," Kenny said, "there must be a way that we can get Max to come to America and live with us. With his frequent arrests, it will be hard to gain an exit permit for him but we could try."

We did. But the official advised us, "In Canada, Max is covered by health insurance and we take care of him no matter what happens. If you take him to America, you will be responsible for all his actions. Our assessment of Max is that he is an alcoholic who will not change. As his alcoholism advances and he wants beer or cheap wine, he will lie or even steal if he has the opportunity. If he gets into a squabble or fight, you could be legally held responsible for monetary damages. It is regrettable, but these are the facts. I must advise you against taking him home. I will make it easier for you by denying your request for now and any other time you ask."

We thanked the officer for being truthful. Before we were to leave for home, we took Max out for dinner. He was restless, sometimes talkative, and then somberly quiet. Kenny paid at the register, Max walked away from me and addressed a young couple who looked surprised as he handed them twenty dollars and said, "Have dinner on me."

Kenny looked shocked, and he offered Max a ride to where he was staying.

"Come on," Max said, "I'll show you my place."

As he directed us, the neighborhoods became more rundown. Uncollected garbage was strewn around the places. Old car wrecks were everywhere. With each block, it became more unsettling for me. Finally he told us to stop at a ramshackle, two story shack. He opened a side door and asked us to follow.

Kenny locked the car and said, "Max, we will see that you get in, but we can't leave the car here."

We stepped onto a dirt floor, and he motioned for us to climb the long rickety ladder that led up to the second floor. We reached the top and stepped into the narrow hall where garbage cans were loaded with smelly garbage and empty beer cans. Max fumbled for his key, and we entered a small room furnished with an iron frame twin bed, a small cupboard, and a wooden board with hooks that held a jacket and a wrinkled pants. The flypaper that hung from the ceiling was blackened by flies.

"There is nothing here that I could offer you," Max said, "but you can sit on the bed if you want."

A bug sat on my shoe. Was it looking for a bite? My skin felt crawly. "No Max we have to leave," I said, "we want to be home before nightfall. But I will give you the photos of Mama and our family. Think of us and let us know where you are."

I hugged him and left the room, and Kenny helped me down the ladder because I could hardly see through the tears I cried for Max.

As we came outside, Kenny exclaimed, "Our car is still here, I didn't know if we would find it in one piece."

"Kenny," I sighed, "I can never come back here and see Max again, I just can't take it. How am I going to tell Mama how Max is living?"

"Annelee, were you surprised when Max gave the couple money?"

"Yes, I never imagined he had that much money on him."

"He didn't. That was my money. I told him to buy food for himself. I couldn't believe it when he handed it to strangers. I guess it is sad, but you shouldn't give drunks money for food. They drink it up. I bet he

regrets right now that he gave it away."
Kenny shook his head and went on, "The
loneliness he must feel when he is sober,
the guilt he thinks he has to carry because
he feels the accident was his fault when
it wasn't."

We rarely heard from Max, and
whenever we tried to contact him, he had
moved again. I wrote to Mama and told
her that Max was drinking heavily. She
was relieved that we had located Max
since she too had not heard from him in
years, but I had added to her worries.
Anneliese, she wrote, it seems Max is
beyond our help. Will alcohol cause his
premature death? I don't want him buried
somewhere where no one will know who

A visit with brother Max in
Winnipeg in 1972.

he once was. He is my son and he should have a decent burial.

Kenny and I promised Mama should that time come, we or Roy would
have his body brought across and we would bury him in one of the
cemetery lots next to us. Soon after, someone called from Winnipeg and
told us that Max was ill and wanted to see us. I couldn't bring myself to
go, so Kenny decided to drive to the given address with his Cousin Eddy.
Guilt-ridden, I went to work feeling I had failed my brother maybe it
was his final wish to see me. Yet the memories and pain of our previous
visit robbed me of the will to see him in his alcoholic state. I waited
anxiously to hear from Kenny and I was relieved when he came home
the next day.

"Annelee, I am glad you were not with us," he recalled. "Eddy and I
located the address. The whole neighborhood was shacks and garbage. It
looked unsafe and Max's place was a shack with the door wide open and
off its hinges. Skinny dogs and cats roamed through the neighborhood. I
told Eddy to stay with the car, but if I wasn't out in fifteen minutes to
come in after me. I entered. The place reeked of stale alcohol and urine
and I faced a drunken man sitting on the floor. Bugs were sharing his
food remnants and lice were surely nesting in his hair. He was incoherent,

but he told me that Max would be back tomorrow and maybe not."

"I asked him how ill Max was and he said, 'Sometimes bad, sometimes not so bad.' I thought of you. I, too, couldn't take the filthy place any longer so I got out of there. We never saw Max. We stayed at a motel and called the social service official who hadn't seen Max in a week. The woman said that she knew Max, but he could be places they didn't know about. I left my address and phone number, and we decided to come home."

We were notified that Max had died on October 30, 1988, and we had his cremated ashes flown to Grand Forks, North Dakota. Our undertaker had to wait until the box of Max's ashes was checked by custom officials before release. We purchased a beautiful pewter urn. Our family and friends attended the burial ceremony and as we had promised Mama, we buried Max in our family plot. His life began with so much hope and so many dreams, but these were Mama's and Papa's dreams. My little brother Max grew up and he too had dreams. He wanted to make his own future when he left his homeland and immigrated to Canada but a terrible accident, misplaced guilt and alcohol destroyed his dreams.

CHAPTER 31

We Couldn't Mend It

It had been four difficult years. To move on with our lives, we stayed involved within our own family, our friends, and the people near us. Kenny did volunteer work, while I worked steadily on improving our libraries at school, and implementing television and computer access for each classroom. My classroom teaching had been

Brother Werner & I

limited to two classes. However, my student contact remained the same since library research, book selection and checkout often required my assistance. I loved my work, but I knew 1991-1992 would be my final year of teaching and retirement would bring changes that, at times, I didn't feel ready for. I felt blessed because every day of work had also been a day that held new experiences for me and new accomplishments for my students.

Teaching became difficult because the students begged me to stay until they too could graduate. Our good-byes were frequently tearful, but we promised each other that we would stay in touch. During the final week in May the administration officials and teaching staff gave me the usual retirement party while my family and friends were there to extend support during emotional moments. How quickly twenty-two years had passed. It was good that summer vacation started and for a while it seemed life would go on as always come fall.

Kenny was happy to have me home, but feared how I would react when summer vacation was over and another school year started. It had been five years since we had been back to Germany, so Kenny suggested that we return during September 1992. I agreed readily, since Cousin Joey, Cousin Baerbl, her husband Werner and their families had long since asked when we would visit them again. They were so glad to have us, but my brother, Werner, kept his distance. I could not understand why he acted like a stranger when our paths crossed, but I realized the depth of our estrangement when I could not enter the home he and I once shared. As we walked by, his in-laws looked out the windows and they barely responded to our greetings nor did they ask us in.

Cousin Joey said, "Anneliese, your papa loved the home he had built for your mama and I am sure he hoped that it would be handed down to his children and on to future Solch generations. But from what I hear, Werner will sell the home to the highest bidder. I will buy it for my son Stefan so it will stay in the Solch name. Your mama and papa would surely like that, wouldn't they?" I hugged him. He was not just my cousin, he also was my dear friend and I knew that he would do what he had said.

He looked at me, "Anneliese," he said, "I have made plans for tomorrow. Since the East-West Line exists now only in history books, I suggest that we take an early morning excursion to Aunt Lisbeth's hometown, Eger. You remember, the Czechs renamed Eger, and now it is known as Cheb."

We left early the next morning, and Kenny, who remembered our last visit in 1945 asked to drive. We recalled for Cousin Joey how Kenny and the interpreter had brought me to Czechoslovakia where I had witnessed the merciless beatings of the German residents as the Czechs rounded them up for deportation or worse yet, to face the ruthless People's Court.

Cousin Joey broke in, "Anneliese, had I seen what you witnessed that day, I know I would have never crossed into Czechoslovakia, and I assure you that I would have made sure that Aunt Lisbeth wouldn't cross either. That area had been in turmoil and chaos then and it is now. While we are in Cheb, you and Kenny will do well to stay close to me."

My stomach felt queasy as we drove toward the town's center. It seemed time had stood still here since 1945. Homes and business places hadn't seen a coat of paint. Bullet holes were still visible on the outside walls. People wore clothes that had seen years of wear. Many were unkempt, and they seemed extremely poor. Cousin Joey explained that he hired master bakers from Cheb and the surrounding areas because they worked for less than half of what he would have to pay a German master baker. Yet they still made three times more than they could make in Czechoslovakia if they could find a job.

As we approached the market square, Cousin Joey said, "Mikhail, who is one of my master bakers, will meet us here and translate for us if it becomes necessary. He is probably the son of one of the Czechs who in 1945 would gladly have sent us into the sulfur mines, beaten, or even killed us. Now the Czechs come across and beg us for work. How times have changed for them! I can't imagine that now Mikhail would ever hurt me or anyone because he is honest and works hard. Although he tells me that he would never work for a German if he could get equal pay for equal work in Czechoslovakia. Since he must support his family and wants to own a home, he has no other options. Mikhail tells me that he hates the Gypsies and Turks because after the war, they took possession of the vacated German homes. Those transients got these completely furnished homes free, but he has to pay for his." Cousin Joey paused, and then he reflected, "It is the damn wars that change people. Even decent people become so filled with hate that they kill for no reason. Some just kill or torture because they were told that they are facing their enemy. As your Papa always said, 'War is insanity and inhumanity of men toward other men.'"

Mikhail met us and we opted to tour the cathedral. We were asked to pay a fee because it was under renovation. Cousin Joey refused and explained that he knew the fee existed for years, but so far he had not seen any renovation progress.

I thought we had entered the town's fair area, when Cousin Joey explained. "These are permanent, wooden sales booths and I heard from my workers that refugees from Laos and Thailand are hired by ruthless vendors to sell their wares." He warned us, "just look, but don't buy!"

I stopped at a row of booths where they sold lovely, knitted sweaters and immediately I was surrounded by a group offering their sweaters at various prices. I couldn't stand the pleading of these poor salesmen and I selected a lilac sweater from one of the men. "Fifteen dollars," he shouted, while others surrounded me and lowered their prices. I grabbed the sweater and I threw the money to the vendor so I could get away. Mikhail grabbed me by the arm. He shouted at the group and they left.

Cousin Joey reproached, "Anneliese, only groups and businesses buy from these people. They are desperate. If they don't meet the quotas that they must sell they are punished. About six months ago, an employee apparently kept some money that he should have turned in. A hired shooter came by, grabbed the poor man and pulled him out to the middle of the square. Then in front of everyone, he shot him and walked away. When the Czech police came, no one had seen anything nor did anyone know about the shooting that they had witnessed. We are getting out of here before they accost you again."

We drove by Aunt Lisbeth's former home which since 1947 had been occupied by Gypsies. The high fence wall lay in pieces here and there. The landscaped yard was overgrown with weeds; the house was barely visible through the tall trees and bushes that hadn't been trimmed in years. Adults were going in and out. They yelled at the children who played in old cars and wagons while others sat on the ground and teased their dogs or ran back and forth. Nothing had the beauty and cleanliness that was once common throughout the area.

Now I understood why Aunt Lisbeth had constantly refused to reenter Cheb and I too knew that I would not return to Czechoslovakia because it evoked too many horrific memories and too much pain. All I wanted now was to return to the safety and normalcy of my hometown. We arrived at Cousin Joey's home where my former classmates and friends, Marerl, Ella, Bertl and Annemarie were waiting.

"Kenny, you and Anneliese are coming with us." Bertl explained, "Kenny, our husbands will give you a tour of the area while we have a class reunion with Anneliese. Three of our husbands speak English. Kurt and Egon have business connections in America so you are in good hands."

The men whisked Kenny away and we entered the restaurant on the market square where shouts and clapping greeted me. Fourteen former classmates expressed how glad they were to see me. We recalled schooldays and the horrid fourth grade nun, who always reprimanded,

"Anneliese, you will never amount to anything, never!"

We recalled absent

Kenny & Werner -1992
They had been soldiers on opposite
sides. Once enemies - now friends.

classmates who had married and sought a better life in far away towns but only three of us had ventured out to other countries. It made me reminiscent of my life in America where my German past was dead because the only one who knew my family was Kenny. My classmates affirmed that they could not have lived like that.

Ella reflected, "When you left in 1947, some of us thought you wanted a better life than we had here, but now I know you must love that man because otherwise you would have come back and worked in the telegraph office. You know, times have changed and you could have a good life here too."

"Ella," I answered, "I am now at home in America. Kenny, my children, and the friends I have made are what gives my life meaning. Would you believe it, I am glad that we came, but I am also anxious to return to Minnesota where we live."

We spent time at my cousin Baerbl's home where her husband Werner and Kenny went for long walks and relived World War II. They had been soldiers on opposite sides, but now they could visit, share memories, walk side by side, and strengthen the friendship that had begun when they came to visit us in Ada, in 1983. We returned to Adolf's home in Niederroth, near Munich, where as planned, we would spend several days before our flight home.

CHAPTER 32

1992 – VA Hospital Becomes Lifeline

We were glad our journey was ending because Kenny's stomach pains became more frequent and were of longer duration. He also confided,

"Annelee, I am starting to feel my age. My stomach ulcers are bothering me. Lately my lower abdomen hurts, I have problems with urination and breathing is more difficult. At first I blamed it on the change of climate, food and change of hours in Germany, but I am glad to get home and learn what causes these sudden flair ups."

Once we were home, Kenny was anxious to return to the VA Medical Center in Fargo and gain reassurance from his doctors that his health was not declining. The day-long visit involved a complete health exam and x-rays. We knew that Kenny's lungs had been severely damaged by chemicals as he readied and water- proofed all the C-Company's vehicles and gear for the Omaha Beach Landing in 1944. Kenny, never one to complain, had also ignored the increasing difficulties to climb stairs or the steep inclines to castles and chalets in Germany.

He told the doctor, "After the war, my health just wasn't the same as it had been before I was drafted. After 1945, I was periodically ill throughout the years but lately, I do less than ever. Yet I am always tired, even after a rest I am still tired. What is going on with me?"

The doctor's prognosis was factual but not encouraging. "Kenny, we will do everything we can for you. Medicines will help, but what you can do will be greatly limited by the asthma attacks that will increase in frequency and duration, especially if you overexert."

From 1992 on, neighbors and friends helped without being asked.

They were there as midnight emergency trips to the VA clinic became a necessity. Mary Rose, the receptionist, the nurses, the doctors, Mark Rye the pulmonary specialist, and Gloria Engel the physician's assistant, all pulled together as a team and their expertise kept Kenny functioning. During March 1995, Kenny was diagnosed with colon cancer and he was scheduled for immediate surgery. He told me that he had confidence in his doctor. Then he voiced his fears and worries.

"Annelee, what kind of life will I have? What will the future hold for you and me? If the colon cancer is advanced the doctor wants my permission to immediately perform a colostomy and, most likely, it will be a permanent one. I don't know how I will live with a bag on my side filling up with my bowel waste. What if I can't control the discharge? Will the bag expel an unpleasant odor? What if I need you to help me? What kind of life will that be?"

I understood that it was hard for Kenny, who was a proud, private man, to deal with having a natural function taken from him and replaced with a bag. Now the unknown loomed before us again.

"Kenny," I pleaded, "you won't survive colon cancer without the surgery. Have the surgery and then we will get through this day by day. Don't worry."

I did not tell Kenny that I had just learned that on the day of his surgery, I was scheduled for laser treatment on my right eye because the eye specialist had discovered an aneurysm. I needed to depend on a driver. My friend, Betty, drove me to the clinic and took care of me. I had wanted to cancel, but Kenny's doctor assured me that the surgery could take four hours, and as long as Roy was present, I could easily have the laser treatment because Kenny would be still under anesthetics when I returned. I was concerned for Roy keeping vigil alone, but I didn't need to worry.

When we returned, Marvin our friend and neighbor, was in the waiting room with Roy. He smiled and explained, "I drove in because Joyce and I didn't want Roy to wait alone for the outcome of the surgery."

It was past noon when Dr. M. came toward us and explained that a colostomy had been necessary to assure and prove with additional tests that Kenny would now be cancer free. "Kenny is emotionally strong," he said, "He will adjust and there are many good days ahead for you."

Sometimes, I thought, to get anything at all in life, you will have to take second best and adjust. Because of the permanent colostomy, Kenny's hospital stay was prolonged. We formed a bond with other patients and their families. Everyone had their own struggle. Some could cope and help others while some blamed God and asked, "Why me?"

Kenny had his own struggle and fear. The specialist came and taught him the correct bag application. She helped several times and then told Kenny,

"Since you know the procedure, you will take care of your own function."

Kenny looked at me and pleaded, "Annelee, will you help me?"

I knew my answer, but yet it was so hard to say, "No, Kenny, you can do that, I will be there for you in an emergency, but otherwise you will be on your own. So it is best if you try and see how you get along while you are still in the hospital."

The stoma care nurse clinician instructed Kenny. "Close the bathroom door. We will be right outside." She turned to me, "Annelee, you handled Kenny's request the right way. I deal with wives who help their husbands at all times, but after a while the wives resent the husband's dependency and problems arise that could have been avoided. Unless a patient is otherwise helpless, a colostomy can and should be taken care of by the patient because he/she can live a normal lifespan."

The adjustment took time so we lived and coped. During ongoing exams we learned that Kenny had stayed cancer free. During fall 1996, Kenny's emphysema attacks were of longer duration and hospitalization was frequent. I spent my days driving to Fargo, visiting with Kenny and returning home in the evening. The thought of winter driving made me shudder. I hoped that Father Winter would be kind – but nature's fury was waiting.

CHAPTER 33

1997 - Nature's Fury Unleashed

It was November 16-17 when an early winter blizzard named Andy struck with 15-25 mph wind and 13.6 inches of snow closed the roads and kept everyone homebound. By March 1997, we had endured six blizzards and the accumulated ninety-eight inches of snow set an all time record. While other states named hurricanes, the weather bureau had just named the seventh blizzard Gust who settled in with a 15.7 inches snow record. The stress of the never ending snowfall brought on emphysema attacks, and several times Kenny needed to return to the VA hospital in Fargo. Our neighbors, Marvin, Duane, Art, Kenneth and Jack faced the brutal weather and they always cleared our driveway before they did their own. They took turns and drove fifty miles to the Medical Center at the VA while I sat in the back seat with Kenny. I worked his breathing equipment while he was gasping and fighting for each breath. Our drivers stayed until Kenny was hospitalized and breathing on his own. When I spoke of payment, they steadily refused.

"We do this for Kenny because if he could, he would do the same for us. Don't mention payment again."

Throughout these most difficult weeks, I suggested to Kenny that we should move to Fargo so he would be able to gain emergency care within minutes, but he declined.

"No Annelee, I want to be near my neighbors and friends because there is nothing better than that anywhere. Don't worry if I shouldn't make it in. I would sooner leave this world surrounded by friends and near you than in a hospital."

I understood his decision and hoped spring would bring better days. On April 5, the blizzard Hannah held many forces of nature. Unrelenting, she carried snow, pelted us with icy winds and ultimately brought the 100 Year Flood to our region. On Saturday, the evening of April 5, freezing rain coated power lines, 2000 poles snapped like match sticks as cities and farms were plunged into darkness. Since we lacked a back-up generator, within hours our home turned freezing cold. I lit candles in the living room, gathered down covers, fetched flashlights and hoped they would provide dim light throughout the night. Mummy like we sat wrapped in the down covers until morning. The sump pump had quit running and I scooped pail after pail into the drain until I felt as cold as the water. But Kenny became my main concern. As the winter storm raged outside, he started to hyperventilate and I became frightened. Unknown to us, Jack, the American Legion commander, had volunteered to check on Kenny who by now needed emergency hospitalization. Our local hospital was two blocks from our home. Kenny was transported there on a tractor because the blinding snow storm, icy roads and 70 miles per hour wind bursts created snow drifts too high for cars to navigate safely. There was no room for me to go along. By now our battery radio was dead. Cut off from the outside world, I felt lost and unsure what I should do. I gathered an additional flashlight, went back to the basement and scooped water because the inactive sump pump caused some flooding. It was close to 5:00 p.m. when someone knocked until the back door windowpane rattled. I opened the door and barely recognized Jack. His eyelids were coated with ice, his cheeks were deep red from cold, and his clothing was covered with icicles and snow. I asked him to come into the kitchen, but he shook his head and over the gusts of wind shouted,

"Annelee, take Kenny's meds. They need you at the hospital to tell them what he needs to take as the night goes on. Get a warm coat and wear a long scarf, mittens and boots."

Dressed so I could barely move, he secured me on the tractor. The two block ride became treacherous as Jack navigated around huge snow drifts and blocks of ice. Even though Jack was constantly blinded by swirling snow, he kept going until he reached the entrance door of the hospital. I was shivering. My teeth were chattering while snow and ice were falling from my outerwear. I wondered if I would ever feel warm again. The nurse organized Kenny's medications and after we double checked the order, I turned to leave.

She blocked my way. "Annelee, you can't leave," she explained. "We have orders to keep everyone right here. The dikes are breaking. Water is rushing into town from all sides and visibility is near zero."

I wanted to protest, but water gushed in through the door and as it reached past my ankles, I stepped onto a foot stool. Nurses and men rushed in and announced that they would move all patients to the second floor of the nursing home. Those who could walk with help were taken first. Others were carried up the two flights in chairs while beds from the nursing home were filled with patients who were helpless and seriously ill. Light was provided by an emergency generator as we sat and waited, hoping for calm by morning.

Monday's dawn was breaking when the nurses opened an emergency exit and explained that the building was no longer safe, and the evacuation to the Twin Valley Nursing Home was implemented. Able-bodied patients followed directions, stepped onto the makeshift ramp and entered the bus. Kenny, wrapped in blankets, worked his breathalyzers and shivered as he struggled to enter the bus. An icy sea hid the wheels of the bus, and after a slow rocky start, the driver navigated his way while sheets of ice rocked the bus from side to side. I feared we would take an ice-cold bath in the waters around us before we reached our destination. As we neared Twin Valley, the water surged down hill against the bus. We passed this onslaught and we were on rain soaked but safe ground. Young people who had been my students rushed toward me,

"Mrs. Woodstrom, don't worry. You are safe now." They reassured me, "we'll take care of Kenny. Come in. We have breakfast ready for everyone."

Once inside, the warmth and the aroma of the hot breakfast items brought momentarily a feeling of normalcy while we reunited with other flood victims who shared their stories. Kenny's condition worsened. Marilyn, my long-time Twin Valley friend, volunteered to drive us to the VA hospital, but Pastor Helen Beth's four-wheel drive was considered the safest vehicle for the treacherous roads. Kenny suffered from exhaustion. Tomorrow, Tuesday, April 8th, was our 50th Wedding Anniversary. Kenny bemoaned the fact that we had twelve dollars between us, and he was dressed in a hospital gown and a robe.

"Annelee, I have never thought that after fifty years of marriage it would come to this? I am ill. You have the burden of caring for me, and now you even have to wear borrowed clothes."

"Kenny," I tried to console him, "that doesn't matter. It matters that you get well. Then we will deal with what lies ahead."

When the hospital staff learned of our 50th Anniversary Day, Mark the respiratory specialist, whisked us away to his favorite restaurant near the VA hospital where several nurses and caretakers were waiting to help us celebrate. These people made our 50th Wedding Anniversary special and unforgettable. Upon Kenny's release a week later, Dawn, one of the nurses, offered us her home until we could safely return to Ada. The owner of a car rental agency called and offered us a car to drive home, cost free.

I remembered Mama's words of wisdom. "When darkness overwhelms you and you think you can't go on, it is then that from somewhere help comes along."

It was Friday, April 11, when Joyce, my friend and neighbor called.

"Annelee, we are back in Ada. The conditions here are terrible. Think of the worst and it is worse than that! The National Guard moved the ice to the side of the streets in stacks six to seven feet high."

I broke in, "Have you been in our home?"

"Yes," she hesitated, but then went on. "Your home had about seven feet of water in the basement, but you lucked out because you don't have any bathroom sewage covering the floors. We do. When you add the oil leak we had to that, you can imagine the stench. We can't live in our home so we will stay at the lake until we have heat and light."

We knew that we could not live in our home, and we wondered where we could stay but then our friends called. Corral and Francis Gibson wintered in Arizona, so they offered us their home in Twin Valley.

"Annelee, how is Kenny holding up? It must be extremely stressful for him. Just go to our home. We asked our neighbors to turn on the heat and check the lights. Television and food are also waiting for your arrival."

Since we were just fifteen miles from home, I suggested that we return briefly to Ada and check the flood damage. Before we arrived in Ada, I made Kenny promise that he would stay upstairs and let me check the basement. Uneven, thick ruts of ice covered the driveway, so we gingerly crawled and walked until we reached the backdoor. The upstairs was untouched by flood waters, but it smelled musty and I hesitated before I opened the basement door. A foul odor penetrated my nostrils and the water soaked carpet squeaked as I went down the stairs to face devastation I had not imagined. In the family room, the cabinets were ripped off the walls and the cabinets' contents were strewn in all directions. Some rested atop the sofa that lay on its side. The easy chairs had turned the round table upside-down while the wooden chairs had formed a pyramid that could topple any time soon. The bookcase on the south wall was bulging with wet, swollen books, and the photo albums that held much of Sandy's life gave off a putrid smell and now held a grayish mass of images I could not recognize. I sat on pile of rubble and cried bitter tears. I felt that Sandy had died again in a cruel finality. The photo albums, photo slides, and her school memorabilia that had held memories of her growing up were now gray masses of wet, stinking paper. Album after album that held these precious photos was crumbling in my hands. All we would have left now were memories stored in our brain and the love of her being would remain in our hearts.

Kenny called down, "Annelee, what are you doing? Are you coming up?"

I pulled myself up and walked to the stairs, "Kenny I just want to look at the bedrooms and I'll be up."

As I navigated to the back bedrooms, tipped over furniture blocked my way until I made space to enter. The paneling still showed the watermark along the window. Drawers emptied of their contents were on the stripped beds. Kenny's bowling ball that had been stored behind louver doors in the closet had come to rest in the middle of the bed. The louver doors were intertwined with wet, dirty clothes, the only items that added color throughout the rooms. The bathroom and shower were covered with human waste, and the door was ripped from its hinges. I stepped on soggy food packages in the laundry room because the 15 cubic foot freezer had tipped and spewed its contents. The washer and dryer were pushed into the storage room and rested there covered with Christmas decorations that I had collected ever since we were married. The Christmas tree stood straight up like it was waiting to be decorated, while canned food was lying near the tree stand. The smell was unbearable at times and I knew it was no place for Kenny to enter and view. We returned to Twin Valley for the night, I called Roy and shared the devastation of our home.

"Mom, don't worry," he said, "Titus and I will be up in the morning my friends, Fred and Tom also offered their help."

The next morning, Titus, Roy and his friends arrived before noon. He recalled, "We couldn't believe the countryside. After Fergus Falls we frequently drove through water and we had to take several detours. As we came closer to Ada, we had to prove to the National Guard that we had carpenter tools with us and we were planning to work."

We had met Tom and Fred before and we were thankful for their volunteer help. Titus urged, "Let's go down and look at the damage." Minutes later I heard them exclaim from the basement, "We need a system to attack this mess."

Within hours, the front lawn was hidden under piles of debris. Water soaked mattresses, appliances, wet, heavy carpet and padding cut into manageable pieces, Christmas decorations, photo albums and my collection of books all that had been part of our lives for years, lay now in a pile waiting for the numerous trucks to take to the garbage dump.

Grandson Titus, Roy and his friends stayed in Ada for three days and worked tirelessly. They rested their tired bodies in their van or on the living room floor. They also cleaned the garage where Kenny's collection of tools, the car, lawn mower, snow blower and several other items needed to be cleaned and sanitized.

All this time, volunteers from churches and organizations streamed in from neighboring towns and from far away. They helped where they were needed. Daily, the Salvation Army served three meals to seven hundred displaced residents while the Red Cross provided cleanup kits, temporary housing costs, clothing and whatever the displaced population needed.

Volunteers came and the teaching staff from Twin Valley worked tirelessly. Our basement needed sanitation several times before a new hot water heater, furnace, a new electric panel, and a washer and dryer could be installed. As the cement foundation started to dry out, we learned that our home had structural damage because the basement walls were cracked beyond repair. We found that expenses mounted and our savings receded faster than the flood waters. Without donations from several organizations and the ten year FEMA loan, we would not have financially survived

"Annelee, I am going on eighty-one," Kenny lamented. "Now we have to borrow 10,000 dollars from FEMA and dip into our savings. I'll be ninety-one before we pay the loan off. I know I will never live that long. I will leave you with a debt. How will you manage?"

"Kenny, we need to fix the basement walls. At least we have a home, we are better off than the people who can never return to their homes." I pleaded, "Please don't worry. We will do what we can."

During the summer of 1997, we secured a contractor and he and his crew promised that they would have our home restored by Christmas Eve. Ada was saturated with builders, painters, plumbers and crane operators all trying to erase the horrendous flood damage. While the high school and hospital were demolished, the infrastructure of the city was replaced and upgraded. Residents restored and made their homes livable while a new high school and hospital were in the planning stages. Our contractor and his crew worked hard. They ripped off the front porch and the patio, braced the house with huge timber beams, dug an eight foot ditch around the house and worked on reinforcing the basement in sections until the basement could once again hold the house securely.

Kenny's sister, Irene, came from California and offered her help. Since I was often involved with the completion of the basement, I was thankful that she and Kenny could spend afternoons together and reminisce about times past or play their favorite card games. Our good friends Marvin and Joyce helped when needed. Hilde and Harold stopped by and spent time visiting or playing cards. The visitation Pastor Torgney and his wife Lila became our friends, and Roy, Linda and family came home whenever they could. Every day we could see that Kenny's health was failing. The emergency trips to the VA became an almost weekly occurrence, and a motorized wheelchair was now a necessity.

As Christmas came, we experienced again the goodness of the people around us. The furniture that we had salvaged from the flooded basement had been in storage at the upholstery shop. A group of handymen helped the owner, while he upholstered sofas and chairs for others. The men refinished our furniture, fixed the lamps and delivered all of it on the afternoon before Christmas Eve. Stanley, the boss of the basement crew, asked me to come down and inspect their work. The basement walls were painted a soft off-white. The windows had matching blinds while the cabinets and doors were stained pecan and varnished. The restored furniture and bedding were in place and even the light fixtures and paintings were hung. We felt a bond between us because we had mastered months of uncertainty, hard work and worries. Now it had come together. The traces of the flood were gone, and we knew that in ten years we would be debt free. We had scars, but we had survived the hundred year flood disaster.

October 1996

May-August 1997

Where are the streets and lawns?

I couldn't stop the tears and my appreciation knew no bounds, "If only Kenny could come down and see the wonderful work you have done," I said.

"Don't you worry," one of the men said, "Go up and see how Kenny is feeling. We will be up shortly."

I tried to describe our completed basement to Kenny, "If only I could see it," he uttered. "But even with your help I can't master the stairs."

"I'll take photos tomorrow," I promised.

"Now photos won't do, will they Kenny?" Stanley who had come up from the basement remarked. He went on, "We will carry you downstairs. We'll put you in a chair, tie you in, and show you what we have done. Don't worry, Kenny, we will be very careful."

Bowling ball in bag rests in bed.

Several crew members helped as they carried Kenny down the steps into the family room where they placed him in a chair. They carried Kenny from room to room and showed him the new louver doors on each closet, the new light fixtures, cabinets and appliances. Wrapped in a

Family Room

warm blanket, Kenny looked, touched and could not thank the men enough while tears were in everyone's eyes. They had turned on the electric heat. I brought coffee, a plate of sausages, bread and various cheeses, and we had our first lunch in our restored basement. I could not believe how happy Kenny was. His eyes had a sparkle I had not seen for months. He talked with the men, ate a hearty lunch, and at his insistence they toured the basement again and answered his many questions. They carried Kenny back up and placed him in his chair. We shook hands and wished everyone a blessed Christmas. I followed them to the door and expressed my appreciation again.

"Don't thank us, Annelee. This is Christmas like it should be." Stanley pondered, "I feel good because Christmas is here for me today." We hugged and I too felt the Christmas Spirit of 1997.

Roy and Linda, and our grandchildren, Freya, Titus and Liv arrived on Christmas Eve. They too were pleasantly surprised to see their downstairs sleeping quarters restored and they were touched by the goodness of Stanley's crew. The Spring Flood of 1997 had brought so much devastation and it was a stressful period in our life. But we had also experienced the caring and goodness of people we had never met. Kenny felt good that Christmas Eve and he said,

"I'm a lucky man. I have my family. They love me and take such good care of me. My neighbors and friends have and do help when we need it. Tonight I know my life holds so many blessings. It truly is a Christmas I will never forget."

CHAPTER 34

To Say Good-bye

New Year 1998 was a quiet celebration because Kenny lost movement and strength. The VA Medical Center contacted the Norman County First Care Nursing Association, and Kenny received daily home nursing care. It was good to have these caring professionals because without their help Kenny would have been in a nursing home. One evening we had retired for the night, but Kenny was restless and could not sleep. We talked quietly when he suddenly turned toward  me and said, "Annelee, I am getting weaker every day, and I don't know how long I can go on. Since I saw how you handled all the devastation during the flood, dealt with FEMA, with money matters, worked with the building contractor, I know you will be all right when I have to leave." I tried to break in, but he went on, "It is okay. I was luckier than most people because I had you. We had some difficult times, but we had a good life. I want you to know that I always loved you every day. You were and you are my life. Don't say anything now. I just needed to say that because I feel my strength is going. Come, lie close and let me hold you. Just be still."

I lay close to him and cried until I had no tears left. I knew he had done what he needed to do. He had said his good-bye. Now he had fallen asleep. The next morning he was at peace with himself and I was glad because he had a good day. He joked with the Home Care nurses and the neighbors as they stopped by. The phone rang. It was Dennis our nephew, and he said that he was flying in from Herndon, Virginia to be with Kenny and help when and where he was needed.

Dennis arrived and Kenny was elated. He and Dennis talked the same language when it came to mechanics. Kenny wanted to make sure that we would have a backup generator if we had another electric failure. Dennis found what we needed, and while Kenny watched from the patio window, Dennis made sure that the generator worked if the need arose. With the help of some neighbors, they drove Kenny through the area and he was glad and relieved because the Flood of 1997 had lost its grip. During Sunday night, Kenny became quite ill and he was admitted at the Fargo VA Emergency Medical Center. Dennis drove back to Ada to rest. He returned and relieved me. I drove home late Monday evening and on Tuesday morning Kenny's nurse called.

"Annelee, this is Myrtle, and I am here with the director of nursing,"

"How is Kenny," I interrupted.

"He is as well as he can be," the director of nursing said. "The reason for my call, however, is different. Kenny insists that I tell you to call the children home. He tells us that he is not coming home again, and before he dies, he wants to talk with Roy and his family. We think you have time. Even this weekend would be okay, but Kenny insisted that we make the call."

"Thanks for letting me know how Kenny feels. Please tell Dennis I'll be in shortly."

Dennis met me in the waiting room of the hospital, "Annelee, Kenny insists for everyone to be near him. I am glad you are back. Why don't you go and talk with Kenny. He is asking for you."

I couldn't change Kenny's mind, so I called Roy and they arrived on Wednesday. Kenny talked with Roy and Linda, and then with Titus and Liv.

Kenny wished that Freya would be here too. Freya, who was now living in Atlanta had booked her flight so we told Kenny, "Freya will arrive on Friday."

"Good," Kenny sighed relieved, "then I will wait for her."

Freya's arrival brought such joy to Kenny. He was so glad to have his family near him. The grandchildren had decorated his hospital room with posters that told how much they loved Grandpa and photos brought forth memories of times past. We changed off for meals, but otherwise we stayed by Kenny's side. The nurses brought in a bed chair so Dennis or I could spend the night. We were grateful for these hours when we could share our innermost thoughts and I am glad that one night I told Kenny what he meant to me.

"Kenny, surely, it was not always easy for you to live with me. You were always steadfast in what you believed. I called it stubborn sometimes, remember? But you were good for me." He reached for my hand, "Kenny, let me go on. It took a long time for us to gain the best in marriage that was there for us. I am glad we were together when Sandy died. I know we could not have survived alone, but together we got through the worst time of grief."

"When I was young and newly married I wished that we would be rich. I didn't know it then, but I know now that we were rich throughout the years we worked together. We had more than a lot of rich people I know. Kenny, I love you more than you will ever know. Thanks for being you because you helped me become what I am now." I reached for and held his hand until he fell asleep.

The doctors and the staff were surprised how Kenny expressed exactly what was important to him. He told them, "Please don't send my friends away, I want to visit with them." The week passed and on Monday, our friends, Joyce and Marvin came. We always could depend on them, and it didn't need to be said because it had been like that for the past four decades. Kenny smiled after they left and said, "Annelee, I know our friends will be there for you, so reach for them when you need help."

On Tuesday noon, our pastor was visiting. Janet and Gordon were near, and we thought Kenny was sleeping when he suddenly asked,

"Why am I back? I was in heaven. It was so beautiful. Sandy, Ma and Dad were waiting for me and there is Eddy. Don't you see him, Annelee?"

"No, Kenny, I don't," I said.

"Well, you must need different glasses. They are right there, waiting for me."

Janet told me later that she was so moved by the special time they were given to share with Kenny before he died. She said that all the way

home she thought about Kenny and his hours of peace and acceptance of
leaving what he so dearly loved on earth. Janet wrote the following
poem that very evening:

Today I witnessed the presence of God
We stood around Ken's bed and listened as this
Gentle man taught us about death and dying.
He had fought his enemy with hammers and tongs ...
His vigorous activity born of the love of life.
His body finally said, "no more."

We watched as he drifted through his past and saw a
Young, blond German girl on a bicycle — the one
He told his buddies he would someday marry.
He looked at her now and called her "a champion."

"Don't close the door, stay with me till I leave"
He drifted —until he heard the soft voice of Freya,
His granddaughter urging him to sip some malted milk.
He made a joke - - a quick rebound –
That keen sharp wit yet so alert.
He drifted –
His eyes opened – "I thought I was in heaven, I was with
        Sandy; I want to go."
"Soon dad, soon."

His eyes found Gordon's — "thank you my friend.
        I'm glad
You are here so I can say it."
This man whose life was one of service, of friendship,
Now thanking friends.
Each visitor included in his psalm of thanks.

"Annelee, where are you? I want to see your face."
That dear face of 50 years so precious to him still.

The past, the future, the present merging together
In the mystery of life and death.
Sister, nephew, family, friends stand by as Ken's load
Of living freight wanes and gives him flight.
He had been given a glimpse of heaven and
        He is eager to go.

I look at my friend and recall some words in
A poem "The Ship"

I stand and watch the ship until at length
She is only a ribbon of white just where the sea
And the sky come together and mingle with each other.
Then somebody at my side says:
"Here she is gone!"
Gone where! Gone from my sight that is all.
Her diminished size is in me not in her, and just at
The moment we say 'she is gone' there are other
        Voices taking up the glad shout;
"There she comes!"
That is what we call death,
That is what we call Life Eternal

Ken, you have given us a gift today
We have seen death through your eyes, it gives us
The strength and faith to say good-bye.

Wednesday and Thursday Kenny drifted in and out of what he called his deep sleep. When he was awake, he talked with us and told us how much he appreciated the life he was allowed to live. Kenny was at peace, and sometimes it seemed he just awoke to briefly talk completely lucid, and then he would drift and be out of our reach. Friday morning the nurse came in and told us,

"Go for breakfast and I will ready Kenny for the day."

We came back. The nurse told Dennis who had walked in ahead of me, "Kenny left us. He just slept away and wouldn't come back again.

This time he stayed in the heaven he always told us he saw."

I was angry at first, Kenny, I thought, we were with you day and night, and then you leave us when we are not there for your final good-bye. Dennis put his arms around me, "Annelee this is probably the way Kenny wanted to go on his final journey—alone—without us trying to keep him here."

Kenny was buried on February 10, 1998. He had a military honor guard. His family, his friends and neighbors, and numerous people from the VA hospital, came from far away. They came to say good-bye to a man who truly was a Gentleman Soldier.

CHAPTER 35

A Tribute to My Gentleman Soldier and
All the Soldiers Who Fought in Wars

For those fortunate to have never been on a battle field anywhere, I would like to give insight to what the soldiers who fight for their country were, and presently, are asked, to endure. Kenny was on the frontline for eleven months. The following is what he recalled when he was asked to tell a committee about his war experiences.

He had said to me, "Annelee, I can't talk about the hell I went through, if I can't get a disability card for Veteran's Hospital care...so be it."

I encouraged him, "Kenny, you tell me, and I will type while you talk."

Kenny on right.

Kenny's health had been severely impaired by fighting for eleven months on the Western fronts. He incurred life-long damage to his lungs and was afflicted with bleeding ulcers. Every soldier who fought and faced the enemy could probably tell you, "The mental anguish will always live within me. It can be silent at times, but it is never still."

The following are Kenny's recollections: As I remember he checked in a small book for dates and other facts. The booklet was lost in the 1997 Flood.

INDUCTION AND MILITARY SERVICE PRIOR TO EUROPE

Kenneth Woodstrom 37172821. I was inducted April 2, 1942, at Fort Snelling, Minnesota, and the following Sunday I was sent to Camp Barkley, Texas, Company C, 352nd Infantry, 90th Infantry Division.

The old 90th Division was reactivated as the Texas Oklahoma Division, which consisted entirely of new recruits from all over the United States. I had been classified as a mechanic.

Our first regimental commander, Colonel Patrick, was one of the officers of high rank that I got to talk with. He instructed me during basic training on how to be 1st scout in a combat situation.

However, since I had been a mechanic in a Ford garage for the previous seven years, I was sent to the motor pool. Mr. Williams, a civilian advisor tested me and stated that while others would be going to school for additional training, I would be going to work immediately at the motor pool. While our company was taking physical training to become combat ready, I worked in the motor pool from morning until late at night.

September 1942, although I never marched even once in the morning marches it was the rule that all men had to partake in a long alert call and march twenty miles. I was taken from the motor pool and asked to march with all my combat equipment on my back. I had worked all day long in the motor pool and after just a couple hours of sleep, I had to report for the march by 2:00 a.m. By sun-up it was very hot, and since I was not conditioned to march, I passed out later that morning and I awoke in the hospital at Camp Barkley where I was hospitalized for several days.

After returning from Louisiana maneuvers to Camp Barkley, I again was sent to the motor pool where I repaired and condition – that was to water proof with chemicals – all trucks and Jeeps. I was again excused from all combat training. One morning, my first sergeant came to the motor pool and said that every man had to run the obstacle course and then run three additional miles. I was ordered to go back to my quarters to get my full pack and equipment and come to the obstacle course. By now, the rest of the company was waiting for me to run the obstacle course and then take the three mile run. Again, it was extremely hot. I asked for water, but they wouldn't give me any. I passed out, and I woke up again in the hospital.

On April 2, 1943, our company was able to knock off twenty-five miles in less than eight hours, carrying full field pack and equipment. At this time we received our first furloughs.

September 1943. We were going west to Arizona-California maneuvers. Our company was in charge of taking care of the camp, and I was in charge of taking care of the motor pool. By December 6, 1943, we were combat ready, and our company was shipped from California to Fort Dix, NJ.

After I had been home on furlough, I was told to report to the dispensary. At the time I was unaware that I was there to be reclassified. After several days I asked to be returned to my company because I knew that they were alerted to ship out and I wanted to stay with the company where I knew the men. I was returned to them and we were immediately moved to Camp Kilmer, NJ.

SERVICE IN EUROPE 1944-1945

On March 23, 1944, we embarked on the British ship Dominion Monarch. For thirteen days we sailed the ocean before we docked in Liverpool, England. On April 4th, 1944, our First Battalion was quartered at Gadsacres. I immediately went to work at the motor pool working seven days a week until dark, again water proofing and getting Jeeps and trucks ready to run under water in the Channel. On May 13, 1944, the regiment moved sixty-four miles nearer to the English Channel to Camp Race Horse where we had our first experience with planes and bombs.

During June 1944, again, without any training, I was made the 50 caliber machine gunner for our company and at the same time, I was also in charge of our Jeeps. We were ordered to leave the ship, we went on barges and then drove ashore immersed in water while deafening submarine alerts were sounded constantly.

By June 8, we were fighting on the Normandy Beaches. At dawn the sight of the invasion – real war with life and death next to each other —

was an indescribable experience for me. My first sergeant who had trained so well and had told us repeatedly how important training was for living longer was killed the next day.

He had just told me, "Woody, if you keep the vehicles running and ammunition supplies coming up, we will end this war in a hurry."

BY JUNE 3, OUR REGIMENT HAD SEVEN HUNDRED AND THREE CASUALTIES AND ONE HUNDRED AND THIRTY-THREE DEAD. THE SMELL OF DEAD WAS EVERYWHERE AND DEAD SOLDIERS WERE PILED UP LIKE CORDWOOD. Our regimental objective was to cut off Cherbourg Peninsula.

It was on July 1, my twenty-eighth birthday, before we had a chance to wash, shave, and change into clean clothes. We hardly knew each other because dirt was covering our long hair and whiskers. Out of 212 men in our company, there were sixty men left. We received replacements.

On July 7, our company and K-Company had repulsed fourteen counter attacks, Dawson and I tried to get bazooka ammunition to the front. It was a dark, cloudy night, and many hair-raising incidences took place. For example, a German soldier was running for cover right next to us as shells were coming in.

I had my rifle on him when Dawson said to him, "You are a German."

"Ja, ja." he answered.

Dawson said to him, "You better keep your hands up."

As more artillery shells came in, he got away from us.

The very same night we took off with the Jeep. Before we started out of the woods, I let the Jeep die so we wouldn't be heard. To keep the vehicle even quieter, I removed the ammunition from my 50 caliber machine gun. But as the moon broke through the clouds, the Germans spotted us and sent up flares. We hit the ground away from the Jeep.

I said to Dawson, "When the flares go out, I'll go back and get the Jeep."

So I crawled to the Jeep and as soon as I started it, I backed it up. The Germans started firing again, and we could see the tracers coming at the Jeep. I lay down in the Jeep and backed right over my buddies legs. I got the jeep into the woods and went back to find Dawson. He was really hurting for a while, but he turned out okay.

After fighting for almost every foot along and around the hedge rows, we cut off the Cherbourg Peninsula. After fifty days of combat, we were transferred from the First to General Patton's Third Army. On July 25, three thousand planes blasted a path two miles wide through the German defenses.

We then fought in the closing of the Falaise-Argentan Gap, moving on Maizieres-les-Metz. Under intolerable conditions we occupied the town jointly with the Germans. I was part of the fighting that had as its main objective to encircle Metz, a fortress, that had been considered as almost impregnable. Outside of Lemans, France, our battalion was cut in two by the Germans and we were cut off from our outfit. After the fighting stopped, Captain Redman had me drive the spearhead Jeep. When we finally made contact that night, we were attacked again and fierce fighting continued throughout the rest of that night. The few of us that were left after that battle lived with physical and mental exhaustion. It was now November 1944, and we were with the first crossing of the Moselle River where unrelenting rain and cold transformed our foxholes into deep pools of icy water.

DECEMBER, 1944, THE SIEGFRIED LINE

During December 1944, we crossed the Saar River with ice on the water. We had to get into the icy water to get our boat across the river. Our clothes froze on us, and our vehicles had to be left across the river. After grueling fighting, I was on a carrying party carrying out our wounded soldiers. I returned to the company and our lieutenant was killed by a shell concussion. Four of us made it back to the pillbox where I fell asleep totally exhausted. Within a few minutes, we had to leave the pillbox to get back to the company. Several of us passed out and woke up in the basement of a house. In the morning, we were taken back to the field hospital. It was there that the doctor asked me for how long I had been on K-rations. I had been on K-rations since 'D-DAY' that was over seven months. The doctor excused me from heavy duty such as carrying parties for a couple of days. The concession, however, did not eliminate or lessen my symptoms being still on the front line.

From the Siegfried line, we moved on to the Battle of the Bulge. Throughout the Battle of the Bulge, I was part of the continuous fighting that finally broke the resistance fighting of the Germans.

It was probably the first week in April. We were in a small village named Merkers. It was said that the Merkers mine was discovered because two American soldiers helped a midwife while she was assisting during the delivery of a baby. Because of the curfew, the soldiers later accompanied the midwife to her home. As they passed the mouth of the salt mines of that region, the woman pointed and said something like "the mines hide gold."

As the soldiers questioned the woman further, they learned weeks earlier huge loads of treasures were brought to Merkers and hidden in the salt mines. The soldiers reported the story to their officers, they questioned the mining officials, and the treasures were found.

Kenny said, "I remember for two days our jeeps were lowered into the mine, then we drove to the mine haft and loaded the jeeps with gold bars. We were about 1200 feet below ground level. That's the only time I really felt safe, because I knew that I wouldn't be shot at. But being underground for two days where it was damp and cold was not easy on my lungs. It was such tedious work. We were told that we bought up billions of German Marks and over a million of American dollars. Then we brought up hundreds of famous paintings and sculptures from all over the world."

Kenny remarked "I'm sure these figures were close, because our Jeeps were loaded several times in each section. I never imagined that so much wealth could be hidden in one place. Some members of the 357th were left behind to guard this treasure. But Dawson and I weren't that lucky. We moved on with our jeep and advanced with the remainder of the company a 120 miles toward Czechoslovakia. The German Army was now disorganized. We took prisoners by the thousands. Often the German soldiers had just gathered in villages and waited for us to arrive so they could surrender. The remainder of the entire German Army was taken prisoner. We learned of the atrocities that had taken place at the Concentration Camp Flossenburg, Bavaria"

"It was hard to imagine that such a beautiful little village like Flossenburg could hold such horror. I do belief in God, but what we saw and experienced throughout the invasion of Western Europe was man-made hell."

THE REGIMENTAL RECORD STATES
THE FOLLOWING FACTS:

The 357th Infantry Regiment had eleven months of continuous combat, a total of 355 days of combat in three countries. The regiment had been in contact with the enemy for 267 of those days. The 357th Infantry had figured prominently in every major phase of the campaigns which led to the defeat of the German Reich. The trying Normandy operations, the break-out, the encirclement and destruction of the German Seventh Army at Falaise, the battles of pursuit across France, the assault crossings of the major river barriers, the capture of Metz, the cracking of the Siegfried line and the ultimate race across Germany into Czechoslovakia were accomplished in these eleven months. The 357th Regiment had 1,080 riflemen, and a total of 953 were killed in action while 143 died of wounds. The dead thus numbered 1,096. In other words, slightly over 100 percent of its authorized riflemen were killed.

Kenny stated that just he and only five of the original men he was inducted with were still part of Company C at the end of the war. He said that there were 1,000 replacements for his regiment.

He went on, "I am positive that my continuous combat experiences took their toll on my physical and nervous system. Ever since I have been bothered by gastric stomach problems, and I have been periodically under doctor's care since 1945."

When the committee asked Kenny how much disability payment he should receive, he said, "I fought for my country. If I get 10% and care at the VA Medical Center I am okay with that."

Kenny was a special man. He was a soldier who gave his all.

I am proud because Kenny was my husband, he was a good father, and he loved his country.

---

1. Marcin Jamkowski "Ghost Ship Found" National Geographic, February 2005, pp. 32-51.
2. Donald Sommerville, WORLD WAR II Day By Day, July 24-August 2, 1943, p. 189.
3. John W. Wright, "Czech Republic" 2006 the New York Times ALMANAC the Almanac of Record. p. 365.
4. Therese Neumann, A Portrait Based on Authentic Accounts, Journals and Documents by Johannes Steiner, Alba House Copyright 1967 by the Society of St. Paul, Staten Island NY 10314.
5. 2007 - School cones are still given to every child on his/her entrance to first grade. The cones hold pencils, color crayons, small books and items the teacher recommends. The students may also find small, favorite items they wished for.

ANNELEE WOODSTROM
Award-winning author of WAR CHILD and EMPTY CHAIRS
www.anneleewoodstrom.com • Email: annelee@loretel.net

Use this form OR print the following form from
www.anneleewoodstrom.com on your computer printer,
complete the necessary information on the printed form
and mail, with your check or money order, to:

ANNELEE WOODSTROM
PO BOX 5 • ADA, MN 56510

ORDER FORM

Annelee, please send the following books to:

Name: _____

Street Address: _____

City: _____ State:_____ Zip Code:_____

WAR CHILD **$21.06***
Multiply by number of books ordered   X _____
Total for this book .... $_____

EMPTY CHAIRS **$22.00***
Multiply by number of books ordered .... X _____
Total for this book .... $_____
TOTAL DUE FOR THIS ORDER .... $_____

*NOTE: PRICES SHOWN INCLUDE SALES TAX,
SHIPPING AND HANDLING CHARGES

Mail this form along with your check or money order.
OR ORDER BY CREDIT CARD

Bill my: ❏ Visa   ❏ MasterCard   Expires_____

Card #_____

3 Digit Code on Back of Card_____

Signature _____

Daytime Phone Number_____